BBC
Bitesize

Bitesize
Pearson Edexcel
GCSE (9-1)
FRENCH
REVISION GUIDE

24

Series Consultant:
Harry Smith

Author:
Liz Fotheringham

GCSE French / **Contents**

Contents

☑ Tick off each topic as you go.

How to use this book

Use the features in this book to focus your revision, track your progress through the topics and practise your exam skills.

 Features to help you revise

Each bite-sized chunk has a **timer** to indicate how long it will take. Use them to plan your revision sessions.

Scan the **audio QR codes** for the listening activities. You can also access these from your ActiveBook or by visiting **www.pearsonschools.co.uk/BBCBitesizeLinks**.

Complete **worked examples** demonstrate how to approach exam-style questions.

Aiming higher boxes give you tips for getting the best grades.

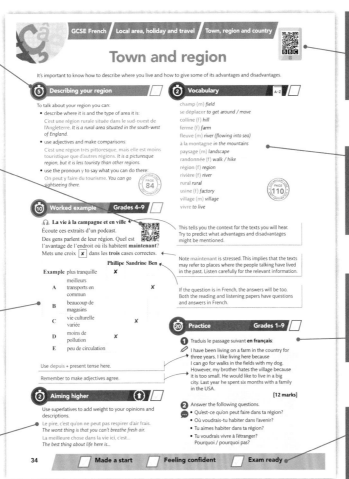

Scan the **QR codes** to visit the BBC Bitesize website. It will link straight through to more revision resources on that subject.

Key words and phrases are translated for each topic. Stamps refer you to the relevant **vocabulary** and **grammar** sections.

Test yourself with exam-style practice at the end of each page and check your answers at the back of the book.

Tick boxes allow you to track the sections you've revised. Revisit each page to embed your knowledge.

 Exam focus features

The *About your exam* section at the start of the book gives you all the key information about your exams, as well as showing you how to identify the different questions.

You will also find green *Exam skills* and red *Strategies* pages. These work through extended exam-style questions and provide techniques for approaching each exam paper.

 ActiveBook and app

This Revision Guide comes with a **free online edition**. Follow the instructions from inside the front cover to access your ActiveBook.

You can also download the **free BBC Bitesize app** to access revision flash cards and quizzes.

If you do not have a QR code scanner, you can access all the links in this book from your ActiveBook or visit **www.pearsonschools.co.uk/BBCBitesizeLinks**.

☑ **Made a start**   ☑ **Feeling confident**   ☑ **Exam ready**   **iii**

Your French GCSE

Your GCSE French exam tests your knowledge of French and your ability to communicate in speech and writing across a range of contexts.

About the exam papers

You will have to take **four papers** as part of your GCSE French qualification. Each paper is equally weighted and worth 25% of the total marks.

Paper 1
Listening
Questions in English and French

Paper 2
Speaking
Role play, picture-based task and conversation

Paper 3
Reading
Questions in English and French, translation into English

Paper 4
Writing
Writing tasks and translation into French

For each activity in this Revision Guide, these icons will show you which paper you are revising for.

 Paper 1 Listening   Paper 2 Speaking   Paper 3 Reading   Paper 4 Writing

What you need to know

The papers cover five themes. You need to understand and use vocabulary from all of them.

Theme 1: Identity and culture
Topic 1: Who am I?; **Topic 2:** Daily life; **Topic 3:** Cultural life

Theme 2: Local area, holiday and travel
Topic 1: Holidays; **Topic 2:** Travel and tourist transactions; **Topic 3:** Town, region and country

Theme 3: School
Topic 1: What school is like; **Topic 2:** School activities

Theme 4: Future aspirations, study and work
Topic 1: Using languages beyond the classroom; **Topic 2:** Ambitions; **Topic 3:** Work

Theme 5: International and global dimension
Topic 1: Bringing the world together; **Topic 2:** Environmental issues

Your exam dates

Find out the date and time of each of your GCSE French papers and write them in this table.

	Date	AM or PM?
Paper 1		
Paper 2		
Paper 3		
Paper 4		

Foundation and Higher tier

There are two tiers for each paper: Foundation and Higher.

You can sit either Foundation or Higher, as long as all four skills are the same tier. You must sit all four papers in the same exam series.

Foundation tier papers cover grades 1–5. Higher tier papers cover grades 4–9.

Revising for your exam

- Get into the habit of revising some vocabulary every day.
- Make a revision plan and make sure that you allow yourself enough time to cover everything you need to know.

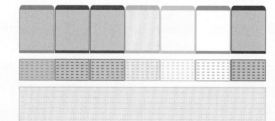

- Listen to spoken French on a regular basis.
- Practise speaking on your own or with a friend.
- When you revise nouns, don't forget to learn the gender.
- Use the revision guide to see how words are used in context.

Paper 1: Listening

Paper 1 tests your ability to understand spoken French and to respond to questions in both French and English.

 Listening exam key facts

In the listening paper, you will be expected to understand and respond to different types of spoken French.

Duration: 35 minutes (45 minutes Higher tier)

Number of marks: 50 marks

Percentage of exam: 25%

The exam includes 5 minutes' reading time of the paper before the audio is played.

The questions are in two sections:

Section A – questions in English with multiple-response or short answers in English (Foundation tier); questions in French with multiple-response answers in French (Higher tier).

Section B – questions in French with multiple-response answers in French (Foundation tier); questions in English with multiple-response or short answers in English (Higher tier).

 In the exam

- You will hear different extracts of spoken French and will need to respond to questions about each extract.
- Each extract will be played twice.
- You can make notes at any time.
- Each question will have a theme or topic, such as 'News report' or 'Les Jeux Olympiques'.
- You will need to identify the gist or main points of what is said, including specific details and the speakers' opinions .
- For all of Section A you will be expected to answer in **English**. All of Section B will be in **French**. Read the question carefully to be sure which language to use.

 Exam explainer

Some questions are multiple choice. You need to select the correct option.

During your 5 minutes' reading time, and the pauses before the audio is played, try to predict what words you might hear for each scenario.

Put a cross in the correct box.

Special occasions in France
You listen to a podcast sent to you by a French exchange student.
Listen to the recording and put a cross ✖ in the correct box.

The heading sets the context for the audio clip and tells you what kind of language to expect.

For this task, you need to understand the overall gist of what you have heard. You will not need to understand every word.

Your friend is talking about...

☐	a music event
☐	a religious event
✖	a sport event
☐	a fashion event

She thinks the event is...

☐	easy
☐	challenging
☐	too busy
☐	fun

[2 marks]

In your exam, the invigilator will play each audio clip. In this book, you can scan the QR codes to play them or go to www.pearsonschools.co.uk/BBCBitesizeLinks.

You will be given an example question that has been answered correctly. Use this example to help you 'tune in' to the recording.

In this question you need to give details from the extract you hear. You can make notes as you listen to the audio clips to help you answer.

Recycling
You hear a radio discussion programme about recycling. Listen to the discussion and answer the following questions **in English**.

(a) What does Michelle find difficult to recycle?

_____

Almost all the question parts are worth one mark, so you only need to give a simple answer for each one.

(b) What is the reason for this?

_____

[2 marks]

 Made a start   **Feeling confident**   **Exam ready**

Paper 2: Speaking

In your speaking exam, you will be expected to communicate effectively for a variety of purposes.

 Speaking exam key facts

Duration: 7–9 minutes (10–12 minutes Higher tier)
Number of marks: 70 marks
Percentage of exam: 25%

The speaking exam will be conducted by your teacher. It will be recorded and then marked by an Edexcel examiner. The speaking exam has three tasks: role play (15 marks), picture-based task (24 marks) and general conversation (36 marks).

Preparation time

- You will be given a role play card and a picture stimulus. You will have 12 minutes to prepare them, and you will be supervised during this time.
- You are allowed to make notes and can take these into the exam with you.
- You will have to hand these notes to your teacher before the start of the general conversation.
- You are not allowed to use a dictionary.

 Task 1: Role play

Vous êtes dans un hôtel en France. Vous parlez avec un(e) employé(e).

1. Chambre – nombre de personnes
2. Chambre – où
3. !
4. Cuisine française – opinion
5. ? piscine

! means you will have to answer an unpredictable question.

? means you need to ask a question.

You will be given a card with five prompts to prepare for a role play scenario. The role play will last 1½–2 minutes.

You will be assessed for communication only and will be awarded up to 2 marks per task for successfully conveying the message.

At Foundation tier you will only need to use the present tense or a familiar conditional tense. You will need to ask one question and respond to one unpredictable question.

At Higher tier you must ask two questions, respond to one unpredictable question and one in the past tense.

Up to 5 further marks are awarded for knowledge and creative use of language.

 Task 2: Picture stimulus

Regarde la photo et prépare des réponses sur les points suivants:

- la description de la photo
- familles nombreuses – ton opinion
- activités récentes en famille
- fêtes en famille dans l'avenir
- rapports familiaux

You will be given a picture stimulus with either five bullet points (Foundation tier) or four bullet points and an unpredictable question (Higher). Use these bullet points to prepare your responses. This part of the exam will last 2–3 minutes. Marks are awarded for:

- communication and content: 16 marks
- linguistic knowledge and accuracy: 8 marks.

You will be asked at least one question where you will need to give and explain your opinion.

For the first question, you will need to describe what you can see in the photo.

 Task 3: General conversation

The general conversation has two parts and covers two themes you didn't talk about in the picture-based task. The general conversation will last 3½–4½ minutes at Foundation tier, and 5–6 minutes at Higher tier. The time will be split equally between the two parts.

Part 1: You will choose this theme and will talk about a topic from within it for up to one minute. You will then have a short conversation on this and possibly other topics within the theme.

Part 2: The second part of your conversation will cover the other theme and will be more spontaneous.

Marks are awarded for communication and content (12 marks), interaction and spontaneity (12 marks) and linguistic knowledge and accuracy (12 marks).

Paper 3: Reading

Paper 3 tests your ability to understand and respond to written French.

 Reading exam key facts

Duration: 45 minutes (1 hour Higher tier)
Number of marks: 50 marks
Percentage of exam: 25%

The questions are in three sections:

- **Section A** – six questions in English with multiple-response / short answers in English.
- **Section B** – three questions in French with multiple-response answers in French (Foundation tier); two questions with multiple-response answers and one question requiring a short answer in French (Higher tier).
- **Section C** – translation from French into English (a minimum of 35 words for Foundation tier and 50 words for Higher tier).

Section C is worth 14% of the total marks for Paper 3 (7 marks at both Foundation and Higher tier).

> You may be asked to read a short passage of French and answer in English.

> You only need to give two details.

 Exam explainer

La musique

Complète chaque phrase en utilisant un mot de la case. Il y a des mots que tu n'utiliseras pas.

> adore classique comprendre déteste ennuyeuse folklorique jazz jouer intéressante monotone rock rythmique supporter

> **@theo_s** Mon copain dit que la musique rock est ennuyeuse et je suis totalement d'accord. Je trouve ça nul!

> **@Caro_K** Écouter de la musique classique ne me dit rien. C'est monotone! Mais c'est tout de même vrai que les musiciens ont beaucoup de talent.

> **@JeSuisSophie** Le jazz est ma musique préférée. Je peux écouter ça toute la journée!

Exemple: @JeSuisSophie _adore_ le jazz.

1. Selon @theo_s, la musique rock n'est pas _____ .
2. @Caro_K admire les gens qui jouent de la musique _____ .
3. @Caro_K ne peut pas _____ la musique classique.

 Exam explainer

Le Journal d'une femme de chambre **by Octave Mirbeau**

Read this extract. Célestine describes her new employment.

> Aujourd'hui, 14 septembre, à trois heures de l'après-midi, par un temps doux, gris et pluvieux, je suis entrée dans ma nouvelle place. C'est la douzième en deux ans. Bien entendu, je ne parle pas des places que j'ai faites durant les années précédentes. Il me serait impossible de les compter (...)
>
> L'affaire s'est traitée par l'intermédiaire des Petites Annonces du *Figaro* et sans que je voie Madame. Nous nous sommes écrit des lettres, ç'a été tout (...) Les lettres de Madame sont bien écrites (...) elles révèlent un caractère méticuleux.

(a) What was the weather like the day she started her new job? Give two details. **[2 marks]**

(b) Where did Célestine find out about her new job? **[1 mark]**

> For questions only worth one or two marks you will need to give short and concise answers.

> You will not need to use all the words in this type of multiple-response task.

> The exam will include extracts of varying lengths from a range of sources, including authentic sources such as tweets, text messages, emails, websites, instructions, public notices, advertisements, brochures, guides, letters, newspapers, reports and magazines. There will also be extracts from literary sources.

 Exam focus

- You will be expected to identify the gist of a text, as well as details and points of view.
- You will be expected to work out the meaning of some unfamiliar language, using your knowledge of the context, language and grammar.
- You will be expected to make inferences (read between the lines) for some texts and to draw conclusions.
- There will only be an example answer if this is necessary to help you understand how to answer a particular question.
- You are not allowed to use a dictionary.

Paper 4: Writing (Foundation)

Paper 4 tests your ability to communicate in written French. This page explains the requirements for the Foundation tier.

Writing exam key facts

Duration: 1 hour 10 minutes
Number of marks: 60 marks
Percentage of exam: 25%
You are not allowed to use a dictionary.

The Foundation paper has four questions.

You must answer all of the questions. Questions 1, 2 and 3 are in French and you must answer in French.
For Question 4, you must translate 5 sentences into French. The translation into French is worth 12 marks (20% of the total marks for Writing).

Exam explainer – Writing (Foundation) Grades 1–5

1 Le parc

Tu visites un parc en France. Tu partages cette photo avec tes amis.

Écris une description de la photo et exprime ton opinion sur le parc.

Écris 20–30 mots environ **en français**. **[12 marks]**

Question 1 assesses your ability to describe and explain.

You are assessed on communication and content (6 marks), and linguistic knowledge and accuracy (6 marks).

2 Au travail

Vous travaillez dans un hôtel et vous devez écrire un mail pour répondre aux questions d'un(e) client(e) qui veut les informations suivantes:

- où se trouve l'hôtel
- types de chambres disponibles
- l'heure de disponibilité de la chambre
- activités possibles en ville

Il faut écrire en phrases complètes.

Écrivez 40–50 mots environ **en français**. **[16 marks]**

In Question 2, you will need to use the formal register to write an email or short message.

You have to respond in French and write 40–50 words.

You will be assessed on the communication and content of your answer (8 marks) and on linguistic knowledge and accuracy (8 marks).

3 Mon collège

Écris un mail. Tu **dois** faire référence aux points suivants:

- ton collège et ses élèves
- les aspects positifs et négatifs de ton collège
- une visite scolaire récente
- où tu veux faire tes études dans l'avenir.

Il faut écrire en phrases complètes.

Écris 80–90 mots environ **en français**. **[20 marks]**

In Question 3, you will have a choice of two tasks. Each task will give you a different scenario and four bullet points. You should write about each of the bullet points and will need to use past, present and future tenses.

You should use the informal 'tu' form for this task.

You will be assessed on the communication and content of your answer (12 marks), and its linguistic knowledge and accuracy (8 marks).

You will be given five sentences in English to translate into French. The sentences will be ordered in increasing level of difficulty.

There are two marks per sentence for three of the sentences and three marks per sentence for the remaining two sentences, so 12 marks in total.

4 La vie quotidienne

Traduis les phrases suivantes **en français**.

(a) My sister is small. **[2 marks]**

(b) At school I hate science and PE. **[2 marks]**

...

(e) I played video games at my house with my friends. **[3 marks]**

  Made a start **Feeling confident** **Exam ready**

Paper 4: Writing (Higher)

Paper 4 tests your ability to communicate in written French. This page explains the requirements for the Higher tier.

Writing exam key facts

Duration: 1 hour 20 minutes
Number of marks: 60 marks
Percentage of exam: 25%

The Higher paper has three questions. Question 3 on the Foundation paper and Question 1 on the Higher paper are the same.

You must answer all of the questions. Questions 1 and 2 are in French and you must answer in French. For Question 3, you must translate an English text into French. The translation into French is worth 20% of the total marks for Writing (12 marks at Higher tier).

You are not allowed to use a dictionary.

Aiming higher

For the highest marks, your response to the task should be relevant, detailed and cover each element of the task.

You should use a wide range of vocabulary and grammatical structures, including more complex structures, such as relative clauses and après avoir + past participle. Your response should include the past, present and future tenses and you must make sure that what you're writing is accurate in terms of spelling and grammar.

Exam explainer – Writing (Higher) Grades 4–9

In Question 1, you will have a choice of two tasks. Each task will give you a different scenario and four bullet points. You should write about each of the bullet points and will need to use past, present and future tenses.

You should use the informal 'tu' form for this task.

1 Mon collège

Écris un mail. Tu **dois** faire référence aux points suivants:

- ton collège et ses élèves
- les aspects positifs et négatifs de ton collège
- une visite scolaire récente
- où tu veux faire tes études dans l'avenir.

Écris 80–90 mots environ **en français**. **[20 marks]**

You will be assessed on the communication and content of your answer (12 marks), and on linguistic knowledge and accuracy (8 marks).

2 Le bénévolat

Un magazine français cherche des articles sur le bénévolat pour son site internet.

Écrivez un article sur une activité bénévole que vous avez faite récemment pour intéresser les lecteurs.

Vous **devez** faire référence aux points suivants:

- pourquoi vous avez participé à cette activité bénévole
- votre opinion du bénévolat
- les activités bénévoles les plus importantes
- une autre initiative bénévole que vous comptez faire dans l'avenir.

Justifiez vos idées et vos opinions.

Écrivez 130–150 mots environ **en français**.

[28 marks]

In Question 2 you will have a choice of two tasks. You will be asked to write a report, an article, a letter or similar for a specific purpose. You must use the formal (vous) register and write about each of the bullet points.

Your answer with be assessed for communication and content (16 marks) and for linguistic knowledge and accuracy (12 marks).

3 Les vacances d'hiver

Traduis le passage suivant **en français**:

To celebrate Christmas, all my family came to my house. My parents prepared a special meal and we watched films. I received a new book. It is useful for my homework. Next week, for New Year's Eve, I would like to go to a party in the town centre. I think it will be exciting!

[12 marks]

In Question 3 you will need to translate a passage of English into French. It will be about 50 words long.

Your answer is assessed for your ability to convey the key messages (6 marks) and your ability to apply grammatical knowledge and structures (6 marks).

Understanding rubrics

Revise the French instructions you will find on your exam papers.

② About rubrics

The 'rubrics' are the instructions that are given for tasks on the exam papers. Always read them carefully and make sure you understand what you have to do. Occasionally, there may also be an example to help you understand what to do.

The rubrics will be in French on the writing paper, on the picture stimulus card and in section B of the reading paper. On the listening paper the rubrics are in French in section B (Foundation) and section A (Higher).

⑤ Following instructions

Question types

Mets une croix dans la case correcte. *Put a cross in the correct box.*

Choisis entre... *Choose between...*

Complète les phrases en choisissant un mot ou des mots dans la case. *Complete the sentences by choosing a word or words from the box.*

Il y a des mots que tu n'utiliseras pas. *There are some words that you won't use.*

Lis ce mail / ces descriptions / cet article. *Read this email / these descriptions / this article.*

Regarde la photo et prépare des réponses... *Look at the photo and prepare answers...*

Answering

Réponds aux questions en français. *Answer the questions in French.*

Traduis les phrases suivantes en français. *Translate the sentences into French.*

Traduis le passage suivant en français. *Translate the following passage into French.*

Quelle est la ville / personne correcte? *What is the correct town / Who is the correct person?*

Il n'est pas nécessaire d'écrire des phrases complètes. *It is not necessary to write in full sentences.*

② Instructions for writing tasks

Écris une description de la photo. *Write a description of the photo.*

Exprime ton opinion / Exprimez votre opinion sur le sport / la musique / les visites scolaires. *Express your opinion about sport / music / school trips.*

Écris / Écrivez 20–30 mots environ en français. *Write about 20–30 words in French.*

Écris / Écrivez une réponse / une lettre / un article. *Write a response / a letter / an article.*

Justifiez vos idées et vos opinions. *Justify your ideas and opinions.*

⑤ Vocabulary A–Z

case (f) *box*
croix (f) *cross*
fois (f) *time*
idée (f) *idea*
juge (m) *judge*
lecteur (m) *reader*
mot (m) *word*
opinion (f) *opinion*
phrase (f) *sentence*

point (m) *point*
réponse (f) *answer*
chacun *each one*
chaque *each*
entre *between*
il faut *it is necessary to / must*
en français *in French*
plusieurs *several*
suivant *following*

Verbs

choisis *choose*
écris *write*
exprime *express*
lis *read*
mets *put*
réponds *answer*
traduis *translate*

convaincre *to convince*
faire référence à *to refer to*
intéresser *to interest*
justifier *to justify*
utiliser *to use*

All the verbs in this column are in the **tu** form of the imperative.

⑩ Practice

What does each of the following rubrics mean in English?

1 Attention! Chacun des mots peut être utilisé plusieurs fois.

2 Il faut écrire en phrases complètes.

3 Écrivez une lettre pour convaincre les juges.

4 Écrivez un article pour intéresser les lecteurs.

5 Mets une croix ✘ dans la case correcte.

6 Tu dois faire référence aux points suivants.

Made a start | Feeling confident | Exam ready

Numbers

You will need a good understanding of numbers as they appear in a variety of contexts.

  Cardinal numbers 1–100

1	un	21	vingt-et-un
2	deux	22	vingt-deux
3	trois	23	vingt-trois
4	quatre	24	vingt-quatre
5	cinq	25	vingt-cinq
6	six	26	vingt-six
7	sept	27	vingt-sept
8	huit	28	vingt-huit
9	neuf	29	vingt-neuf
10	dix	30	trente
11	onze	40	quarante
12	douze	50	cinquante
13	treize	60	soixante
14	quatorze	70	soixante-dix
15	quinze	71	soixante-et-onze
16	seize	72	soixante-douze
17	dix-sept	80	quatre-vingts
18	dix-huit	81	quatre-vingt-un
19	dix-neuf	90	quatre-vingt-dix
20	vingt	100	cent

30–39, 40–49 and 50–59 follow the same pattern as 20–29.

71–79 are like saying *sixty eleven*, *sixty twelve*, etc.

80 is literally *four twenties*. For 81–99, add 1–19 to quatre-vingt.

! There is an **s** on **quatre-vingts** for 80, but not for 81–99.

 More numbers

101 cent-un
200 deux-cents
205 deux-cent-cinq
750 sept-cent-cinquante
1.000 mille
1.000.000 un million

Percentages are expressed as pour cent:
dix pour cent 10%

Adding -aine to a number means *about*:
une dizaine de poires *about 10 pears*
une douzaine *a dozen*
un certain / grand nombre de *a certain / great number of*

In French you use a full stop or a space to indicate thousands. A comma (virgule) is used to represent a decimal point: 10,5% (*10.5%*)

  Ordinal numbers

1st	premier / première	1er (m) / 1re (f)
2nd	deuxième / second(e)	2ème
3rd	troisième	3ème
4th	quatrième	4ème
5th	cinquième	5ème
6th	sixième	6ème
7th	septième	7ème
8th	huitième	8ème
9th	neuvième	9ème
10th	dixième	10ème

Ordinal numbers agree with the noun, but only premier and second have a feminine form, for example la Première Guerre mondiale.

Second(e) is used when talking about the second item of two things only, whereas deuxième is used when talking about the second item in a longer list.

Ça coute cent-quatre-vingt-quinze euros.

 Practice   Grades 1–5

 You hear a radio report giving the results of a survey about leisure habits.

Listen to the recording and put a cross **✗** in each one of the **three** correct boxes.

		37%	63%	75%	84%
Example	Going on social networks	✗			
A	Going to the cinema				
B	Listening to the radio				
C	Meeting up with friends				
D	Shopping				
E	Surfing the net				
F	Playing sport				
G	Watching TV				

[3 marks]

 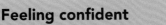

The French alphabet

You will need to be able to understand and say the letters of the alphabet in order to spell things out loud.

② About the French alphabet

French uses the same letters of the alphabet as English, but they are pronounced differently. Make sure you are able to recognise them when spoken, and that you know how to say them. You may need to be able to spell out:

- your name or a place name
- a web address
- your address or email address
- a common French acronym.

② How to say the French alphabet

A – ah	H – ash	O – oh	V – vay
B – bay	I – ee	P – pay	W – doobleh vay
C – say	J – jhee	Q – kuh	X – eeks
D – day	K – kah	R – air	Y – ee-grek
E – euh	L – ell	S – ess	Z – zed
F – eff	M – emm	T – tay	
G – jhay	N – enn	U – oo	

⑤ Common abbreviations

bac: baccalauréat (m) *school leaving exam*

CDI: centre de documentation et d'information (m) *resource centre*

CES: collège d'enseignement secondaire (m) *secondary school*

DOM: départements d'outre-mer (m pl) *French departments overseas*

EPS: éducation physique et sportive (f) *PE (physical education)*

HLM: habitation à loyer modéré (f) *council / social housing*

RN: route nationale (f) *main road*

SDF: sans domicile fixe (m) *homeless person*

SNCF: société nationale des chemins de fer français (f) *national rail service*

SVP: s'il vous plaît *please*

TGV: train à grande vitesse (m) *high-speed train*

TVA: taxe sur la valeur ajoutée (f) *VAT (value added tax)*

UE: Union européenne (f) *European Union*

VTT: vélo tout terrain (m) *mountain bike*

SAMU: service d'aide médicale d'urgence (f) *emergency medical services*

> Le SAMU is actually pronounced as a word, not as individual letters.

② Punctuation and symbols

You may need to know the following punctuation marks:

´ accent aigu (m)

` accent grave (m)

^ accent circonflexe (m)

¨ tréma (m)

ç c cédille (f)

- trait d'union (m)

' apostrophe (f)

. point (f)

, virgule (f)

@ arrobase (f)

_ tiret bas (m)

ABC majuscule

abc minuscule

⑤ Worked example | Grades 1–5

① Donne-moi ton adresse courriel.

💬 Adélaïde_Roussel@tricolore.fr

② Comment ça s'écrit?

💬 ah majuscule day miniscule euh accent aigu ell ah ee tréma day euh tiret bas air majuscule oh minuscule oo deux ess euh ell arrobase tricolore (comme le drapeau) point eff air

You can also use the link word **comme** when spelling something out, e.g. **A, comme Afrique**.

⑮ Practice | Grades 1–5

① While in France you hear some conversations. What are they about?

🎧 Listen to the recording and put a cross ✗ in each one of the **four** correct boxes.

Example	A high-speed train	✗
A	A bicycle	
B	Council / social housing	
C	Homeless people	
D	Resource centre	
E	Emergency services	
F	A school subject	
G	A main road	

[4 marks]

② Answer the following questions.

💬
- Comment t'appelles-tu?
- Comment ça s'écrit?
- Quelle est ton adresse?
- Et ton adresse mail?

 Made a start   Feeling confident   Exam ready

Dates

You need to know how to say the date, and talk about months and days to describe events or important occasions.

⑤ How to say the date

In French, the days of the week and the months of the year are all masculine, and are written with a lower case letter. You use cardinal numbers (deux, trois, quatre, cinq…) when talking about dates, except for the first of the month, which uses the ordinal number, premier.

Quelle est la date d'aujourd'hui / de ton anniversaire?

What is the date today / of your birthday?

(Aujourd'hui) c'est le douze janvier.

*(Today) it's **the 12th of January**.*

C'est le lundi premier juin.

*It's **Monday the first of June**.*

en juillet *in July*

Le Salon du Chocolat a lieu à Paris au mois d'octobre.

The Salon du Chocolat takes place in Paris during the month of October.

> When you say the day of the week in the date, **le** comes before the day, instead of the number.

⑤ Days and months

Les jours de la semaine – the days of the week

lundi	Monday	vendredi	Friday
mardi	Tuesday	samedi	Saturday
mercredi	Wednesday	dimanche	Sunday
jeudi	Thursday		

Les mois de l'année – the months of the year

janvier	January	juillet	July
février	February	août	August
mars	March	septembre	September
avril	April	octobre	October
mai	May	novembre	November
juin	June	décembre	December

février prochain / dernier *next / last February*

début / fin avril *at the beginning / end of April*

de mai à septembre *from May to September*

PAGE **102**

⑤ Worked example — Grades 1–5

1 Quand est-ce que tu travailles au supermarché?

💬 Je travaille le vendredi soir.

> For something that happens regularly on the same day of the week, you use **le**, e.g. **le vendredi** means *on Fridays*.

2 Quand vas-tu voir tes grands-parents?

💬 Je vais voir mes grands-parents dimanche prochain.

> **prochain** means *next*; **dimanche dernier** *last Sunday*.

3 Qu'est-ce que tu as le mardi matin au collège?

💬 Le mardi matin, j'ai maths et géo.

> To talk about a particular time of day, use **le** + day of the week + time of day, e.g. **le mardi matin / après-midi / soir** *Tuesday morning / afternoon / evening*.

⑤ How to say the year

There are several ways to say the year in French:

La Révolution française a eu lieu en **mille sept cent quatre-vingt-neuf / dix-sept cent quatre-vingt-neuf**.

The French revolution took place in 1789.

Mon grand-père est mort en **mille neuf cent quatre-vingt-dix-neuf / dix-neuf cent quatre-vingt-dix-neuf**.

My grandfather died in 1999.

Ma petite sœur est née en **deux mille treize**. *My little sister was born in 2013.*

Pendant **les années soixante**, les femmes portaient des jupes courtes.

In the sixties women wore short skirts.

⑤ Practice — Grades 1–5

🎧 You hear some information about various French festivals on the radio.

Listen to the recording and complete the sentences. Use the correct date from the box.

1st March	21st April	1st May	17th May
28th May	21st June	28th March	8th December

(8th December struck through)

Example: The fête des Lumières begins on
 8th December .

(a) The last day of the Cannes Film festival is
 _____ .

(b) The fête du citron finishes on _____ .

(c) The fête de la musique is _____ .

[3 marks]

Telling the time

You should be familiar with both the 12-hour and 24-hour clock.

(5) About telling the time

You will need to be able to tell the time in order to understand and talk about:

- arrivals and departures

  Le train part à neuf heures. *The train leaves at nine o'clock.*

  Ma grand-mère arrive à trois heures et demie.

  My grandmother arrives / is arriving at half past three.

- the start and finish of an event

  Les cours commencent à neuf heures moins le quart.

  Lessons begin at a quarter to nine.

  Le concert a fini à neuf heures vingt. *The concert finished at twenty past nine.*

- opening and closing times

  Le musée ouvre à dix heures. *The museum opens at ten o'clock.*

  Les magasins ferment à six heures du soir. *The shops close at six o'clock.*

- a period of time

  J'ai travaillé de huit heures à quatre heures. *I worked from 8 a.m. to 4 p.m.*

The question for most of these situations would begin with À quelle heure...? *At what time...?*

(10) Worked example   Grades 1–9

 Parle-moi de ta journée scolaire.

Ma journée scolaire commence le matin à huit heures et demie quand j'arrive au collège. Normalement, j'ai du temps pour bavarder un peu avec mes copains pendant un quart d'heure parce que le premier cours ne commence qu'à neuf heures moins le quart, mais aujourd'hui, le bus était en retard et je n'ai pas eu le temps. J'ai cours toute la matinée, mais il y a une récréation qui dure vingt minutes, de dix heures cinquante à onze heures dix. Après le déjeuner, j'ai encore deux cours avant la fin de la journée.

Try to use a variety of negative expressions, not just ne...pas. Ne...que means *only*.

Relative pronouns like qui, que and dont are another useful way to show that you can use a variety of structures.

 GRAMMAR LINK PAGE 83

(10) Quelle heure est-il?   A-Z

In French you say the hour first and then the minutes.

7.00 Il est sept heures.

7.10 Il est sept heures dix.

7.15 Il est sept heures quinze **or** et quart.

7.30 Il est sept heures trente **or** et demie.

7.35 Il est sept heures trente-cinq **or** il est huit heures moins vingt-cinq.

7.45 Il est sept heures quarante-cinq **or** il est huit heures moins le quart.

VOCABULARY LINK PAGE 102

These are statements about what the time is in answer to the question: Quelle heure est-il? *What time is it?*

There is no s on heures for the time with une: à une heure cinq.

There is no e on demi with midday (midi) and midnight (minuit): il est midi / minuit et demi.

The 24-hour clock is often used in France. Make sure you know the equivalent 12-hour clock time.

1	2	3	4	5	6	7	8	9	10	11	12
13	14	15	16	17	18	19	20	21	22	23	24

You can add du matin, de l'après-midi or du soir (*in the morning, afternoon, evening*) to the end of a 12-hour clock phrase to make it clear what time of day you are describing.

Je fais de la natation à six heures du soir (or à dix-huit heures). *I go swimming at six in the evening.*

The best answers will use conjunctions like quand to join sentences and make them more complex.

You must say pendant (*during*) in time expressions like this, not pour (*for*) which should only be used when talking about the future.

(5) Practice   Grades 1–5

🎧 Listen to the recording and answer the following questions **in English**.

(a) When does the train arrive?

(b) At what time does the exhibition close?

(c) When does the concert start?

(d) When does your friend go to bed?   **[4 marks]**

 Made a start   Feeling confident   Exam ready

Greetings

There are many ways of greeting people in French, depending on the time of day or year, the occasion and the person to whom you are speaking.

⏱ 10 Forms of address

There are formal and informal ways of greeting and addressing people. You should use the informal form **tu** when talking to someone your own age, a friend, a child or a family member. Use the formal **vous** when talking to an adult or someone you do not know very well. You should also use **vous** when talking to more than one person. You can add **monsieur** or **madame** to your greeting to make it even more polite.

You must also use the appropriate possessive adjective and emphatic pronoun:

Comment s'appelle votre mari / ton frère / ta sœur?
What is your husband / brother / sister called?

Ça va? *How are you?*

Oui, et toi / vous? *Fine, and you?*

Je te / vous présente mon père / ma mère / mes parents.
I'd like to introduce you to my father / mother / parents.

> This question uses the stressed pronoun of the informal **tu** and formal **vous.** See page 82.

Exam focus
You will need to read the instructions carefully in your role play exam and use the correct form of address for the situation.

⏱ 5 Worked example

 Listen to the following extracts from conversations. Write **F** for the use of a formal form of address, and **I** for an informal use.

1	F
2	I
3	I
4	F
5	I

1. - Mademoiselle, je vous présente ma femme.
   - Enchantée, madame.
2. Salut, Gaëlle! Quoi de neuf?
3. Allô, c'est toi, Marc?
4. Bonjour madame, comment allez-vous?
5. Coucou Lyse, ça va?

This is what you say when answering the phone. You don't use **Allô** as a general greeting though, or when you are with someone in person, in which case you would say **Salut** or **Bonjour**.

⏱ 10 Vocabulary

Greetings for certain occasions
bon appétit *enjoy your meal*
bon voyage *have a safe journey*
bon anniversaire *happy birthday*
bonne année *Happy New Year*
bonne chance *good luck*
bonnes vacances *have a good holiday*
Joyeux Noël *Happy Christmas*
Joyeuses Pâques *Happy Easter*

Saying goodbye
For goodbyes in person or on the phone you can use:
- Au revoir *Goodbye*
- À bientôt *See you soon*
- À demain *See you tomorrow!*
- À tout à l'heure *See you later*

Writing a letter or email
For informal letters and emails, you can start with:
- Cher Paul / Chère Christine *Dear Paul / Christine*
- Salut à tous! *Hi everyone*

For formal letters and emails you should start with:
- Monsieur / Madame *Dear Sir / Madam*
- Messieurs / Mesdames *Dear Sirs / Madams*

For informal letters and emails, you can end with:
- Amicalement *best wishes* (used between friends)

For formal letters and emails, you should use:
- Cordialement *regards*
- Veuillez agréer, Monsieur / Madame, l'expression de mes sentiments distingués.
  Yours sincerely / faithfully

⏱ 5 Practice — Grades 1–5

 While in France you overhear snippets of conversations. Complete the sentences. Use the correct word or phrase from the box.

> Christmas   New Year   at an airport
> Happy Birthday   good night   good morning
> at a restaurant   in a hospital

Example: This conversation takes place __at an airport__ .

(a) This person is _____ .

(b) This is at _____ .

(c) This person is saying _____ . **[3 marks]**

 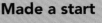 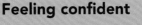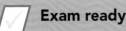

BBC

Opinions

You will need to be able to recognise points of view, express your own opinions and give reasons for them.

⑤ Vocabulary
 A–Z

Introducing opinions
je crois que *I believe that*
je pense que *I think that*
je trouve que *I think / find that*
à mon avis *in my opinion*
d'après moi / lui *in my / his opinion*
pour moi *for me*
personnellement *personally*

> Adverbs like **totalement** *(totally)* or **tout à fait** *(completely)* can add weight to an opinion.

 GRAMMAR LINK PAGE 82

Expressing agreement and disagreement
je suis d'accord *I agree*
je ne suis pas d'accord *I don't agree*
moi aussi / moi non plus *me too / me neither*

> When expressing your opinion, you should aim to back it up with a reason using *because* (**parce que** or **car**) or expand on your answer using expressions like **cependant** (however).

Expressing emotions
ça m'énerve *that gets on my nerves*
ça me fait rire *that makes me laugh*
ça me rend triste *that makes me sad*
ça me plaît *I like it*
ça m'est égal *that's all the same to me*
ça ne me dit rien *that doesn't interest / appeal to me*
ça suffit *that's enough*
ce n'est pas la peine *it's not worth it*

VOCABULARY LINK PAGE 102

Expressing the opposite point of view
par contre / en revanche / d'un autre côté *on the other hand*
au contraire *on the contrary*
pourtant *however*

On dit qu'il y a trop d'ordures, pourtant on ne recycle pas assez. *They / People say there is too much rubbish, however we don't recycle enough.*

② Expressing likes and dislikes

Give an opinion by using these expressions which are followed by a noun or verb in the infinitive.

j'aime *I like*　　　　je déteste *I hate*
je n'aime pas *I don't like*　　je préfère *I prefer*

J'aime jouer au football. Je déteste aller chez le dentiste.

⑩ Worked example　　Grades 1–9

✏ Write a paragraph in response to this bullet point.
• films – opinions

À mon avis, les films de science-fiction ne sont pas du tout réalistes. Cependant, ils sont souvent très passionnants et divertissants et je peux admirer les effets spéciaux. Par contre, je déteste absolument les films d'horreur parce qu'ils me font peur.

> Learn plenty of useful adjectives like **passionnant** *(exciting)* and **divertissant** *(amusing)* to express positive opinions. Remember to make adjectives agree.

> Use **À mon avis** to introduce your opinion.

⑩ Practice　　Grades 4–5

👓 Your French friend has shown you the following messages about sport.

> **@noah_K** On dit que le tir à l'arc est un sport très ennuyeux mais je ne suis pas d'accord. Je trouve ça absolument fascinant.

> **@karim** J'adore la boxe parce que les boxeurs sont très forts, mais c'est un sport tout de même dangereux.

> **@selim_O** Je ne suis pas d'accord avec les gens qui disent que le cricket est nul. À mon avis, c'est un sport totalement passionnant.

> **@Loulou** Nager dans les lignes d'eau ne me dit rien. C'est tout à fait monotone!

Who says what about sport? Write either **Noah**, **Karim**, **Selim** and **Loulou**. You can use each person more than once.

Example: ____Karim____ likes a dangerous sport.

(a) _____ is not interested in a sport that involves repetitive actions.

(b) _____ likes a team sport that some people find boring.

(c) _____ does not share other people's views on archery.

(d) _____ likes a sport that involves strong people.

(e) _____ has a negative view of swimming.

[5 marks]

Asking questions

You will have to ask questions during the role play and the general conversation in your speaking exam.

(5) How to ask a question

You will have to be able to ask questions about many topics and understand any questions you are asked.

There are several ways of asking a question:

1 Using Est-ce que...?

This turns a statement into a question.
Il est travailleur. *He is hard-working.*
Est-ce qu'il est travailleur? *Is he hard-working?*

2 You can combine est-ce que with a question word.

Pourquoi est-ce que tu ne t'entends pas avec ton frère? *Why don't you get on with your brother?*

3 You can invert the subject and the verb and use a hyphen between them.

Peux-tu m'aider? *Can you help me?*

Comment vas-tu au collège? *How do you get to school?*

> To avoid two vowel sounds appearing next to each other, add a **t** with hyphens to the verb and subject inversion to make pronunciation easier.
> **Pourquoi a-t-elle…?** *Why has she…?*

4 You can use intonation to make a statement sound like a question; just make your voice go up at the end of the sentence.

Il est travailleur? *Is he hard-working?*

(10) Worked example — Grades 1–9

💬 Look at the following question prompts from a role play. What question(s) could you ask?

1 ? Aller en ville – transport *(arranging to meet a friend)*

Comment est-ce qu'on va en ville (ce soir)? / On se retrouve à l'arrêt de bus?

2 ? Aller en ville – transport *(staying at a hotel on the outskirts of a town)*

Comment est-ce qu'on peut aller en ville? / Est-ce qu'il y a un bus pour aller en ville?

(2) Exam focus

Your question must have a verb in it to score full marks. Don't forget that you will need to ask your teacher a question in the general conversation too. Remember to use **vous** when addressing them. In the role play you may need to use **tu**, depending on the context.

(2) Question words

qui *who*
qu'est-ce que *what*
qu'est-ce qui *what*
quand *when*
où *where*
pourquoi *why*
comment *how*
combien *how much / how many*
quel(s), quelle(s) *which*

> In **qu'est-ce que**, **que** is used for the **object** in a question:
>
> Qu'est-ce que tu fais? *What are you doing?*
>
> In **qu'est-ce qui**, **qui** is used for the **subject** in a question:
>
> Qu'est-ce qui manque? *What is missing?*

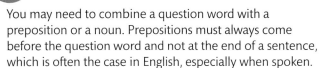

PAGE **103**

(5) Using prepositions and nouns

You may need to combine a question word with a preposition or a noun. Prepositions must always come before the question word and not at the end of a sentence, which is often the case in English, especially when spoken.

Avec qui vas-tu en vacances? *With whom are you going on holiday? / Who are you going on holiday with?*

Dans quelle région est-ce que tu vas passer tes vacances? *In which region are you going to spend your holiday? / Which region are you going to spend your holiday in?*

À quelle heure est-ce qu'on va se retrouver? *At what time are we going to meet? / What time are we going to meet at?*

This task requires you to ask *how* you get into town, but your answer must fit the context.

Here, **on** has the sense of *we – How shall we get into town?*

Here, **on** has a broader meaning – *How can one / you get into town?*

Asking whether there is a bus is an alternative way of completing the task.

(10) Practice — Grades 1–9

💬 What questions could you ask for the following scenarios?

- ? Heure du concert (at a box office)
- ? Végétarien (in a restaurant with the waiter)
- ? Projets pour les vacances (talking to a friend)
- ? Tarifs pour les étudiants (museum entry)

Describing people

You need to be able to give personal information, describe appearances and personalities, and talk about your role models.

⑤ Describing appearance

You will need to use the verbs avoir, être and porter (*to wear*) to describe your own or someone else's appearance and personality. This is also an opportunity to show that you know a range of adjectives and how to use them.

VOCABULARY LINK **PAGE 106**

Je suis assez mince et de taille moyenne. J'ai les cheveux roux, longs et ondulés, et les yeux bleus. J'ai des taches de rousseur sur le visage. Je ne porte pas de lunettes. Je ressemble un peu à ma mère mais elle est plus petite et a les cheveux très bouclés. Ma meilleure amie est jolie et grande. Elle porte des vêtements cool et elle est très gentille.

I am quite slim and medium height. I have long red wavy hair and blue eyes. I've got freckles on my face. I don't wear glasses. I look a bit like my mother but she is smaller and has very curly hair. My best friend is pretty and tall. She wears cool clothes and is very kind.

⑤ Giving personal information

In a role play task you may be asked for some other personal details:

Quel âge as-tu / avez-vous? *How old are you?*

J'ai quinze ans, mais dans un mois, j'aurai seize ans. *I am fifteen, but in a month's time I will be sixteen.*

Quelle est ta / votre date de naissance? *What is your date of birth?*

Je suis né(e) le 22 avril 2001 (deux mille un). *I was born on April 22nd 2001.*

Tu es / Vous êtes de quelle nationalité? *What is your nationality?*

VOCABULARY LINK **PAGE 109**

Je suis anglais(e). *I am English.*

⑩ Worked example — Grades 4–5

 Read Jacob's email to his new pen pal.

> Salut, je m'appelle Jacob. J'ai les cheveux blonds et les yeux bleus. Je suis grand et très musclé et j'adore jouer au foot et aller à la salle de gym. Malgré mon apparence, je suis parfois un peu timide et je n'aime pas parler avec les gens que je ne connais pas. Cependant, avec mes amis, je suis très bavard.

What do you learn about Jacob in the email?

Put a cross **✗** next to each one of the **two** correct statements.

A Jacob thinks that people might get the wrong impression about his character from his appearance. **✗**

B Jacob says he feels comfortable talking to people he hasn't met before. ☐

C Jacob has green eyes. ☐

D Jacob enjoys being active. **✗**

⑤ Talking about personality

Quelles sont tes / leurs qualités personnelles? *What are your / their personal qualities?*

Je suis gentil(le) et patient(e). *I am **kind** and **patient**.*

Il / Elle est égoïste et jaloux / jalouse. *He / she is **selfish** and **jealous**.*

GRAMMAR LINK **PAGE 75**

Les gens qui m'inspirent sont les gens qui font toujours de leur mieux. *The people who inspire me are the ones who always do their best.*

> You can use adjectives that describe positive personal qualities to talk about your role model.

> Malgré means *in spite of*. Jacob says that his character is different from what people might expect from his appearance.

> Jacob says he doesn't like talking to people he doesn't know. Je n'aime pas parler avec les gens que je ne connais pas. Use connaître to talk about knowing a person or place and savoir to talk about knowing how to do something.

⑩ Practice — Grades 4–5

🎧 Your exchange partner is talking to some friends about what they look for in their ideal partner. What qualities do they look for? Listen to the recording and put a cross **✗** in each one of the **three** correct boxes.

		Léo	Adèle	Farouk
Example	sense of humour	✗		
A	generosity			
B	good physique			
C	kindness			
D	patience			
E	talkative			
F	shyness			

[3 marks]

Family

You will need to be able to talk about your family, and any activities you do together, as well as family life in general.

⑤ Introducing your family ✓

To talk about your family, you will need to use possessive adjectives and the verbs avoir and être.

GRAMMAR LINK PAGE 77

Voici ma **famille**. Mes **parents** sont divorcés alors me voilà avec ma **mère** devant mon **beau-père**. Il a un **fils** avec ma mère, mon **demi-frère**, et j'ai aussi une **sœur cadette**.

*This is my **family**. My **parents** are divorced so you can see me with my **mother** in front of my **stepfather**. He has a **son** with my mother, my **half-brother**, and I also have a **younger sister**.*

⑩ Worked example   Grades 4–9 ✓

💬 Answer the following question.

Qu'est-ce que tu as fait avec ta famille le week-end dernier?

Le week-end dernier, nous sommes allés voir mes grands-parents parce que c'était l'anniversaire de ma grand-mère. Elle a maintenant soixante-dix ans. Elle est un modèle pour moi parce qu'elle est toujours très active. Nous étions douze personnes à la fête car nos cousins étaient venus aussi. Le déjeuner était vraiment excellent et après, nous avons chanté «Joyeux anniversaire!» Nous nous sommes tous bien amusés. J'adore passer du temps en famille.

⑤ Aiming higher ⬆ ✓

Look for opportunities to extend your sentences by using a relative clause or the pluperfect tense.

Nous avons mangé un excellent repas que ma grand-mère avait préparé. *We ate an excellent meal that my grandmother had prepared.*

You could also use après avoir + past participle

Après avoir mangé un excellent repas, nous avons chanté... *After eating an excellent meal, we sang...*

② Family life   A–Z ✓

famille monoparentale (f) *single-parent family*
belle-mère (f) *stepmother*; beau-père (m) *stepfather*
adopté(e) *adopted*
aîné(e) *elder / older*; ma sœur aînée *my older sister*
cadet(te) *younger*; mon frère cadet *my younger brother*
célibataire *single*
séparé(e) *separated*
divorcé(e) *divorced*
jumeau (m) / jumelle (f) *twin*
garder les enfants *to look after the children*
Je suis fils / fille unique. *I'm an only child.*
famille nombreuse (f) *large family*
modèle (m) *role model*

VOCABULARY LINK PAGE 106

Exam focus 📌

Use a variety of verbs. In the Worked example answer there are four examples of verbs in the perfect tense; each is different and they include verbs conjugated with avoir and être as well as a reflexive verb: Nous nous sommes tous bien amusés. The imperfect and present tenses are also used.

Listen out for a time marker in a question; you can use it to start your answer, giving you a bit of thinking time.

You could extend this sentence to give a reason, e.g. parce que nous nous entendons tous très bien (*because we all get on well*).

⑩ Practice   Grades 4–9 ✓

✏️ Un magazine français cherche des articles sur la vie familiale en Angleterre.

Écrivez un article sur votre vie familiale pour intéresser les lecteurs.

Vous **devez** faire référence aux points suivants:

* activités typiques en famille
* une fête familiale récente
* les avantages et désavantages d'une famille nombreuse
* votre famille idéale dans l'avenir

Justifiez vos idées et vos opinions.

Écrivez 130–150 mots environ **en français**.   **[28 marks]**

 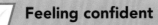

Friends and relationships

Talk about relationships between you, your friends and family, and say how you feel about different people.

⑤ What you need to know

To talk about relationships you should know how to:

- Use reflexive verbs:

  Je m'entends bien avec mes parents.

  I get on well with my parents.

   GRAMMAR LINK PAGE **95**

- Give a reason for a good / bad relationship:

  Ils me permettent de sortir.

  They let me go out.

  Je dois faire trop de ménage.

  I have to do too much housework.

- Use adjectives to describe personality types:

  Il / elle est paresseux(euse) / égoïste / têtu(e) / généreux(euse) / travailleur(euse).

  He / she is lazy / selfish / stubborn / generous / hard-working.

- Express your opinions and feelings:

  Ce n'est pas juste! It's not fair!

See page 6 for more on opinions.

② Vocabulary

s'amuser *to have fun*
s'entendre avec *to get on with*
s'énerver *to get annoyed*
se disputer avec *to argue with*
se fâcher contre *to get angry with*
se fâcher avec *to fall out with*
se fier à *to trust*
s'inquiéter (au sujet de) *to worry (about)*
se mettre en colère *to get angry*
se moquer de *to make fun of*
conflit (m) *conflict, argument*
dispute (f) *argument*
de mauvaise humeur *in a bad mood*
gâter *to spoil*
critiquer *to criticise*
faire des remarques sur *to comment on*
déranger *to disturb*

VOCABULARY LINK PAGE **106**

⑩ Worked example Grades 4–9

✏ Décrivez votre vie de famille.

> The verbs and adjectives all agree with their subjects.

Ma vie de famille est extrêmement difficile parce que je ne m'entends pas bien avec mes parents. Ils sont trop sévères car je ne peux pas sortir le soir avec mes copains. Par conséquent, je me dispute souvent avec eux. Hier, je me suis aussi fâché(e) avec mon petit frère parce qu'il a refusé de promener le chien. Je pense qu'il est vraiment paresseux. À mon avis, mes parents le gâtent trop.

Show you know how to use direct object pronouns. Similarly, you could say of your parents: **je les trouve agaçants / gentils** *I find <u>them</u> annoying / kind.*

This extract from a longer answer contains a good variety of vocabulary and shows that you can express an opinion and give reasons for it. It uses both present and perfect tenses with time phrases and conjunctions.

⑩ Practice Grades 4–9

👓 Read Marc and Dominique's comments about friendship.

> **Marc:** On se dispute de temps en temps, car mes copains pensent que je passe trop de temps à la maison – ce qui n'est pas du tout vrai. Je me dispute quelquefois avec mon meilleur ami à l'école parce qu'il est très bavard et qu'il me dérange quand je veux travailler.

> **Dominique:** Je m'entends bien avec mes amies et elles ont confiance en moi. Elles savent que je suis travailleuse et que je ne veux pas sortir avec elles tous les soirs, alors elles me laissent faire mes devoirs tranquillement. Cependant, elles m'énervent parfois quand elles font des remarques sur ce que je porte.

Answer the following questions **in English**.

(a) Why do Marc and his friends not get on from time to time?

(b) In what way does Marc's best friend sometimes annoy him?

(c) What do Dominique's friends accept about her?

(d) When does she get annoyed with her friends?

[4 marks]

Made a start ☑ Feeling confident ☑ Exam ready

When I was younger

You should be able to talk about your childhood and compare it with the present.

 Talking about your childhood

To talk about when you were younger you should use the imperfect tense to:

- describe yourself: **Quand j'avais** six ans, j'**étais** très timide et j'**avais** les cheveux longs. *When I **was** six I **was** very shy and **had** long hair.*
- make comparisons: Mon ancienne école **était** plus petite que mon école actuelle. *My old school **was** smaller than my school now.*
- express likes and dislikes: À l'âge de sept ans, je **détestais** les bananes. *At the age of seven, I **hated** bananas.*
- say what you could and couldn't do: Je **ne pouvais pas** sortir seul. *I **couldn't** go out on my own.*

You may not know what **mouches** (f) **mortes** (*dead flies*) are, but you could work it out using the context and your knowledge of key verbs (**mourir / mort** *to die / dead*).

François uses the noun **voisin(e)** *(neighbour)* as an adjective – *neighbouring farm* (**ferme** (f)).

François watched (**je la regardais**) his mother, rather than helped her.

You can infer that François and his family lived in the countryside from the reference to the farm.

François mentions l'**escalier** *(stairs)* du **grenier** *(attic)* so the house must have more than one storey.

 Vocabulary

âge (m) *age*
bébé (m) *baby*
enfant (m / f) *child*
enfance (f) *childhood*
école (f) **primaire** *primary school*
jouet (m) *toy*
liberté (f) *freedom*
naissance (f) *birth*
peluche (f) *soft toy*
poupée (f) *doll*
jouer à cache-cache *to play hide and seek*
seul(e) *alone*
adolescent(e) (m / f) *teenager*
adulte (m / f) *adult*

 Worked example **Grades 4–9**

👓 *Le Grand Meaulnes* by Alain-Fournier

Read the extract. François is describing how he used to spend his time after school.

> Quand il faisait toujours jour je restais au fond de la mairie, enfermé dans le cabinet des archives plein de mouches mortes, et je lisais assis sur une vieille chaise, à côté d'une fenêtre qui donnait sur le jardin.
>
> Lorsqu'il faisait noir, et les chiens de la ferme voisine commençaient à hurler et que la fenêtre de notre petite cuisine s'illuminait, je rentrais enfin. Ma mère avait commencé de préparer le repas. Je montais trois marches de l'escalier du grenier; je m'asseyais sans rien dire et, la tête appuyée aux barreaux froids de la rampe, je la regardais allumer son feu dans l'étroite cuisine où vacillait la flamme d'une bougie.

Put a cross ✗ in the correct box.

1 François used to spend his time after school…

✗	A	reading
	B	playing in the garden
	C	killing flies
	D	walking his dog

2 François also spent much of his time…

	A	with his neighbour
	B	helping his mother in the kitchen
✗	C	alone
	D	with his pets

3 François and his family used to live…

	A	in a house with a big kitchen
✗	B	in the countryside
	C	next to a library
	D	in a single storey house

 Practice

💬 Answer the following questions.

- Qu'est-ce que tu aimais faire quand tu étais petit(e)?
- Comment allais-tu à l'école à l'âge de sept ans?
- Qu'est-ce que tu rêvais de faire quand tu étais petit(e)?
- Qu'est-ce que tu ne pouvais pas faire quand tu avais cinq ans?

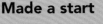

Food

When you talk about food, you need to be able to say what you like and dislike, and to talk about healthy eating habits.

⑤ Talking about food

When you talk about food you will need to be able to use the following :

- the partitive article:

Je mange **des** céréales le matin et **du** pain le soir.

> These words aren't used in English here, but they must be used in French.

- the correct gender of food-related nouns:
  le fromage, la viande, une banane
- adverbs of frequency and negative expressions:
  Je mange **très rarement** de la viande. *I rarely eat meat.*
  Je **ne** mange **jamais** de biscuits. *I never eat biscuits.*
- expressions of liking and disliking, including reasons:
  Je n'aime pas manger de frites parce qu'elles contiennent trop de matières grasses. *I don't like eating chips because they contain too much fat.*

GRAMMAR LINK PAGE 73

⑩ Worked example — Grades 4–9

1 Qu'est-ce que tu aimes manger? C'est bon ou mauvais pour la santé?

J'aime manger des cochonneries, mais je sais qu'elles sont mauvaises pour la santé parce qu'elles contiennent trop de sucre et de matières grasses.

2 Est-ce que tu manges équilibré?

Normalement, j'ai une alimentation très équilibrée, c'est-à-dire que chaque jour, je mange au moins cinq portions de fruits et de légumes, deux portions de produits laitiers et que je ne mange pas trop de viande. Cependant, je suis sorti(e) hier avec des copains et on a mangé des hamburgers et des frites.

C'est-à-dire means *that is to say* and is another way of explaining and developing your answer.

Using **cependant** (*however*) enables you to introduce a different tense into your answer.

② Vocabulary A–Z

alimentation (f) **équilibrée / saine** *balanced / healthy diet*

cochonneries (f pl) *junk food*

féculent (m) *carbohydrate / starchy food*

matières grasses (f pl) *fat*

plat à emporter (m) *ready meal*

protéine (f) *protein*

produit laitier (m) *dairy product*

restauration rapide (f) *fast food*

sucreries (f pl) *sweet things*

vitamine (f) *vitamin*

cela contient beaucoup de vitamines *that contains a lot of vitamins*

consommer *to eat*

contenir *to contain*

éviter *to avoid*

VOCABULARY LINK PAGE 108

Talking about quantities

verre (m) **de / (d'eau)** *a glass of (water)*

portion (f) **de** *a portion of*

10 grammes (m) **de** *10 grams of*

tranche (f) **de** *a slice of*

cuillerée (f) **de** *a spoonful*

> **Mais je sais** means *but I know* and is a useful way of extending your answer and adding more detail.

⑩ Practice — Grades 1–5

🎧 Listen to the advice given by a dietician. Complete the sentences. Use the correct word or number from the box.

50	75	100	125	150	200	~~bread~~
carrots	fish	fruit	meat	peas	potatoes	

Example: For breakfast you can eat 50 grams of ___bread___ .

(a) For lunch you can eat _____ grams of meat or _____ grams of fish.

(b) Apart from _____ you should eat _____ grams of vegetables.

(c) In the evening you should limit yourself to _____ grams of _____

[6 marks]

Meals

You need to be able to talk about meals and to say what your favourite meal is and why.

⑤ Talking about meals

Talking about meals gives you the opportunity to use different tenses, as well as likes and dislikes.

Normalement, au petit déjeuner, je mange du pain.
*I normally **eat** bread for breakfast.*

Pour le goûter, j'ai mangé une pomme.
*For an afternoon snack, **I ate** an apple.*

Dimanche prochain, on mangera chez mes grands-parents.
***We'll be eating** at my grandparents' house next Sunday.*

Je préfère le goûter parce que j'aime les aliments sucrés.
I prefer afternoon snacks because I like sweet food.

⑩ Worked example | Grades 1–5

✎ Tu vas participer à un échange scolaire. Tu envoies cette photo à ton partenaire français(e).

Écris une description de la photo **et** exprime ton opinion sur les repas.

Écris 20–30 mots environ **en français**.

Me voici avec ma famille dans la cuisine.
Le petit déjeuner est mon repas préféré et nous mangeons toujours du pain et des croissants.
Je pense que c'est un repas sain parce qu'on boit du jus d'orange.

Use words like **parce que** and **et** to link together your description and ideas.

The verbs in the answer above are all different and are a mix of the **nous**, **je** and **on** forms. This shows that you know how to conjugate verbs in different forms.

Exam focus 📌
You must express your opinion in the photo task on the Foundation paper.

② Vocabulary | A–Z

aliment (m) *food*
petit déjeuner (m) *breakfast*
déjeuner (m) *lunch*
goûter (m) *(afternoon) snack*
casse-croûte (m) *snack*
dîner (m) *dinner*
Au dîner, on mange... *For dinner, we eat...*
goût (m) *taste*
boire *to drink*
manger *to eat*
déguster *to savour*
faire la cuisine *to cook*
préparer *to prepare*
épicé *spicy*
piquant *spicy*
sucré *sweet*
salé *salty / savoury*
savoureux *delicious / tasty*

VOCABULARY LINK
PAGE 108

⑤ Aiming higher ⬆

- Include more complex structures such as **après avoir / être** + past participle.
  Après avoir mangé cet énorme repas, je voulais m'endormir.
  After eating that enormous meal, I wanted to go to sleep.

- Use expressions such as **être en train de** *to be (in the process of) doing something*:
  Nous sommes en train de prendre le petit déjeuner. *We are eating / We are in the process of eating breakfast.*

- Show you know about past participle agreements with a preceding direct object:
  On a mangé les pommes que j'avais achetées au marché. *We ate the apples that I had bought at the market.*

⑩ Practice | Grades 1–9

💬 Answer the following questions.

- Quel est ton repas préféré? Pourquoi?
- Est-ce qu'il est important de bien manger au petit déjeuner?
- Quel repas est le plus important, à ton avis? Pourquoi?

Shopping

To talk about shopping, you should be able to describe the product, as well as the facilities where you live and whether or not you shop online.

 Buying things

Use adjectives, including demonstrative adjectives, when talking about things you want to buy:

Je voudrais acheter / échanger **ce** pull vert, **cette** chemise blanche et **ces** chaussettes noires.
*I would like to buy / exchange **this** green jumper, **this** white shirt and **these** black socks.*

Use intensifiers when giving your opinion:

Il / elle est **trop** / **assez** grand(e) / petit(e) / cher / chère. *It's **too** / **quite** big / small / expensive.*

GRAMMAR LINK
PAGE
80

Il est **trop** grand!

 Vocabulary A–Z

cadeau (m) *present*
caisse (f) *till*
carte (f) bancaire *bank card*
chercher *to look for*
compte (m) *account*
dépenser *to spend money*
échanger *to exchange*
économiser *to save*
fermer *to close*
livraison (f) gratuite *free delivery*

mode (f) *fashion*
moyen (m) de paiement *means of payment*
offrir *to offer*
ouvrir *to open*
panier (m) *basket*
prix (m) *price*
portefeuille (m) *wallet*
porte-monnaie (m) *purse*
réduire *to reduce*
réduit *reduced*

retourner *to return*
soldes (m pl) *sale;* en solde *in the sales*
vendeur (m) / vendeuse (f) *shop assistant*
vitrine (f) *shop window*
vos commandes (f) *your orders*
bon marché *cheap*
cher / chère *expensive*
démodé *old-fashioned*

VOCABULARY LINK
PAGE
110

 Worked example Grades 1–5

You can talk about any clothes item.

1 Vous parlez avec un(e) vendeur(euse) dans une boutique de mode.

1. Vêtement désiré
2. Description du vêtement (**deux** détails)
3. ? essayer
4. !
5. Moyen de paiement

You could mention a different colour, size or style.

You might ask Est-ce que je peux l'essayer?

1. Je cherche un pull

2. Je voudrais un pull bleu de taille moyenne.

3. Où est la cabine d'essayage?

4. Il est très beau. Je le prends.

5. Je paie par carte bancaire.

In your preparation time, think about what the unpredictable question might be. This answers the question Comment est-ce que vous le trouvez? You could also express a negative opinion, such as Il est trop grand.

You could also say je paie en espèces *(with cash)*

2 Answer the following question.

Est-ce que tu aimes faire du lèche-vitrines?

J'adore la mode mais je n'ai pas beaucoup d'argent, alors j'aime faire du lèche-vitrines avec mes copains. Normalement, nous allons en ville le week-end. Samedi dernier, nous avons vu de très beaux vêtements dans les grands magasins et les boutiques indépendantes.

 Practice Grades 4–9

You hear a discussion about online shopping.

Answer the following questions **in English**.

(a) What is the main advantage of shopping online? **[1 mark]**

(b) What does the speaker see as a disadvantage? **[2 marks]**

  Made a start **Feeling confident** **Exam ready**

Social media

You should be confident in talking about using social media and the advantages and disadvantages of using it.

⑤ Using social media

Use the verb pouvoir to say what you can do with social media.

GRAMMAR LINK PAGE 87

- Je **peux** rester en contact avec ma famille en utilisant les réseaux sociaux. *I can stay in contact with my family by using social networks.*
- On **peut** tchatter et discuter de n'importe quoi. *You can chat and discuss anything.*
- C'est un outil utile pour les entreprises qui **peuvent** informer leurs clients sur leurs produits. *It's a useful tool for businesses who can inform their customers about their products.*

② Vocabulary A–Z

avantage (m) *advantage;* inconvénient (m) *disadvantage*
dangereux *dangerous*
face à face *face to face*
forum (m) *chat room*
mettre en ligne *to upload*
outil (m) *tool*
partager des photos *to share photos*
passer du temps *to spend time*
réseau social (m) (pl réseaux sociaux) *social network*
rester en contact *to stay in contact*
site internet / web (m) *website*
télécharger *to download*
utiliser *to use*

VOCABULARY LINK PAGE 109

⑩ Worked example Grades 1–5

1 Quand vas-tu sur des réseaux sociaux?

💬 Je vais tous les jours sur les réseaux sociaux, du matin au soir, tout le temps, même en cours. J'y suis tout à fait accro!

2 Quels réseaux sociaux est-ce que tu préfères? Pourquoi?

💬 Je préfère les réseaux sociaux où on peut mettre des photos en ligne, car je pense que c'est génial de voir ce que font mes amis.

You could also introduce a perfect tense here: ce que mes amis ont fait.

Use the pronoun y to say *I am addicted* **to them**.

⑤ Aiming higher ⬆

Use the following expressions to present an argument:

d'une part ... d'autre part *on the one hand ... on the other hand*

en revanche *on the other hand*

cependant; pourtant *however*

⑩ Practice Grades 7–9

🎧 Ton amie française et ses copains parlent des réseaux sociaux. Que pensent-ils?

Mets une croix ✗ dans les **trois** cases correctes.

[3 marks]

		Laurent	Aysha	Albert
Exemple	Parfois on passe tellement de temps dans le monde virtuel qu'on oublie le monde réel.	✗		
A	Il faut savoir que les pirates informatiques essaient toujours d'obtenir tes coordonnées personnelles.			
B	C'est amusant de poster des photos en ligne.			
C	Je serais plus organisé sans les réseaux sociaux.			
D	J'utilise les réseaux sociaux pour communiquer avec des gens que je vois rarement.			
E	J'utilise les réseaux sociaux pour rester en contact avec des gens que je vois régulièrement.			
F	Beaucoup de gens mettent des images en ligne sans penser aux conséquences.			

You could avoid repeating sur les réseaux sociaux by using y here – J'y vais tous les jours.

Mobile technology

You will need to be able to talk about how you use the internet and your mobile device.

(5) Online activities

Avec mon portable ou ma tablette, je peux envoyer des textos ou des mails, surfer sur Internet pour obtenir des renseignements, faire des achats en ligne, télécharger et écouter de la musique, regarder des vidéos, tchatter avec mes copains, mettre des photos en ligne et passer des coups de fil.

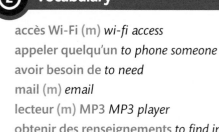

With my mobile phone or tablet, I can send texts or emails, surf the web to find information, shop online, download and listen to music, watch videos, chat with my friends, upload photos and make phone calls.

Exam focus

This answer covers size, colour and what you do with your phone. The vocabulary in this answer could be adapted to answer a similar question about a tablet or computer.

Une marque très connue means a *well-known brand*.

(10) Worked example   Grades 1–9

1 Décris ton portable. / Fais-moi une description de ton portable.

Mon portable est un téléphone intelligent avec un écran tactile. Il est assez grand et argenté. C'est une marque très connue. Il y a une quarantaine d'applis dessus que j'utilise régulièrement, comme l'appareil photo et une appli pour retoucher les photos.

2 Est-ce que les portables sont nécessaires, à ton avis?

À mon avis, les portables sont une partie indispensable de notre vie quotidienne. Ils fonctionnent comme réveil, horloge, carnet d'adresses, agenda, lampe torche, calculatrice ainsi qu'ordinateur et outil pour faire des recherches sur Internet. Quand je sors le soir, mes parents ne s'inquiètent pas parce qu'ils savent que je peux les appeler.

3 Comment as-tu utilisé ton ordinateur le week-end dernier?

J'ai utilisé mon ordinateur pour faire mes devoirs et pour faire des recherches en ligne.

Develop your answer by using quand and parce que.

This response shows that you can use verbs in the singular and plural, and in the first and third persons, as well as reflexive verbs and pronouns correctly.

(2) Vocabulary

accès Wi-Fi (m) *wi-fi access*
appeler quelqu'un *to phone someone*
avoir besoin de *to need*
mail (m) *email*
lecteur (m) MP3 *MP3 player*
obtenir des renseignements *to find information*
ordinateur portable (m) *laptop*
sauvegarder *to save*
tablette (f) *tablet*
transporter *to transport*
Wi-Fi (m) *wi-fi*
vérifier *to check*

VOCABULARY LINK
PAGE **109**

(10) Practice   Grades 4–5

Your French friend shows you some comments about technology on a forum.

Fatima	Je peux utiliser la technologie pour rester en contact avec ma famille en Espagne, mais parfois, il y a une mauvaise connexion.
Léon	Pour moi, un grand avantage est que je ne suis plus obligé de regarder les émissions de télé au moment où elles sont diffusées. D'autre part, je pense qu'il y a des jeunes qui passent trop de temps à jouer à des jeux en ligne.
Nora	Ce que je trouve vraiment bien, c'est que je n'ai plus besoin d'emporter des tas de livres quand je pars en vacances. En plus, les achats en ligne sont normalement moins chers.
Guy	Le problème du harcèlement en ligne devient de plus en plus sérieux.

Who says what about mobile technology? Write either **Fatima**, **Léon**, **Nora** or **Guy**. You can use each person more than once.

Example: _____Nora_____ spends less money buying things online.

(a) _____ is worried about the amount of time spent gaming online by some people.

(b) _____ likes taking a lot of reading material on holiday.

(c) _____ finds that technology can sometimes be unreliable.

(d) _____ likes being able to watch programmes at a more convenient time.

(e) _____ is concerned about cyberbullying.

(f) _____ uses technology to communicate with relatives.   **[6 marks]**

French customs

Knowing about French customs and traditions can help you understand the context of some reading and listening texts.

⑤ Christmas traditions in France

Au réveillon, on mange un grand repas en famille. On mange des fruits de mer comme des huîtres, et comme dessert, il y a la bûche de Noël.

On Christmas Eve, families eat a big meal. They eat seafood, like oysters, and there is chocolate log for dessert.

Comme en Grande-Bretagne, on met des cadeaux sous le sapin de Noël. *Like in Great Britain, people put presents under the Christmas tree.*

② Vocabulary A–Z

anniversaire (m) *birthday / anniversary*
cadeau (m) *present*
célébrer *to celebrate*
église (f) *church*
fêter *to celebrate*
messe (f) *mass*
mosquée (f) *mosque*
musulman *Muslim*

Noël (m) *Christmas*
veille (f) de Noël *Christmas Eve*
réveillon (m) *Christmas Eve / New Year's Eve dinner*
Pâques (f pl) *Easter*
poisson d'avril (m) *April Fools' Day*
Toussaint (f) *All Saints' Day*
noces (f pl) *wedding*

VOCABULARY LINK PAGE 113

⑩ Worked example — Grades 4–9

👓 Read this short article about religion in France.

> Le catholicisme est la religion la plus importante en France, pourtant de plus en plus de gens déclarent qu'ils n'ont aucune religion. Beaucoup de Français ne vont à l'église qu'à l'occasion des grandes fêtes religieuses de l'année, c'est-à-dire à Pâques et à Noël. Quant aux autres religions, le nombre de musulmans et de mosquées en France augmente, alors que le nombre de juifs et de synagogues diminue.

Answer the questions **in English**.

❶ What does this article say about trends in church attendance?

It's decreasing, as many French people only go to church at Christmas and Easter.

❷ What does it say about Islam and Judaism?

The numbers of Muslims and mosques are increasing and the numbers of Jews and synagogues are decreasing.

⑮ Practice — Grades 1–9

❶ You are listening to a podcast about customs and traditions in France. What is mentioned?

Listen to the recording and put a cross ✖ in each one of the **three** correct boxes.

Example	French tradition of good food	✖
A	Christmas festivities	
B	Easter traditions	
C	Family celebrations	
D	Mother's Day	
E	Playing a joke	
F	Remembering the Dead	
G	New Year's traditions	

[3 marks]

Use your knowledge of French life and culture to predict what vocabulary you need to listen out for.

❷ Regarde la photo et prépare des réponses sur les points suivants:
- la description de la photo
- ton cadeau d'anniversaire idéal
- la fête d'anniversaire l'année dernière
- projets pour fêter le Nouvel An l'année prochaine
- ! (*Est-ce que les fêtes de famille sont importantes?*)

You can repeat some of the given information in your answer to give yourself thinking time: Mon cadeau d'anniversaire idéal serait...

French festivals

You should be aware of events and festivals in France as they may be referred to in spoken and written texts.

(5) La fête des Rois

La fête des Rois est le six janvier. On mange un gâteau spécial qui s'appelle la galette des Rois. On cache une fève dans la galette et la personne qui la trouve est le «Roi» ou la «Reine» et porte une couronne.

Twelfth Night / Epiphany is 6 January. They eat a special cake called 'la galette des Rois'. A charm is hidden in the cake and the person who finds it becomes the 'king' or 'queen' and wears a crown.

(2) Vocabulary

s'amuser *to have fun*
cacher *to hide*
carnaval (m) *carnival*
défilé (m) *parade / procession*
se déguiser *to disguise oneself / dress up (in a costume)*
fête (f) des Mères *Mother's Day*
feu (m) d'artifice *firework*
jour (m) de l'An *New Year's Day*
jour (m) férié *bank holiday*
mondial *worldwide*
(le) Nouvel An *New Year*
réunion (f) *meeting*
Saint-Sylvestre (f) *New Year's Eve*
veille (f) de Noël *Christmas Eve*

VOCABULARY LINK
PAGE
113

(10) Worked example — Grades 4–5

👓 Lis cet extrait.

> La période de carnaval commence le 6 janvier (la fête des Rois) et se termine le Mardi gras. Les carnavals de Rio et de Venise ont une renommée mondiale, mais il y a aussi des carnavals partout en France; les plus célèbres sont ceux de Nice et Dunkerque. Ces fêtes vous donnent l'occasion de vous déguiser, de chanter, de danser et surtout de vous amuser. Souvent, les enfants se déguisent en adultes, les adultes en enfants, les femmes en hommes, les hommes en femmes, etc.

Mets une croix $\boxed{✗}$ dans les **deux** cases correctes.

Ne ... que means *only*. The text mentions the carnivals in Rio (Brazil) and Venice (Italy).

A	Le carnaval n'existe qu'en France.	
B	Le début du carnaval est douze jours après Noël.	✗
C	Le carnaval, c'est le moment d'être heureux!	✗
D	On porte ses vêtements de tous les jours quand on fête le carnaval.	

Le début means *the start*.

(5) La fête nationale française

La fête nationale française est le quatorze juillet. C'est l'anniversaire de la prise de la Bastille pendant la Révolution française en 1789. Il y a des défilés dans les rues des grandes villes et le soir, on peut voir un grand feu d'artifice.

Bastille Day is 14 July. It's the anniversary of the taking of the Bastille during the French Revolution in 1789. There are parades in the streets of big towns and in the evening you can see a big firework display.

L'occasion de s'amuser has the same meaning as this.

This means *everyday clothes*. The text says that carnival is the time to se déguiser (*disguise oneself*).

(5) Practice — Grades 1–9

💬 Answer the following questions.
• Que penses-tu des fêtes françaises?
• Tu es déjà allé(e) à une fête en France? C'était comment?

Reading

You will need to be able to talk about your reading habits.

 5 Talking about reading

When you talk about reading you can:

- say how you like to read books: Je préfère lire des livres imprimés. Les livres électroniques ne m'intéressent pas. *I prefer to read printed books. I'm not interested in eBooks.*
- say what type of books you like and why: J'adore les romans policiers parce qu'ils sont passionnants. *I love detective novels because they are exciting.*
- talk about your reading habits: Normalement, je lis pendant une demi-heure avant de me coucher. *Normally, I read for half an hour before going to bed.*
- use the imperfect tense to compare your reading habits now with how they were in the past: Quand j'étais jeune, je lisais des livres illustrés, mais maintenant, je ne lis que des livres classiques. *When I was little I used to read illustrated books but now I only read classics.*

 10 Worked example **Grades 1–5**

 Regarde la photo et prépare des réponses sur les points suivants:

- **la description de la photo**

Sur la photo, il y a des adolescents qui cherchent des livres dans une bibliothèque. La fille aux cheveux longs et blonds porte un gilet tricoté à rayures bleues et blanches. Elle sourit et tient quelques livres dans ses mains.

> Add more detail by using phrases like **à l'avant-plan** (*in the foreground*) or **à l'arrière-plan** (*in the background*).

- **ton opinion sur la lecture**

À mon avis, la lecture est très importante car on peut s'informer et développer son imagination. J'emprunte souvent des livres à la bibliothèque parce que ça ne coûte rien. J'adore lire des romans historiques mais j'aime aussi lire des romans classiques.

> You could mention whether or not you like reading eBooks.

Vocabulary

bande dessinée (BD) (f) *comic / cartoon*
bibliothèque (f) *library*
biographie (f) *biography*
blog (m) *blog*
écran (m) *screen*
histoire (f) *story*
journal (m) *newspaper*
lecteur électronique (m) / lecteur numérique (m) / liseuse (f) *e-reader*
lecture (f) *reading*
livre électronique (m) / livre numérique (m) *electronic book / eBook*
livre illustré (m) *illustrated book*
magazine (m) *magazine*
roman (m) *novel*
texto (m) *text*
emprunter *to borrow*
lire *to read*
télécharger *to download*

 10 Practice **Grades 1–5**

 Fatima parle de la lecture. Complète les phrases en choisissant un mot ou des mots dans la case. Il y a des mots que tu n'utiliseras pas.

une œuvre de fiction	capacité	soir
électroniques	un lecteur électronique	
imprimés	matin	
un ouvrage non romanesque	légèreté	

(a) Fatima lit régulièrement le _____ .

(b) Pendant son temps libre, elle préfère lire _____ .

(c) Elle lit des livres _____ quand elle n'est pas en vacances.

(d) Parfois, elle apprécie la _____ d'un lecteur électronique.

[4 marks]

Exam focus

Before you listen, use your knowledge of grammar and vocabulary to try to predict which type of word might go in the blanks.

 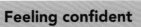

Music

You should know how to talk about your musical tastes.

Discussing music

When you talk about music, you should be able to:

- say what type of music you like:
  J'adore **le rock** mais j'aime aussi **la musique classique**.
  I love **rock** but I like **classical music** too.

- compare musical styles:
  Le rap est **plus** monotone **que** la pop.
  Rap is **more** monotonous **than** pop music.

- talk about your favourite singer or musician and musical experiences:
  Hier, je suis allé à un concert de Grégoire.
  I went to a Grégoire concert yesterday.

- say how you listen to music:
  J'écoute de la musique sur mon portable.
  I listen to music on my mobile phone.

- Use jouer + du / de la / de l' to say you play an instrument:
  Je joue **du** violon / **de la** clarinette / **de l'**accordéon.
  I play the violin / clarinet / accordion.

- Use the present tense + depuis to say how long you have been playing an instrument:
  Ma sœur **joue** de la batterie **depuis** deux ans / septembre.
  My sister **has been playing** the drums **for** two years / **since** September.

- Use pronouns, for example use me when talking about the effect that music has on you.

  La musique classique? J'adore ça parce que ça **me** détend.

 Worked example Grades 1–9

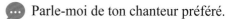

💬 Parle-moi de ton chanteur préféré.

Mon chanteur préféré est un chanteur belge qui s'appelle Stromae. En fait, ce n'est pas son vrai nom, mais il l'a choisi pour lancer sa carrière de chanteur de rap et de hip-hop. Je trouve sa musique très accrocheuse, surtout son premier tube, *Alors on danse*. Je ne l'ai pas vu en concert, mais j'ai regardé ses vidéos sur Internet.

En fait (in fact) is a good phrase to use when you want to clarify something.

The best answers will include a range of tenses and features such as direct object pronouns.

Try to avoid repeating the same verbs. Here you could say Je ne suis pas allé à un de ses concerts, mais... You are then using a verb that takes **être**.

Vocabulary A–Z

chanson (f) *song*
chanter *to sing*
chanteur (m) / chanteuse (f) *singer*
groupe (m) *band*
mélodie (f) *tune*
paroles (f pl) *words / lyrics*
tube (m) *hit*
lent *slow*
vif / vive *lively*

VOCABULARY LINK
PAGE **107**

Exam focus 📌
You should use the perfect and / or imperfect tense when responding to this bullet point.

Exam focus 📌
You should refer to the future here. You could use the conditional to say what you would do if you don't have any future plans.

2️⃣ Expressing opinions about music

Ça me rend heureux / triste. *It makes me happy / sad.*

La chanson a une mélodie vive / inoubliable. *The song has a lively / unforgettable tune.*

Les paroles sont faciles à comprendre. *The words are easy to understand.*

🔟 Practice Grades 1–9

✏️ Laurent, ton ami français, t'a envoyé un mail. Il veut savoir quels sont tes goûts musicaux.

Écris une réponse à Laurent. Tu **dois** faire référence aux points suivants:

- le genre de musique que tu aimes
- pourquoi la musique est importante pour toi
- une expérience musicale récente
- une activité musicale que tu feras dans l'avenir

Écris 80–90 mots environ **en français**. **[20 marks]**

✓ **Made a start**   ✓ **Feeling confident**   ✓ **Exam ready**

Sport

You will be expected to know how to talk about sports you like and why you like them.

 (5) Talking about sport

You should be able to talk about:

- what sports you like doing and why: J'adore le tennis parce que ça demande de bons réflexes. *I love tennis because it requires good reflexes.*
- how often you do a sport: Je fais du roller deux fois par semaine. *I go roller skating twice a week.*
- how long you have been doing a sport: Je fais de la voile depuis deux ans. *I have been going sailing for two years.*
- benefits of your favourite sport: Le footing est bon pour le cœur. *Jogging is good for your heart.*

For team sports use jouer + à: je joue au foot / basket *I play football / basketball.*

For individual sports use faire + de or pratiquer + le / la: je fais du patinage *I go skating*; je pratique l'escrime *I do fencing.*

 (2) Vocabulary **A-Z**

championnat (m) *championship*
se détendre *to relax*
équipe (f) *team*
s'entraîner *to train*
faire partie de *to be a member of*
oublier ses soucis *to forget one's worries*

participer à *to take part in*
respirer *to breathe*
c'est un sport rapide / ludique *it's a fast / fun sport*
sport individuel / d'équipe / nautique (m) *individual / team / water sport*
sportif / sportive *sporty*

VOCABULARY LINK PAGE 108

 (10) Worked example | **Grades 4–9**

 Use the imperfect tense to translate *we were.*

✎ Traduis le passage suivant **en français**:

My favourite sport is tennis and I play twice a week at the sports club with my brother. He prefers football because he likes team sports. Last year we saw lots of cyclists on the road when we were on holiday in the west of France. I think that cycling can be dangerous when there is too much traffic.

Mon sport préféré c'est le tennis et j'y joue deux fois par semaine au centre sportif avec mon frère. Il préfère le foot parce qu'il aime les sports d'équipe. L'année dernière, on a vu beaucoup de cyclistes sur la route quand on était en vacances dans l'ouest de la France. Je pense que le cyclisme peut être dangereux quand il y a trop de circulation.

If you don't know the word for traffic, you could rephrase this using words you do know, such as *a lot of cars.*

The past participle of the verb voir is vu.

Many of these nouns need a definite article (le/la) where they don't in English. Go to page 70 to check the rules. **!**

(10) Practice | **Grades 4–9**

💬 Regarde la photo et prépare des réponses sur les points suivants:

- la description de la photo
- l'importance des événements sportifs internationaux
- un événement sportif que tu as vu récemment
- ton activité sportive pendant tes prochaines vacances
- ! (*Est-ce que tu préfères les sports individuels ou les sports collectifs?*)

Exam focus

! only appears on the Higher-tier picture-based task. It means that you will be asked a question for which you have not prepared. The Foundation picture-based task will show all five of the prompts.

 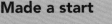 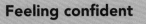

Cinema

You need to know how to say what kinds of films you like and why.

 About cinema

When you talk about films and TV programmes you can use:

- adjectives to express your opinion and give reasons for it:
  J'adore les films de science-fiction parce que les effets spéciaux sont **impressionnants**. *I like science fiction films because the special effects are **impressive**.*

- the comparative and superlative:
  À mon avis, Audrey Tautou est **plus célèbre que** d'autres actrices françaises. *In my opinion Audrey Tautou is **more famous than** other French actresses.*
  C'est **le meilleur film** de cette année. *It's **the best film** this year.*

  GRAMMAR LINK PAGE **76**

- relative pronouns:
  C'est un film **que** j'ai vu trois fois. *It's a film **that** I've seen three times.*
  C'est un film **qui** parle de problèmes sociaux. *It's a film **that** talks about social problems.*

 Vocabulary   A–Z

écran (m) *screen*
avoir horreur de *to hate / can't stand*
j'ai horreur des films d'arts martiaux *I can't stand martial arts films*
comédie (f) *comedy*
effrayant *scary*
faire peur / rire *to scare / to make laugh*
ce film m'a fait rire *the film made me laugh*
être fan de *to be a fan of*
film policier (m) *detective film*
film de guerre (m) *war film*
genre (m) *type (of film)*
réaliste *realistic*
passionnant *exciting*
publicités (f pl) *adverts*
vedette (f) *(film) star*

 VOCABULARY LINK PAGE **107**

 Worked example   Grades 1–5

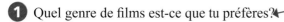

1 Quel genre de films est-ce que tu préfères?

💬 J'aime surtout les films d'action parce qu'ils sont vraiment passionnants. Pourtant, ils sont aussi parfois violents, et je déteste la violence.

2 Quel est le dernier film que tu as vu?

💬 Le dernier film que j'ai vu était *La La Land*, une comédie musicale. Je l'ai vu avec ma famille le week-end dernier. J'ai trouvé ça absolument génial car il s'agit de deux personnes qui veulent réaliser leurs rêves.

The same question might be phrased slightly differently: **Quelle sorte de films aimes-tu? Pourquoi?**

The best answers go beyond a simple response: they give a specific example of the kind of film and might mention the last time you saw that kind of film.

Using the object pronoun in **je l'ai vu** is a feature of the best answers. However, try to avoid repeating the same verb. For example, you could say **Je suis allé(e) le voir.**

 Talking about a film

Le thème du film est la guerre et la paix. *The theme of the film is war and peace.*

Il s'agit d'un vieil homme et de sa petite fille. *It's about an old man and his granddaughter.*

L'action se déroule dans la banlieue de Paris. *The action takes place in the suburbs of Paris.*

La musique est / était... *The music is / was...*

Les effets (m) spéciaux sont / étaient... *The special effects are / were...*

C'est un film réalisé par... *It's a film directed by...*

Les acteurs principaux sont... *The main actors are...*

Je recommanderais ce film parce que... *I would recommend this film because...*

 Practice   Grades 4–9

🎧 Listen to this podcast about a recent film.
Answer the questions **in English**.

(a) How did the speaker first hear about the film?

[1 mark]

(b) In what way are the opening shots of the film memorable?

[1 mark]

(c) How did the speaker feel when he saw the scene between the young man and his mother?

[1 mark]

  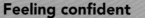

Television

You will need to know how to talk about the kind of television programmes you like and why.

 (5) Your television viewing habits

Use frequency adverbs here:

Normalement, je regarde la télé le matin quand je prends mon petit déjeuner.
__Normally__, I watch TV in the morning when I am having breakfast.

J'allume la télé **tous les jours** pour regarder les infos.
I switch on the television __every day__ to watch the news.

Je ne regarde que **deux heures** de télé **par jour**.
I only watch __two hours__ of television __each day__.

Give reasons:

J'aime regarder des émissions de télé-réalité parce qu'elles me font rire.
I like to watch reality TV programmes because they make me laugh.

Je trouve les documentaires très utiles car il est important de s'informer sur ce qui se passe dans le monde.
I find documentaries very useful as it's important to find out what's happening in the world.

(5) Worked example | **Grades 1–5**

 Regarde la photo et prépare une réponse sur le point suivant:

- la description de la photo

Sur la photo, il y a une famille qui regarde la télé. Ils sont assis ensemble sur le canapé et regardent la même émission. Je pense que c'est une émission divertissante, comme un jeu télévisé par exemple.

(5) Aiming higher

Use the imperfect tense to talk about what you used to watch, and use pronouns to refer to things you have already mentioned:

Avant, **je regardais** beaucoup de dessins animés. Cependant, maintenant, je **les trouve** bêtes. *Before, I used to watch a lot of cartoons, however I find them stupid now.*

(2) Vocabulary A–Z

s'abonner à *to subscribe to*
actualités (f pl) *news*
animateur (m) *host*
chaîne (f) *television channel*
dessin animé (m) *cartoon*
divertissant *entertaining*
documentaire (m) *documentary*
émission (f) *TV programme*
émission de télé-réalité *reality TV programme*
fan de *fan of*
feuilleton (m) *soap (opera) or drama*
infos (f pl) *news*
s'intéresser à *to be interested in*
jeu (m) **télévisé** *game show*
météo (f) *weather forecast*
programme (m) *channel*
série (f) *series*
télécommande (f) *remote control*
télé (f) **de rattrapage** *catch-up TV*
télévision (f) **sur demande** *on-demand TV*

 VOCABULARY LINK **PAGE 107**

(5) Comparing TV programmes

À mon avis, les documentaires sont plus éducatifs que les jeux télévisés. *In my opinion, documentary programmes are more educational than game shows.*

> Remember to use the definite article for things that you are comparing.

Add detail by explaining further: **parce que les membres de la famille sont heureux et qu'ils sourient.** *because the family members are happy and are smiling.*

(10) Practice | **Grades 1–9**

 Answer the following questions.
- Quelles émissions est-ce que tu regardes régulièrement?
- Quels sont les avantages des films à la télé?
- Voudrais-tu participer à une émission de télé-réalité?
- Qu'est-ce que tu as regardé à la télé hier?

Holiday plans and preferences

Being able to say what you like to do on holiday and where you like to go is important.

 Talking about holiday plans

To talk about your holiday plans use:

- the future tense:
  Cette année, j'irai en Espagne avec mes copains pour deux semaines. *This year, I **will go** to Spain with my friends for two weeks.*
  Nous ferons du camping à la montagne parce que nous voulons faire de l'escalade. *We **will camp** in the mountains because we want to go climbing.*

- the conditional:
  Si j'avais beaucoup d'argent, je logerais dans un hôtel quatre étoiles au lieu d'une auberge de jeunesse. *If I had a lot of money, I **would stay** in a 4-star hotel instead of a youth hostel.*

GRAMMAR LINK PAGE **93**

 Worked example   **Grades 4–5**

👓 Lis les commentaires postés sur un forum au sujet des vacances.

> Je m'intéresse plutôt aux activités culturelles, alors je préfère les grandes villes plutôt que la campagne. Le camping n'est pas mon truc, surtout quand il pleut! **Gabrielle**

> Mon frère adore faire du canoë-kayak ou de l'escalade en vacances mais moi, je déteste ça. Je préfère me détendre et me bronzer sur la plage. **Joël**

> Mes vacances idéales seraient sur des pistes couvertes de neige dans les Alpes. **Nicole**

> Normalement, je passe mes vacances dans un gîte rural en Bretagne, mais cette année j'irai en Grèce pour faire de la voile. Mes vacances idéales seraient sur une île tropicale où je pourrais faire du ski nautique et de la plongée sous-marine. **Mamadou**

Qui est la personne correcte? Choisis entre **Gabrielle**, **Joël**, **Nicole** et **Mamadou**.

(a) _____Nicole_____ adore les vacances aux sports d'hiver.

(b) _____Mamadou_____ rêve de passer ses vacances dans un endroit chaud où on peut être actif.

(c) _____Gabrielle_____ a l'intention de visiter des musées pendant ses vacances.

(d) _____Mamadou_____ fera quelque chose de différent cette année.

(e) _____Joël_____ n'aime pas tellement les vacances actives.

Vocabulary A–Z

avoir l'intention de *to intend to*
croisière (f) *cruise*
à l'étranger *abroad*
en plein air *in the open air / outdoors*
faire une excursion *to go on an outing*
location (f) de voitures *car hire*
monument (m) *monument*
passer *to spend* (*time*)
repos (m) *rest*
au bord de la mer / d'un lac *by the sea / a lake*
à la campagne *in the countryside*
à la montagne *in the mountains*
près d'une plage *near a beach*
vacances (f pl) *holidays*

VOCABULARY LINK PAGE **108**

The last sentence means *I prefer to relax and sunbathe* and is similar in meaning to *I am not very active.*

Des pistes couvertes de neige means *slopes covered with snow.*

 Aiming higher

Use conjunctions such as pourtant, cependant and d'un autre côté to introduce different tenses:

J'aime les vacances en famille en camping. Pourtant, si j'avais le choix, je passerais une quinzaine sur une île tropicale.

Use expressions such as avant de and afin de:

J'irai en Espagne afin de perfectionner mes compétences linguistiques.

Visiting museums is a cultural activity (activités culturelles).

This means *will do something different.* Key words to look out for are normalement and mais.

 Practice   **Grades 1–9**

💬 Answer the following questions.
- Est-ce que tu préfères les vacances d'été ou les vacances d'hiver?
- Comment seraient tes vacances idéales?
- À ton avis, est-ce que les vacances sont importantes? Pourquoi / pourquoi pas?
- Quel type de vacances préfères-tu et pourquoi?

Holiday experiences

You should be able to describe your holiday, what you did and what it was like.

⑤ Talking about past events

Use both the imperfect and perfect tenses to describe what you did on your holiday:

Quand il y **avait** du soleil, nous **sommes allés** à la plage où nous **nous sommes bronzés**. *When it **was** sunny, we **went** to the beach where we **sunbathed**.*

Use a variety of time phrases:

L'année dernière *Last year*; en août *in August*; pendant les vacances *during the holidays*; il y a six mois *six months ago*.

② Vocabulary

se bronzer *to sunbathe*
décoller *to take off (in a plane)*
découvrir *to discover*
donner sur *to overlook*
foule (f) *crowd*
faire du tourisme *to go sightseeing*
lunettes (f pl) de soleil *sunglasses*
paysage (m) *landscape*
sable (m) *sand*
séjour (m) *stay*
trajet (m) *journey*
visite guidée (f) *guided visit*

VOCABULARY LINK PAGE 108

⑤ Worked example — Grades 1–5

🖉 Tu es en vacances et tu écris à ton ami(e) français(e).

Tu dois faire référence aux points suivants:
- comment tu trouves le logement et le temps
- les activités que tu as faites
- pourquoi les vacances sont importantes
- tes projets pour les vacances chez toi

Écris 80-90 mots environ **en français**.

Make sure that you cover all the bullet points from the question and structure your different sentences around them.

Salut, ça va? Me voici avec ma famille dans le sud de la France dans un camping super qui est situé au bord de la mer. Tous les jours il y a du soleil et il fait très chaud, alors hier je me suis bronzé et j'ai fait de la natation. À mon avis les vacances sont importantes parce qu'on a la chance de se détendre. Quand je rentrerai chez moi, j'aurai encore deux semaines de vacances. Je vais retrouver mes amis et on va sortir ensemble. **Ben**

Check that you have the correct verb endings and spellings, and that adjectives agree. Also check your word count meets the requirements of the question.

⑩ Practice — Grades 4–9

① Read the following account of a holiday.

> Normalement, j'aime les vacances actives et je vais souvent à la montagne où je peux faire des randonnées et de l'escalade. Quand il ne pleut pas, c'est formidable d'être en plein air! Cependant, cette année, j'ai décidé de faire une croisière en Méditerranée. Chaque jour, on a découvert un nouvel endroit, ce qui a été une expérience très enrichissante. Bien sûr, tout était inclus, y compris les repas, et on pouvait faire de l'exercice dans la piscine ou dans la salle de sport à bord. Le seul problème, c'est que j'avais parfois le mal de mer. **Guy**

What is one advantage and one disadvantage of the type of holiday Guy went on **this year**? **[2 marks]**

② Your exchange partner and her friends are talking about holiday experiences in class. What is each person talking about? Listen to the recording and put a cross ☒ next to each one of the **three** correct contexts.

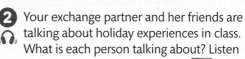

		Abdou	Francine	Hervé
Example	Sightseeing	✗		
A	An accident			
B	A theft			
C	Beach activities			
D	Buying a souvenir			
E	Travel documents			
F	The weather			
G	A visit to a theme park			

[3 marks]

Before you listen, try to predict which words you need to listen out for and jot them down.

Travel and transport

Look at language for describing journeys you've been on, how you travel regularly, and arranging to use public transport.

5 Talking about travel

You will need to be able to:

- say how you travelled to a place and what the journey was like: **On est allés en Écosse en voiture. Ce n'était pas très confortable car le voyage a duré six heures.** *We went to Scotland by car. It wasn't very comfortable because the journey lasted six hours.*

- use the pronoun **y** to mean *there*: **Nous y allons en train / avion / bateau / car.** *We go **there** by train / plane / boat / coach.*

- Compare means of transport:

L'avion est **plus** rapide **que** le train.

10 Worked example — Grades 4–9

 Vous parlez avec un employé dans une gare à Paris.

> 1. Billets de train – où et type
> 2. ? Tarif étudiants
> 3. ? Quai + heure
> 4. !
> 5. Cuisine française - opinion + raison

- Je peux vous aider?

1. Je voudrais un aller simple pour Marseille, s'il vous plaît.

- Ça fait vingt euros.

2. Est-ce qu'il y a un tarif réduit pour les étudiants?

- Oui, il y a une réduction de vingt pour cent, alors ça fait seize euros.

3. Le train part de quel quai et à quelle heure?

- Il part à quatorze heures du quai numéro 3. Qu'est-ce que vous avez fait en France jusqu'ici?

4. J'ai fait un stage pour améliorer mon français.

- C'est bien, ça! Et qu'est-ce que vous pensez de la cuisine française?

5. Je l'adore, surtout les gâteaux parce que j'aime les aliments sucrés.

You must ask a question here.

This question will be in the past tense. Your answer should also use the past tense.

2 Vocabulary — A–Z

aéroport (m) *airport*
agence (f) de voyages *travel agency*
attacher sa ceinture *to put on one's seat belt*
autoroute (f) *motorway*
durer *to last*
guichet (m) *ticket office*
horaire (m) *timetable*
passer par le péage *to go through the toll gate*
quai (m) *platform*
salle d'attente (f) *waiting room*

VOCABULARY LINK PAGE 108

Exam focus

With this scenario you may also need to:

- Ask whether you have to change train / bus: **Est-ce qu'il faut changer de train / bus?**

- Ask for the arrival time of a train / bus: **Le train / bus arrive à quelle heure?**

Note where this role play is set. Don't ask for a ticket to Paris. You could mention any other French town.

10 Practice — Grades 4–5

1 While in France you overhear some people talking about journeys they have made. How did they travel and what problems did they have? Complete the sentences. Use the correct words or phrases from the box.

air	car	cheap	coach	~~expensive~~
flight	illness	late	lost luggage	rail	sea
~~taxi~~	traffic	train	weather	

Example: My _____taxi_____ was ___expensive___ .
(a) The _____ was _____ .
(b) Travelling by _____ resulted in _____ .
(c) The _____ was comfortable but my trip was spoilt by _____ .
(d) My journey by _____ was affected by _____ . **[8 marks]**

2 Answer the following questions.
- Comment vas-tu au collège?
- Quel est ton moyen de transport préféré? Pourquoi?
- Est-ce que tu es allé(e) en France? Décris ton voyage.
- Comment voyagerais-tu si tu avais le choix?

Accommodation

You need to be able to talk about your holiday accommodation and to give your opinion about where you stay.

⑤ Accommodation

When you talk about accommodation you can mention:

- the location: **Le camping est situé non loin de la gare.** *The campsite is located not far from the station.*
- what your accommodation is / was like: **C'est / c'était un gîte / hôtel charmant, mais aussi un peu démodé.** *It is / was a charming holiday cottage / hotel but also a bit old-fashioned.*
- what your room is / was like: **Ma chambre est / était sale.** *My room is / was dirty.*

⑩ Worked example — Grades 4–9

💬 Vous parlez avec le / la réceptionniste d'un hôtel en France.

> 1. Chambre désirée (**deux** détails)
> 2. Choix de l'hôtel - raison
> 3. ! ◄
> 4. ? Repas heure
> 5. ? Piscine

- Bonjour, je peux vous aider?
1. Oui, je voudrais une chambre à deux lits avec balcon s'il vous plaît.
- Bon. Pourquoi avez-vous choisi notre hôtel? ◄
2. J'ai choisi votre hôtel parce que je voulais loger dans un hôtel au centre-ville.
- Très bien. Quand est-ce que vous êtes arrivé en France?
3. Je suis arrivé(e) il y a une semaine.
- Excellent, vous avez la chambre numéro 313 au troisième étage.
4. Merci. Le petit déjeuner est à quelle heure?
- De sept à neuf heures du matin.
5. Et est-ce qu'il y a une piscine?
- Oui, elle est en plein air dans le jardin.

> Alternative types of room could include different facilities (**avec Wi-Fi / douche / salle de bains / vue sur la plage**) or location (**au rez-de-chaussée / premier étage**).

⑤ Accommodation problems

L'ascenseur était en panne. *The lift was out of order.*

Il y avait un chantier de construction en face. *There was a building site opposite.*

La connexion Wi-Fi / la télévision ne fonctionnait pas. *The wifi connection / television wasn't working.*

Il n'y avait pas d'eau chaude. *There was no hot water.*

② Vocabulary

balcon (m) *balcony*
chambre (f) **familiale** *family room*
clé (f) *key*
climatisation (f) *air conditioning*
coffre-fort (m) *safe*
douche (f) *shower*
étage (m) *floor*

au deuxième étage *on the 2nd floor*
au rez-de-chaussée *on the ground floor*
logement (m) *accommodation*
robinet (m) *tap*
vue (f) **sur la mer** *view of the sea*

VOCABULARY LINK
PAGE **109**

⑤ Asking about hotel facilities

Est-ce qu'il y a une piscine / un ascenseur? *Is there a swimming pool / lift?*

Est-ce que vous offrez la pension complète ou la demi-pension? *Do you offer full board or half board?*

> The unpredictable question here could be: **Comment êtes-vous venu(e) dans notre ville aujourd'hui?** You will need to use the perfect tense.

> Alternative answers to this could include **j'ai lu beaucoup de bonnes recommandations en ligne** *(I read a lot of good reviews online)*, or **le tarif n'est pas trop cher** *(the room rate is not too expensive)*.

⑤ Practice — Grades 4–5

🎧 You hear some of your French friends talking about where they have stayed on holiday. Listen to the recording and put a cross [✗] next to each one of the **three** correct statements.

		Nadia	Bertrand	Alice
Example	I was extremely happy with the hotel.	✗		
A	I liked the heated pool.			
B	I was happy with the location of my room.			
C	I disagree with the reviews I saw.			
D	I would hesitate to stay in this hotel again.			
E	My room was not clean.			

[3 marks]

Dealing with problems

You should know how to ask for help and deal with problems like lost property and theft.

 Talking about problems

Situations you may have to talk about include:

- reporting a loss: J'ai perdu mon passeport / mon portefeuille / mon porte-monnaie / ma montre. *I've lost my passport / wallet / purse / watch.*
- reporting a theft: On m'a volé mon appareil photo. *My camera has been stolen.*

GRAMMAR LINK PAGE **100**

- complaining about something: Cet objet est cassé / endommagé. *This item is broken / damaged.* La facture n'est pas correcte. *The bill is wrong.* Il y a une erreur. *There's a mistake.*
- asking for something to be put right: Est-ce que vous pouvez remplacer...? *Can you replace...?* Vous pouvez me rembourser...? *Can you reimburse me...?*

 Vocabulary

assurance (f) *insurance*	sac (m) à dos *backpack*
bureau (m) des objets trouvés *lost property office*	vol (m) *theft*
	assurer *to insure*
délai (m) *waiting time*	échanger *to exchange*
faute (f) *mistake / fault*	livrer *to deliver*
formulaire (m) *form*	se plaindre *to complain*
garantie (f) *guarantee*	rapporter / ramener *to bring back*
panne (f) *breakdown*	
plainte (f) *complaint*	remplir *to fill*
reçu (m) *receipt*	rendre *to give back*
perdre *to lose*	

 Worked example **Grades 4–9**

💬 Vous êtes au commissariat de police. Vous parlez avec l'agent de police.

1. Objet volé + description
2. Vol – lieu + heure
3. !
4. ? Formulaire
5. ? Revenir quand

Mention the stolen item and give a description of it.

You have to say where and when the item was stolen.

The unpredictable question (!) will be in the perfect tense at Higher tier.

When you see ? you must ask a question related to the cue words: *Can I have a form to fill in?*

You could also say Quand est-ce qu'il faut revenir? here.

- Quel est le problème?
1. On m'a volé mon portefeuille. Il est en cuir noir.
- Donnez-moi d'autres détails sur le vol.
2. Ça s'est passé ce matin dans la rue.
- Qu'est-ce que vous avez fait après le vol?
3. Je suis retourné(e) à mon hôtel.

- D'accord, je note ça.
4. Est-ce que je dois remplir un formulaire?
- Oui, voilà.
5. Quand est-ce que je dois revenir ici?
- Demain, s'il vous plaît.

 Practice **Grades 4–9**

👓 Lis ces messages.

Fabrice: Quel désastre! Le pire c'était que je ne pouvais plus envoyer des SMS ou prendre des photos. En plus j'avais oublié de l'assurer.

Alyse: Alors, moi, je suis allée au commissariat de police. J'ai dû remplir des formulaires et faire une description du coupable.

Khalid: Quant à moi, j'ai dû retourner au magasin parce que la montre que j'avais achetée ne fonctionnait pas. Heureusement j'avais mon ticket de caisse et on m'a remboursé tout de suite.

Claire: Et moi... Malheureusement le vélo électrique que j'avais loué est tombé en panne après quelques kilomètres et j'ai dû attendre au moins une heure pour avoir un vélo de remplacement.

Qui est la personne correcte? Choisis entre **Fabrice**, **Alyse**, **Khalid** et **Claire**. Chaque nom peut être utilisé plusieurs fois.

Exemple: _____Fabrice_____ ne sera pas remboursé pour sa perte.

(a) _____ a dû montrer son reçu.

(b) _____ a perdu du temps à cause de son problème.

(c) _____ a été victime d'un vol.

(d) _____ a perdu son portable.

(e) _____ avait acheté un objet endommagé.

[5 marks]

Directions

You need to be able to ask for and give directions.

⑤ Giving directions

To understand and give directions you will need to be able to use:

GRAMMAR LINK PAGE 96

- the imperative in both the **tu** and **vous** forms:
  prends la première rue à droite *take the first road on the right*; **va jusqu'aux feux** *go up to the traffic lights*; **continuez tout droit** *continue straight ahead*; **tournez à gauche** *turn left*; **traversez le pont** *cross the bridge*

- prepositions:
  à côté de l'hôtel de ville *next to the town hall*; **au bout de la rue** *at the end of the road*; **jusqu'à la gare** *as far as the station*; **en face du centre commercial** *opposite the shopping centre*

- ordinal numbers:
  la première / deuxième / troisième rue à gauche *the first / second / third road on the left.*

⑤ Vocabulary

à pied *on foot*
en voiture *by car*
tout droit *straight ahead*
c'est tout près *it's very near*
loin *far*
carrefour (m) *crossroads*
feux (mpl) *traffic lights*
panneau (m) *sign*
place (f) *square*
rond-point (m) *roundabout*
rue (f) *street / road*
trottoir (m) *pavement*

You should also know key vocabulary for places around town.

VOCABULARY LINK PAGE 110

Au carrefour, tournez à droite.

⑩ Worked example   Grades 4–9

💬 Vous êtes dans un office de tourisme en France. Vous parlez avec l'employé(e).

1. Monument désiré à visiter – raison ←
2. ? Directions + distance
3. ! ←
4. ? Restaurant – recommandation
5. Cuisine préférée + raison

- Bonjour, qu'est-ce qui vous intéresse dans notre ville?
1. Je voudrais visiter le château parce que j'aime l'histoire.
- Notre château est très intéressant.
2. Où est le château? C'est loin?
- Pas trop loin. Comment êtes-vous venu(e)?
3. Je suis venu(e) en train.
- Alors, pour le château, il y a un bus ou vous pouvez y aller à pied.
4. Qu'est-ce que vous recommandez comme restaurants?
- Ça dépend – qu'est-ce que vous voulez manger?
5. J'aime la cuisine italienne parce que j'adore les pizzas.

⑤ Asking for directions

You can ask for directions in several ways:

- **Excusez-moi, pour aller au parc / à la gare / aux Champs Élysées?** *Excuse me, how do I get to the park / the station / the Champs Élysées?*
- **Où est le musée / l'hôpital / le bureau de change?** *Where is the museum / hospital / money exchange?*
- **Où se trouve(nt)…?** *Where is / are…?*
- **Où est / sont…?** *Where is / are…?*

Choose a monument you know.

When you see **!** you will have to answer a question you haven't prepared for. At Foundation tier, it will be in the present tense. At Higher tier, it will be in the perfect tense. Listen carefully to what you are asked. **Comment** means *how*.

⑩ Practice   Grades 4–9

🎧 Your exchange partner is giving you some advice for a day trip you are about to go on. Listen to the recording and answer the following questions **in English**.

(a) Where should you go first of all?   **[1 mark]**
(b) What must you do to get there?   **[2 marks]**
(c) How far is it?   **[1 mark]**

 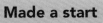 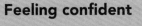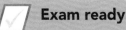

Eating out

You should know the language you need for ordering and talking about a meal out. See also Food (page 12) and Meals (page 13).

(2) In a restaurant

You need to know how to ask for things in a restaurant:

Je voudrais la carte / l'addition, s'il vous plaît.
I'd like the menu / bill, please.

J'ai besoin d'un couteau / une cuillère / une fourchette / un verre. **I need** a knife / spoon / fork / glass.

Qu'est-ce que vous avez comme plats végétariens?
What kind of vegetarian dishes **do you have?**

La bouillabaisse, qu'est-ce que c'est? **What is** 'bouillabaisse'?

Est-ce que le service est compris? **Is** service included?

(2) Talking about your food

appétissant *appetising*
acide *acidic*
amer / amère *bitter*
dégoûtant *disgusting*
délicieux / délicieuse *delicious*
frais / fraîche *fresh*

 PAGE 108

La soupe n'était pas appétissante car elle était froide et manquait de sel. *The soup wasn't appetising because it was cold and lacked salt.*

(10) Worked example   Grades 1–5

💬 Vous parlez avec un serveur / une serveuse dans un restaurant.

> 1. Réservation + heure et nom
> 2. Position de la table.
> 3. Quoi manger (**deux** détails).
> 4. !
> 5. ? Wi-Fi

- Bonsoir, je peux vous aider?

1. J'ai une réservation pour une table à sept heures au nom de Miles.

- Bon. Où est-ce que vous voulez vous asseoir?

2. Je voudrais une table près de la fenêtre.

- D'accord. Qu'est-ce que vous désirez comme entrée et plat principal?

3. Je prends l'assiette de crudités et le poulet rôti.

- Pourquoi est-ce que vous dînez dans notre restaurant, ce soir?

4. Le menu n'est pas trop cher!

- Ah bon!

5. Est-ce qu'il y a accès au Wi-Fi ici?

Alternatives are: **dans le coin** *in the corner;* **sur la terrasse** *on the terrace.*

Make sure that your answer is appropriate. You would need to say something different if you were asked: **Qu'est-ce que vous désirez comme dessert?**

Other possible answers include:

Votre restaurant est près de mon hôtel. *Your restaurant is near to my hotel.*

Il y a beaucoup de recommandations sur Internet. *There are lots of recommendations on the internet.*

You could also ask **Quel est le mot de passe Wi-Fi?**

(5) Practice   Grades 4–5

👓 Read the following report.

> Selon un sondage sur les habitudes des Français au restaurant, 21% des hommes mangent au restaurant chaque semaine contre 12% des femmes. Pour 45% des gens sondés, un bon restaurant est un endroit où on peut passer un moment convivial. Pour 19%, il faut que le service soit accueillant et amical, et pour 11% un repas copieux est le plus important. Quant à un mauvais restaurant: pour 20%, c'est un établissement trop bruyant, pour 22%, c'est un temps d'attente trop long et le pire pour 29%, c'est un mauvais rapport qualité / prix.

Answer the following questions **in English**. You do not need to write in full sentences.

(a) What percentage of people surveyed thought that friendly staff are the mark of a good restaurant?

(b) How do 20% of people surveyed characterise a bad restaurant?

(c) What do 11% of people think is important?

(d) What characterises the worst restaurants according to the report?   **[4 marks]**

✓ **Made a start**   ✓ **Feeling confident**   ✓ **Exam ready**

Shopping on holiday

You should know how to buy things that you need on holiday such as food, gifts and souvenirs.

⏱ 5 Giving directions

To buy food, you can:

- ask what is available: **Avez-vous des melons?** *Do you have any melons?* **Est-ce qu'il y a des fraises?** *Are there any strawberries?*

GRAMMAR LINK PAGE **80**

- say what you would like: **Je voudrais un kilo / cinq cents grammes de porc.** *I would like a kilo / 500 grammes of pork.*
- say what you need: **J'ai besoin d'une bouteille d'huile d'olive.** *I need a bottle of olive oil.* **Il me faut un paquet de pâtes / chips.** *I need a packet of pasta / crisps.*
- comment on the quality of the produce: **Le poisson est très frais.** *The fish is very fresh.* **Les pêches sont très bonnes.** *The peaches are very good.*

⏱ 5 Vocabulary 🔖 A–Z

cadeau (m) *present;* collier (m) *necklace*
carte (f) postale *postcard;* timbre (m) *stamp*
distributeur (m) d'argent *cash machine*
mode (m) d'emploi *instructions for use*
mode (m) de paiement *payment method*
porte-clés (m) *keyring;* sac (m) *bag*
réduction (f) *reduction*
réparation (f) *repair*
service (m) *service*
garantir *to guarantee*
marcher / fonctionner *to work*
négocier *to bargain / haggle*
ramener *to bring back*

⏱ 10 Worked example   Grades 1–9

✎ Ton ami(e) français(e) veut savoir si tu fais des achats en vacances. Écris un mail. Tu dois faire référence aux points suivants:

- ce que tu aimes acheter en vacances
- les avantages et inconvénients des achats de souvenirs
- une expérience récente dans un magasin ou au marché en vacances
- ce que tu achèteras dans l'avenir.

Écris 80-90 mots environ **en français**.

You could say that some souvenirs are difficult to transport. **Il est difficile de transporter des objets fragiles comme ceux en verre.**

You could say that you will only buy gifts for your family in the future. **Dans l'avenir, je n'achèterai que des cadeaux pour ma famille.**

Exam focus 📌
Read the bullet points carefully and make sure that you use the correct verb tenses.

Salut! Quand je suis en vacances, j'aime bien acheter des petits objets comme des vases ou des porte-clés parce que je veux avoir un beau souvenir de mes vacances. Cependant, ils sont parfois inutiles et je devrais en acheter moins. Récemment, j'étais en Turquie et le dernier jour de mon séjour, on est allés au grand marché. Je voulais acheter un joli tapis mais le vendeur a demandé un prix incroyable. Alors, j'ai dû négocier avec lui et finalement j'ai payé une somme plus basse. Je pense que j'achèterai moins de souvenirs dans l'avenir et que je prendrai plutôt des photos.

⏱ 20 Practice   Grades 1–9

1 Yves is talking about his holiday purchases. Listen to the recording and answer the following questions **in English**.

🎧 **(a)** Where did Yves do his shopping? **[1 mark]**
(b) What did he buy his father? Give **two** details. **[2 marks]**
(c) Why couldn't he buy a present for his mother? **[1 mark]**

2 Regarde la photo et prépare des réponses sur les points suivants:

💬
- la description de la photo
- manger en vacances – préférences
- visite récente d'un marché
- cadeaux que tu vas acheter
- ton opinion sur les marchés de rue.

✓ **Made a start**   ✓ **Feeling confident**   ✓ **Exam ready**

Where I live

You should be able to describe your home and say what you like and dislike about it.

 Talking about your home

To talk about your home you can use:

- prepositions:

  Ma maison est située dans une rue tranquille à côté d'un parc. *My house is located in a quiet street **next to** a park.*

- adjectives and qualifiers:

  Mon appartement est très petit et assez démodé. *My flat is **very small** and **quite old-fashioned**.*

- demonstrative pronouns:

  Ma maison est plus petite que celle de mes cousins. *My house is smaller than my cousins' house. (i.e. **that** of my cousins.)*

   GRAMMAR LINK PAGE **83**

 Vocabulary A-Z

arbre (m) *tree*
fenêtre (f) *window*
fleur (f) *flower*
HLM (habitation à loyer modéré) *low-cost home*
immeuble (m) *block of flats / building*
jardin (m) *garden*
maison (f) individuelle / jumelée / mitoyenne *detached / semi-detached / terraced house*
grenier (m) *attic*
pièce (f) *room*
sous-sol (m) *basement*

VOCABULARY LINK PAGE **110**

 Describing your house

Voici ma maison. Directement en face de la porte d'entrée se trouve la cuisine. Au rez-de chaussée, nous avons aussi un salon ouvert avec salle à manger. L'escalier mène du vestibule au sous-sol où on trouve la machine à laver. Au premier étage, il y a deux chambres: celle de mes parents et ma chambre, ainsi que la salle de bains avec douche et toilettes. Le grenier a été aménagé en deux chambres. À l'extérieur, nous avons un joli jardin avec beaucoup d'arbres et de plantes.

This is my house. Directly opposite the front door is the kitchen. There is also an open plan sitting room and dining room on the ground floor. Stairs lead from the hall to the basement where the washing machine is. On the first floor there are two bedrooms – my parents' and mine, as well as the bathroom with a shower and toilet. The attic has been converted into two bedrooms. Outside we have a pretty garden with lots of trees and plants.

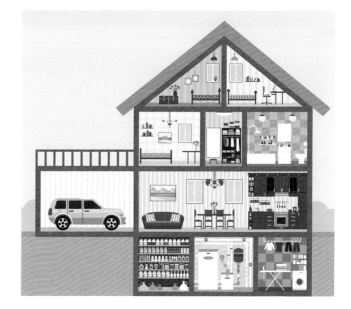

 Worked example Grades 1–9

💬 Depuis combien de temps habites-tu dans ta maison?

Model answer 1

J'habite dans ma maison depuis six ans. Auparavant, nous habitions dans une maison mitoyenne à la périphérie de la ville.

Model answer 2

J'habite dans ma maison depuis mon enfance. Je n'ai connu que cette maison et je l'aime bien, mais si j'avais le choix, j'aurais un bel appartement au centre-ville.

You must answer this question, using the present tense and a period of time.

Use **auparavant** *previously* to extend your answer to where you lived before.

The best answers extend a simple response. Here, the imperfect and the conditional add more detail.

 Practice Grades 1–9

💬 Answer the following questions.

- Que penses-tu de ta maison / ton appartement?
- Comment serait ta maison idéale?

The neighbourhood

You should know how to describe your neighbourhood and express opinions about it.

 Describing your neighbourhood

To describe your neighbourhood you can use:

- the verb pouvoir to say what you can or can't do there:

  On peut y faire des achats / visiter le musée / aller au théâtre. **You can** go shopping / visit the museum / go to the theatre there.

  On ne peut pas aller au parc. **You can't go** to the park.

- adjectives to describe and compare places in town:

  Il y a une église très ancienne qui est plus grande que la cathédrale. *There is an old church that is bigger than the cathedral.*

- opinions: J'aime habiter à Manchester parce que c'est une grande ville agréable. *I like living in Manchester because it is a big, pleasant city.*

- negatives: Il n'y a ni cinéma ni théâtre. *There is **neither** a cinema **nor** a theatre.*

- qualifiers: Il n'y a absolument rien pour les jeunes. *There is **absolutely** nothing for young people.*

 Worked example | **Grades 4–9**

👓 Read these reviews of a town.

> Dans cet espace énorme, on trouve, sous le même toit, une centaine de boutiques où on vend des choses à des prix incroyables. On n'a jamais besoin de sortir avec son parapluie!
>
> Pendant la saison touristique, on peut bien s'y amuser, mais on s'ennuie le reste de l'année.
>
> Trouver une place de stationnement au centre-ville est presque impossible. Cependant, au parc relais à la périphérie, une place de stationnement est garanti.
>
> Pour les tout-petits, il y a plein de choses à faire, avec des aires de jeux et une ferme urbaine, mais pour les ados, il n'y a même pas de club pour les jeunes.

Put a cross | **✗** | next to each one of the **three** correct statements.

Example	The shopping facilities are excellent.	
A	You are guaranteed to find a parking space where you want.	
B	It's a good place to visit all year.	
C	There is a park and ride facility.	✗
D	You need your umbrella when you go shopping.	
E	There is a huge shopping centre.	✗
F	There are good facilities for all ages.	
G	Teenagers would prefer better facilities in the town.	✗

Vocabulary

aire (f) de jeux *play area*
banlieue (f) *suburb*
bruit (m) *noise*
circulation (f) *traffic*
embouteillage (m) *traffic jam*
heure (f) de pointe *rush hour*
quartier (m) *neighbourhood / district*

piste (f) cyclable *cycle lane*
transports (m pl) en commun *public transport*
zone piétonne (f) *pedestrian zone*
animé *lively*
bruyant *noisy*
calme *calm*
pollué *polluted*
tranquille *quiet*

 VOCABULARY LINK PAGE **109**

Aiming higher

Use the imperfect tense to compare where you live now and have lived previously, or what your town is like now and was like in the past.

Avant, j'habitais au centre d'une ville industrielle, mais il y a deux ans, on a déménagé en banlieue. *Before, I lived in the centre of an industrial town, but two years ago we moved to the suburbs.*

Avant, il y avait un grand château mais il est maintenant en ruines. *Before, there used to be a big castle, but now it is in ruins.*

> This comment refers to the shopping facilities, and in particular the great prices and the fact that everything is under one roof (sous le même toit).

> This contrasts the out-of-town parking (park and ride) with that in the centre of town.

> This comment contrasts the facilities for young children with those for teenagers (les ados).

Practice | **Grades 4–9**

✏️ Une société française cherche des articles sur des villes en Angleterre. Écrivez un article pour intéresser les employés de la société qui vont travailler en Angleterre. Vous devez faire référence aux points suivants:

- différents / divers aspects de l'histoire de la ville
- pourquoi on devrait vivre dans cette ville
- les avantages et inconvénients de la vie en ville
- un festival qui aura bientôt lieu dans votre ville.

Justifiez vos idées et opinions.

Écrivez 130–150 environ mots **en français**.　**[32 marks]**

Town and region

It's important to know how to describe where you live and how to give some of its advantages and disadvantages.

 Describing your region

To talk about your region you can:

- describe where it is and the type of area it is:

  C'est une région rurale située dans le sud-ouest de l'Angleterre. It is a rural area situated in the south-west of England.

- use adjectives and make comparisons:

  C'est une région très pittoresque, mais elle est moins touristique que d'autres régions. It is a picturesque region, but it is less touristy than other regions.

- use the pronoun **y** to say what you can do there:

  On peut y faire du tourisme. You can go sightseeing there.

  GRAMMAR LINK · PAGE **84**

 Vocabulary A-Z

champ (m) *field*
se déplacer *to get around / move*
colline (f) *hill*
ferme (f) *farm*
fleuve (m) *river (flowing into sea)*
à la montagne *in the mountains*
paysage (m) *landscape*
randonnée (f) *walk / hike*
région (f) *region*
rivière (f) *river*
rural *rural*
usine (f) *factory*
village (m) *village*
vivre *to live*

VOCABULARY LINK · PAGE **110**

 Worked example **Grades 4–9**

🎧 **La vie à la campagne et en ville**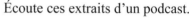

Écoute ces extraits d'un podcast.

Des gens parlent de leur région. Quel est l'avantage de l'endroit où ils habitent **maintenant**? Mets une croix **✗** dans les **trois** cases correctes.

		Phillipe	Sandrine	Ben
Example	plus tranquille	✗		
A	meilleurs transports en commun			✗
B	beaucoup de magasins			
C	vie culturelle variée		✗	
D	moins de pollution	✗		
E	peu de circulation			

This tells you the context for the texts you will hear. Try to predict what advantages and disadvantages might be mentioned.

Note **maintenant** is stressed. This implies that the texts may refer to places where the people talking have lived in the past. Listen carefully for the relevant information.

If the question is in French, the answers will be too. Both the reading and listening papers have questions and answers in French.

Use **depuis** + present tense here.

Remember to make adjectives agree.

 Aiming higher ⬆

Use superlatives to add weight to your opinions and descriptions.

Le pire, c'est qu'on ne peut pas respirer d'air frais. The worst thing is that you can't breathe fresh air.

La meilleure chose dans la vie ici, c'est... The best thing about life here is...

 Practice **Grades 1–9**

1 Traduis le passage suivant **en français**:

✏ I have been living on a farm in the country for three years. I like living here because I can go for walks in the fields with my dog. However, my brother hates the village because it is too small. He would like to live in a big city. Last year he spent six months with a family in the USA.

[12 marks]

2 Answer the following questions.

💬 • Qu'est-ce qu'on peut faire dans ta région?
- Où voudrais-tu habiter dans l'avenir?
- Tu aimes habiter dans ta région?
- Tu voudrais vivre à l'étranger? Pourquoi / pourquoi pas?

Francophone countries

You may need to be familiar with where French is spoken around the world for a range of topics, such as education, music, food, religious customs, festivals (**le Carnaval de Québec**, **la Fête des Masques** in Mali, for example) and holidays.

⑤ Where is French spoken?

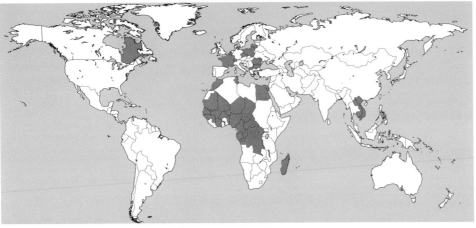

On parle le français dans plusieurs pays d'Afrique de l'Ouest, par exemple au Sénégal, au Mali, au Burkina Faso, au Niger, au Togo, au Cameroun et en Côte d'Ivoire ainsi que dans les pays nord-africains comme le Maroc, l'Algérie et la Tunisie. En Asie du Sud-Est, avant, on parlait français au Vietnam, au Laos et au Cambodge. Le Québec, au Canada, est aussi une région francophone.

French is spoken in several West African countries, for example Senegal, Mali, Burkina Faso, Nigeria, Togo, Cameroon and Ivory Coast as well as North African countries such as Morocco, Algeria and Tunisia. In South East Asia, they used to speak French in Vietnam, Laos and Cambodia. Quebec, in Canada, is also a francophone region.

⑩ Worked example   **Grades 4–9**

👓 Lis ces conseils pour les visiteurs en Guadeloupe, une île des Antilles françaises.

> Essayez d'éviter la saison des pluies entre juillet et novembre en raison du risque d'ouragans. Par contre, le temps sec et chaud de décembre à mai est très agréable.
>
> N'oubliez pas que cet archipel des Caraïbes est un département d'outre-mer français, alors vous pouvez régler vos achats en euros.
>
> Prévoyez suffisamment de temps quand vous vous déplacez car le service de bus et de bateaux entre les îles n'est pas très fréquent. Si vous louez une voiture, sachez que l'état des routes est moins bon qu'en Europe. Prenez votre temps et conduisez prudemment!

❶ Pourquoi n'est-il pas conseillé de visiter la Guadeloupe au mois d'août?

parce qu'il fait mauvais temps

❷ Qu'est-ce que les touristes venant d'Europe n'ont pas besoin de faire s'ils veulent visiter la Guadeloupe?

changer de l'argent

❸ Comment est-ce que l'état des routes pourrait avoir des conséquences sur les déplacements en voiture?

Ils seraient assez lents. ◀ **Moins rapides, plus périlleux** or **moins confortables** would also be possible here.

⑩ Practice   **Grades 4–9**

🎧 You hear a report about school life in Cameroon. Listen to the report and answer the following questions **in English**. You do not need to answer in full sentences.

(a) Why are classes sometimes cancelled in primary schools in Cameroon? Give **two** details.   **[2 marks]**

(b) What is a problem for 69% of primary schools and 73% of secondary schools?   **[1 mark]**

(c) What is the biggest problem for 59% of primary schools and what is the consequence of this?   **[2 marks]**

 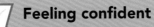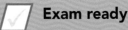

Seasons and weather

There are many contexts in which you may need to be able to talk about the weather and seasons.

 Seasons and weather

You can talk about seasons or the weather to add detail to an answer, or to show that you can use a range of tenses in the following contexts:

- discussing future plans: Demain, il y aura du vent, alors nous pourrons faire de la voile. *Tomorrow **it will be windy** so we can (will be able to) go sailing.*
- talking about a holiday: Quand il pleuvait, nous sommes restés à l'hôtel. *When **it rained**, we stayed in the hotel.*
- describing a photo: Ils sont à la plage et il y a du soleil. *They are at the beach and it is sunny.*
- giving reasons for doing or liking a particular activity: J'adore l'hiver parce que j'aime la neige et le froid. Je peux aussi faire du ski. *I love winter because I like snow and the cold. I can also go skiing.*

> ! Remember these expressions for talking about seasons:
> **en été / automne / hiver** *in summer / autumn / winter*
> But: **au printemps** *in spring*

 Worked example | **Grades 4–5**

 A weather app gives you this information.

région	vendredi	samedi
Pays de Loire	Généralement ensoleillé, mais froid	Le ciel sera très nuageux
Provence	Vent faible, ciel un peu nuageux	Le ciel va s'éclaircir
Normandie	Temps pluvieux et froid	Vent fort, ciel couvert
Alsace	Risque de neige le soir	Temps glacial
Corse	Temps orageux	Risque de précipitations

Choose between **the Loire Valley**, **Provence**, **Normandy**, **Alsace** and **Corsica**. Each region may be used more than once.

Example: Stormy weather is forecast on one day for ____Corsica____.

(a) Snow and ice are forecast for ____Alsace____.

(b) On Saturday, it will be cloudy and windy in ____Normandy____.

(c) There is the possibility of rain in ____Corsica____.

(d) On Friday, it will be sunny in _the Loire Valley_.

(e) Friday's weather will be cold and rainy in ____Normandy____.

(f) Light winds and cloud will give way to bright weather in ____Provence____.

 Quel temps fait-il?

météo (f) *weather forecast*

Several weather expressions use the verb il y a (in different tenses) + du / de la / des:

Il y a du vent / soleil / brouillard / tonnerre *It's windy / sunny / foggy / thundery.*

Il y a de la neige / brume. *It's snowing / misty.*

Il y aura de l'orage. *It will be stormy.*

Il y avait des averses / éclaircies. *There were showers / bright spells.*

You can also use faire and être:

Il fait / fera / faisait doux / beau / mauvais / frais.
The weather is / will be / was mild / fine / bad / fresh.

Le temps est / sera / était nuageux / pluvieux / variable.
The weather is / will be / was cloudy / rainy / variable.

> VOCABULARY LINK PAGE **102**

 Aiming higher ⬆

Use more advanced weather phrases and idioms in your Writing and Speaking exams:

Hier, il pleuvait si fort quand nous sommes sortis que nous avons été immédiatement **trempés jusqu'aux os** et que nous avons dû enlever nos vêtements **mouillés**.

wet | *soaked to the skin – literally to the bone*

 Practice | **Grades 1–5**

🎧 Jules, Vanessa and Ahmed are talking about their favourite seasons. What do they like to do?

Complete the sentences. Use the correct word or phrase from the box.

> climbing walking horse-riding skiing
> sailing swimming ~~sunbathing~~ heat snow
> sun wind cold hot mild

Example: Jules likes the ____heat____ and ____sunbathing____.

(a) Vanessa likes the _____ and _____.

(b) Ahmed prefers _____ weather because he likes _____. **[4 marks]**

You only need to look at the **samedi** column. Don't immediately go for the answer with **nuageux** as there is no mention of wind. Remember that **couvert** means *overcast* and is a synonym for *cloudy*.

My studies

You will need to be able to give your opinions about school subjects and give reasons for them.

⑤ School subjects

To talk about school subjects you should:

- express likes and dislikes with reasons:

  Ma passion, c'est l'histoire parce que je trouve l'étude des événements du passé fascinante.
  My passion is history because I find the study of events in the past fascinating.

- make comparisons:

  Je pense que l'allemand est plus utile que le dessin.
  I think that German is more useful than art.

- use the conditional to express wishes:

  Si j'avais le choix, je n'étudierais pas les maths.
  If I had the choice, I wouldn't study maths.

⑤ Talking about your ability

Je suis très fort en biologie mais assez faible en espagnol. Par contre, mon copain est doué en langues.

I am very good at biology but quite weak in Spanish. On the other hand, my friend is gifted in languages.

> You can extend your answer by saying what someone else's preferences are.

⑤ Worked example | Grades 1–9

❶ Tu préfères les sciences ou les langues?

💬 J'aime les deux car je les trouve faciles. En plus, les profs enseignent ces matières d'une manière stimulante. Cependant, ma copine n'aime pas les langues parce qu'elle les trouve trop difficiles.

❷ Quelles matières as-tu trouvées difficiles cette 💬 année? Pourquoi?

Cette année, j'ai trouvé la technologie difficile parce que je ne suis pas très créatif et qu'il faut avoir de bonnes idées. D'ailleurs, je ne suis pas fort en dessin et on doit produire un plan avec nos idées.

❸ Pourquoi as-tu choisi d'étudier le français?

💬 En fait, je ne l'ai pas choisi car nous devons tous étudier le français. Cependant, je pense que c'est une matière très utile car on apprend à communiquer avec des gens qui parlent une autre langue.

> This answer uses two tenses, adjectives, an impersonal verb and a modal verb.

> This is a detailed response that includes **je**, **nous** and **on** forms of verbs as well as a relative clause (**qui**).

② Vocabulary

apprendre *to learn*
bulletin (m) scolaire *school report*
comprendre *to understand*
cours (m) *lesson*
demander *to ask*
devoirs (m pl) *homework*
échouer *to fail*
emploi (m) du temps *timetable*
études (f pl) *studies*
examen (m) *exam*
matière (f) obligatoire / facultative *compulsory / optional subject*

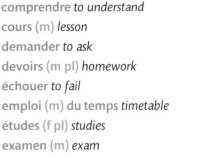

VOCABULARY LINK PAGE **112**

⑤ Talking about subjects and teachers

J'aime mon prof de maths parce qu'il me fait rire.
I like my maths teacher because he makes me laugh.

Je trouve le prof de chimie trop impatient. Il n'enseigne pas bien et on n'apprend rien dans son cours.
I find the chemistry teacher too impatient. He doesn't teach well and we don't learn anything in his lessons.

⑤ Aiming higher ⬆

Phrases like **d'ailleurs** (*moreover / besides*) and **néanmoins** (*nevertheless*) are useful when you want to give a more extended answer to a question or point.

⑤ Practice | Grades 4–9

🎧 Listen to this extract from a radio discussion about school subjects.

Answer the questions **in English**.

(a) What specific subject does the speaker like?
(b) What reason is given for this?
(c) What is their least favourite subject?
(d) What reasons are given for this? (**two** details)

[5 marks]

Exam focus

With longer listening passages, listen for the main points on the first listen, and then for the details on the second listen.

Your school

Knowing how to describe your school and give your opinion on aspects of school life, such as school rules, is important.

⑤ About your school

- The school day:

  La journée scolaire commence à huit heures et demie et finit à quatre heures. *The school day starts at 8.30 a.m. and finishes at 4.00 p.m.*

- What your school is like (size, age, equipment):

  Mon collège est un collège mixte pour environ mille élèves. Il est très bien équipé car il y a des tableaux interactifs dans toutes les salles de classe, un réseau Wi-Fi partout dans les bâtiments et on utilise des tablettes en cours. *My school is a mixed school for about a thousand pupils. It is very well equipped as there are interactive boards in all the classrooms, a wi-fi network throughout the buildings and we use tablets in lessons.*

- Your opinion about school matters, such as rules:

  À mon avis, le directeur est trop strict et les règles sont injustes. *In my opinion, the headteacher is too strict and the rules are unfair.*

- Your opinion about school pressures:

  J'ai peur de rater mes examens. *I am afraid of failing my exams.*

⑩ Worked example   Grades 4–9

 Traduis le passage suivant **en français**:

My school is quite big but the buildings are old. I have to get up early because lessons start at quarter to eight. Normally I go home by bus, but yesterday I had a detention and the bus left without me. In the evening we have to do so much homework! It's not fair!

Mon école est assez grande mais les bâtiments sont vieux. Je dois me lever tôt parce que les cours commencent à huit heures moins le quart. Normalement, je rentre à la maison en bus, mais hier, j'ai eu une retenue et le bus est parti sans moi. Le soir, nous devons faire tellement de devoirs! Ce n'est pas juste!

② Vocabulary   A–Z

activités (f pl) **périscolaires** *extra-curricular activities*
bien équipé *well-equipped*
cantine (f) *canteen*
installations (f pl) **scolaires** *school facilities*
directeur / directrice (m/f) *headteacher*
harceler *to bully*
redoubler *to repeat the year*
retenue (f) *detention*

 VOCABULARY LINK PAGE **112**

⑤ Talking about rules

To say what you are or are not allowed to do, use:

- **devoir**: **Nous devons** porter un uniforme scolaire.
  We have to *wear a school uniform.*

- **permettre + de**: **Il nous est permis** d'utiliser nos portables pendant la récré.
  We are allowed to *use our mobile phones during break.*
  On ne nous permet pas de nous maquiller.
  We are *not* ***allowed to*** *wear make-up.*

- the phrase **il est interdit + de**: **Il est interdit de** courir dans les couloirs. ***You are not allowed to*** *run in the corridors.*

② Comparing French and English schools

En France:

On ne porte pas d'uniforme. *You don't wear a uniform.*

La journée commence vers huit heures. *The day begins at about eight o'clock.*

On n'étudie pas la religion. *You don't study RE.*

On doit redoubler si on ne fait pas assez de progrès. *You have to repeat the year if you don't make enough progress.*

Les grandes vacances durent deux mois. *The summer holidays last for two months.*

⑩ Practice   Grades 1–9

🎧 Jérôme and Nora are talking about their school. Listen to the recording and answer the following questions **in English**.

(a) What negative aspects of his school does Jérôme mention? Give **two** details.   **[2 marks]**

(b) In what way does Nora's school cater for less academic pupils?   **[1 mark]**

     Made a start   Feeling confident   Exam ready

School trips, events and exchanges

You will be expected to be able to describe and talk about school trips and exchanges.

 Talking about trips and exchanges

When you describe trips and exchanges you can:

- use a range of verbs and tenses: Dans trois semaines, je **ferai** un voyage scolaire en Espagne. *In three weeks I **will go** on a school trip to Spain.*
L'an dernier, **on a organisé** un échange avec un collège à Rouen. *Last year an exchange **was organised** with a school in Rouen.*

- talk about the benefits and / or problems with trips:
L'échange m'**a permis** de découvrir une nouvelle culture. *The exchange **allowed** me to get to know a new culture.*
Quelques élèves **avaient** le mal du pays. *Some pupils **were** homesick.*

 Worked example — **Grades 4–9**

✏️ Votre collège partenaire cherche des articles sur des échanges. Écrivez un article sur ce sujet pour leur blog. Vous devez faire référence aux points suivants:

- votre expérience d'un échange
- les aspects les plus mémorables
- l'importance des échanges – votre opinion
- vos intentions par rapport à un échange ou une visite à l'étranger dans l'avenir.

Justifiez vos idées et vos opinions. Écrivez 130–150 mots environ **en français**.

Ma récente visite en France avec l'échange scolaire était ma première expérience d'une visite dans un pays étranger sans mes parents. J'avais peur d'avoir le mal du pays, mais la famille de mon correspondant était tellement gentille et accueillante que je ne me suis jamais senti seul. Pour moi, ça a été une expérience tout à fait enrichissante parce que j'ai eu la chance d'assister aux cours au collège de mon correspondant.

À mon avis, les échanges scolaires sont importants parce qu'on peut découvrir une nouvelle culture et une nouvelle cuisine, et se faire de nouveaux amis. On peut également améliorer ses compétences linguistiques. Au début de mon séjour, j'avais des difficultés à comprendre tout ce que les membres de la famille disaient, mais à la fin de la semaine, ça allait mieux. Puisque je veux toujours perfectionner mon français parlé, je vais faire un stage intensif d'un mois pendant les vacances d'été, en France.

 Vocabulary A–Z

correspondant(e) (m / f) penfriend
différence (f) difference
excursion (f) day trip
expérience (f) experience
groupe (m) scolaire school group
programme (m) programme
similarité (f) similarity
sortie (f) excursion / trip
visite (f) visit
à l'étranger abroad
apprécier to appreciate
organiser to organise
participer to take part in
rencontrer to meet
rester to stay
accueillant(e) welcoming

 Aiming higher ⬆️

Try to avoid repeating vocabulary: école (f) or établissement (m) are synonyms of collège (m).
Include higher-level structures, like the pluperfect: Avant de participer à cet échange, je **n'étais jamais allé** à l'étranger sans mes parents.

> You must use the perfect and imperfect tenses to respond to the first two aspects of the task.

> This paragraph gives reasons for the importance of exchanges and uses the future tense to respond to the fourth bullet point.

Practice — **Grades 1–9**

💬 Regarde la photo et prépare des réponses sur les points suivants:

- la description de la photo
- l'importance des échanges scolaires
- un voyage scolaire que tu as fait
- un événement scolaire auquel tu vas participer
- ! *(Est-ce que tu préfères les échanges scolaires ou les voyages scolaires à l'étranger?)*

Using languages

You should be able to talk about how you use languages.

 Talking about your linguistic skills

You will need to:

- use modal verbs: Je **voudrais** apprendre l'espagnol. *I would like to learn Spanish.*
  Je **ne peux pas** comprendre l'arabe. *I can't understand Arabic.*
  On **doit** pratiquer la prononciation. *You have to practise the pronunciation.*

  GRAMMAR LINK PAGE **87**

- talk about the different aspects of language learning:
  Les exercices d'écoute sont plus difficiles que ceux de lecture. *Listening exercises are more difficult than reading ones.*
  Il faut avoir une bonne mémoire. *You have to have a good memory.*
  Je ne parle pas allemand. *I don't speak German.*

You should know when to use **apprendre** (*to learn*) and **comprendre** (*to understand*) to talk about languages.

 Vocabulary

améliorer *to improve*
communiquer *to communicate*
se débrouiller en *to get by in*
s'exprimer *to express oneself*
prononcer *to pronounce*
compétence (f) linguistique *linguistic skill*
expression (f) orale / écrite *spoken / written communication*

interprète (m / f) *interpreter*
langue (f) étrangère *foreign language*
possibilités (f pl) d'avancement *promotion prospects*
indispensable *indispensable*
couramment *fluently*
rapidement *rapidly*

 Worked example **Grades 4–9**

👓 Read these online comments about the importance of languages.

> Puisque ma mère est française et que mon père est algérien, je parle français et arabe depuis mon enfance. Je trouve ça génial car je peux communiquer avec tous les membres de ma famille. **Yannick**

> Je suis jalouse des gens bilingues parce qu'ils appartiennent à deux cultures différentes. Je voudrais bien faire la connaissance de personnes de l'Amérique du Sud, alors des compétences en langue espagnole seront indispensables. **Laure**

> Pour moi, c'est tout simple. Parler une langue étrangère est le meilleur moyen d'avoir une carrière intéressante n'importe où dans le monde. **Alain**

> Quand on parle une langue étrangère, on a de meilleures chances d'avancement dans sa carrière et, bien sûr, on peut gagner un meilleur salaire. **Nathalie**

Who says what about learning another language? Enter either **Yannick**, **Laure**, **Alain** or **Nathalie**.

(a) ____Alain____ says having language skills enables you to be part of a global workforce.

(b) ____Laure____ wants to get to know other cultures.

(c) ____Nathalie____ says you are more likely to be promoted if you have language skills.

(d) ____Yannick____ says 'being bilingual is part of my heritage'.

 Practice **Grades 1–9**

🎧 You hear some young people contributing to a Belgian radio phone-in programme. Listen to the recording and put a cross ☒ in the correct box for each question.

1 (a) Hélène is interested in learning...

A	a European language	
B	an Asian language	
C	an African language	
D	sign language	

(b) For her the attraction is that...

A	she can use it for her career	
B	she can use it when travelling	
C	it's a challenge	
D	it's something she doesn't find difficult	

2 (a) Jérôme's motivation for learning a language is to...

A	get to know another country better	
B	earn more money	
C	get an interesting job	
D	be able to communicate with his girlfriend	

(b) Jérôme finds learning this language...

A	easy	
B	frustrating	
C	tiring	
D	difficult	

[4 marks]

  Made a start **Feeling confident** **Exam ready**

Ambitions

You should know how to talk about your future plans and ambitions.

⑤ Stating your ambitions

You can use the present tense and the conditional to talk about your hopes and ambitions:

J'ai envie d'aller à l'université. **I want to** go to university.

J'ai l'intention de faire du bénévolat auprès de personnes âgées. **I intend to** do volunteering with the elderly.

Mon but est de gagner beaucoup d'argent. **My aim is to** earn a lot of money.

J'espère faire de bonnes actions. **I hope** to do some good.

Je n'ai aucune intention de vivre à l'étranger. **I have no intention of** living abroad.

Je rêve d'avoir ma propre entreprise. **I dream of** having my own business.

J'aimerais prendre une année sabbatique. **I would like** to take a gap year.

Je ne voudrais pas travailler dans un bureau. **I wouldn't like** to work in an office.

GRAMMAR LINK PAGE 93

⑩ Worked example — Grades 4–9

🎧 You hear an extract from a street survey about plans and ambitions. Listen to the recording and answer the following questions **in English**.

(a) What is the first reason the speaker gives for changing his mind about what he wanted to do in life?

He wasn't good enough at science.

(b) What kind of languages is he particularly interested in?

Languages that use a different alphabet

(c) What has he still got to make up his mind about?

Whether or not to take a gap year

(d) In what way could he use his language skills if he went travelling?

He could get to know other people and cultures.

Think about what possibilities there are for different **kinds** of languages.

Listen carefully and focus on the **first** reason mentioned.

Note down some ideas for this and then listen to see if your ideas are correct.

Think about what this might be, given the context of plans and ambitions.

② Vocabulary

débouché (m) *job prospect / opportunity*
se détendre *to relax*
espoir (m) *hope*
fonder une famille *to start a family*
mettre de l'argent de côté *to save money*
utiliser les langues *to use languages*

VOCABULARY LINK PAGE 112

② Talking about the future

Use the future tense to talk about your definite plans:

Je serai interprète. *I will be an interpreter.*

J'aurai mon propre appartement. *I will have my own flat.*

Je gagnerai un bon salaire. *I will earn a good salary.*

Read the questions carefully and think about the context. Try to predict what the answer might be in each case.

⑤ Aiming higher ⬆

avant de + infinitive (*before doing something*)
après avoir / être + past participle (*after doing* or *after having done* something)

Avant d'aller à l'université, je prendrai une année sabbatique. *Before going to university, I will take a gap year.*

Après avoir fait du bénévolat, j'aurai de nouvelles compétences. *After having done some voluntary work, I will have some new skills.*

Après être allé(e) à l'université, je chercherai un emploi intéressant. *After going to university, I will look for an interesting job.*

⑩ Practice — Grades 1–9

💬 Answer the following questions.

- Tu veux aller à l'université ou commencer à travailler? Pourquoi?
- Est-ce que tu voudrais étudier à l'étranger dans l'avenir? Pourquoi / pourquoi pas?
- Tu voudrais prendre une année sabbatique dans l'avenir? Pourquoi / pourquoi pas?
- Qu'est-ce que tu voulais faire comme travail quand tu étais plus jeune?

Education post-16

You will need to know the language relating to your plans for further education, at school and beyond.

 Talking about your plans

Use the future tense to talk about your future studies:

J'étudierai les sciences. **I will study** sciences.

J'irai au lycée pour étudier pour mon bac. **I will go** to sixth form college to study for my A levels.

Je deviendrai apprenti. **I will become** an apprentice.

Je laisserai tomber les maths. **I will drop** maths.

Je ne porterai plus d'uniforme scolaire. **I will no longer wear** school uniform.

En septembre, j'entrerai en première. In September, **I will go** into Year 12 / Lower Sixth.

J'aurai plus de liberté. **I will have** more freedom.

J'apprendrai une nouvelle langue. **I will learn** a new language.

 Vocabulary

diplôme (m) *degree / qualification*
année (f) sabbatique *gap year*
apprenti(e) (m/f) *apprentice*
avoir l'intention (de) *to intend (to)*
bac(calauréat) (m) *A level(s)*
en seconde *in Year 11*
en première *in Year 12 / Lower Sixth*
en terminale *in Year 13 / Upper Sixth*
étudier *to study*
laisser tomber *to drop*
liberté (f) *freedom*
lycée (m) *sixth form college*

PAGE
112

 Worked example **Grades 4–9**

👓 Lis les commentaires d'un forum sur les études scolaires et l'avenir.

Aimée	Je passerai le bac parce que je suis forte en langues, surtout en anglais et en espagnol. Cependant, j'ai parfois des difficultés en langues anciennes. Si j'avais le choix, je ne ferais plus de maths car c'est une matière qui ne m'intéresse pas, mais malheureusement, ce n'est pas une matière facultative. En ce moment, je pense faire carrière comme interprète.

Marc	En fin de troisième, j'ai décidé de faire un bac pro cuisine parce que les études universitaires ne m'attirent pas. Je m'intéresse au secteur de la restauration et ce bac me prépare pour une carrière, soit de chef de cuisine, soit de directeur de restaurant. Je continue à étudier les maths car on doit savoir bien compter dans le métier que j'ai choisi. Heureusement, c'est une matière que j'aime.

Qui est la personne correcte? Choisis entre **Aimée** et **Marc**.
Chaque nom peut être utilisé plusieurs fois.

(a) Pour _____Marc_____, le bac mettra à l'épreuve ses compétences pratiques.

(b) _____Aimée_____ doit continuer une matière qu'elle n'aime pas.

(c) _____Aimée_____ aura probablement de bonnes notes.

Une matière facultative means *an optional subject.* Don't overlook the first part of the sentence where Aimée says she doesn't like maths.

Marc says he is going to do the bac pro cuisine and mentions that it can prepare him for a career as a chef.

Aimée says she is good (forte) at languages, from which you can infer that she also gets good marks.

 Practice **Grades 1–5**

✏ Traduis les phrases suivantes **en français**.

(a) In September I will study the subjects that interest me the most. **[2 marks]**

(b) I am happy to drop geography because it's boring. **[2 marks]**

(c) Most of my friends intend to go to university. **[2 marks]**

(d) I think you can get a better job if you have been to university. **[2 marks]**

(e) I would like to find a job or an apprenticeship. **[2 marks]**

  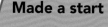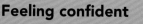

Charity and voluntary work

You need to know how to talk about different types of charities and voluntary work, including fundraising.

⑤ On fait du bénévolat

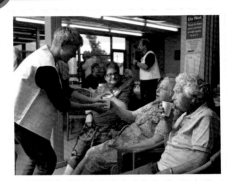

On fait du bénévolat pour différentes raisons, par exemple: pour aider les autres; pour se donner le sentiment d'être utile; et de ne pas se concentrer sur soi-même. D'autres s'engagent pour obtenir de nouvelles compétences ou pour avoir plus de confiance en eux.

There are different reasons for doing voluntary work, for example: to help others; to make oneself feel useful; and not to focus on oneself. Others get involved to gain new skills or confidence in themselves.

Soi is the emphatic pronoun used with **on**. **Soi-même** means *oneself, ourselves*.

② Fundraising activities

 A–Z

aider les autres *to help others*
amasser des fonds *to fundraise*
association (f) caritative *charity*
expérience (f) enrichissante *enriching experience*
faire du bénévolat *to do voluntary work*
manifestation (f) *demonstration*

mondial *worldwide*
participer à la vie de société *to take part in society*
reconnaissant *grateful*
soutenir quelqu'un *to support someone*
solidaire *supportive*
solidarité (f) *solidarity*

VOCABULARY LINK
PAGE
107

⑩ Worked example   Grades 1–9

❶ Fais-tu du bénévolat?

💬 En ce moment, je ne fais pas de bénévolat, mais à l'avenir, je voudrais en faire avec une association caritative qui aide les réfugiés. Je crois que c'est important de penser aux autres.

Use conjunctions like **mais** to introduce a different tense into your answer.

Using the pronoun **en** is a feature of a top answer. The same would apply to **y**.

❷ Est-ce que tu as participé à un événement pour
💬 collecter des fonds?

Don't worry if your answer isn't strictly true. Focus on giving an answer that is varied and accurate.

L'année dernière, notre collège a organisé une journée au profit des victimes de catastrophes naturelles. On a payé une livre sterling pour ne pas porter notre uniforme scolaire, et j'ai participé à un concert pendant la pause-déjeuner.

⑩ Practice   Grades 1–5

🎧 Your French penfriend and her friends are talking about how they raise money for charity. Listen to the recording and put a cross ☒ in the **two** correct boxes.

		Didier	Emma	Guy
Example	Taking part in a charity run	✗		
A	Selling things online			
B	Taking part in a sponsored concert			
C	Raising awareness through social media			
D	Collecting in the street			
E	Washing cars			
F	Baking for a cake sale			

[3 marks]

Jobs and careers

You will need to know how to talk about different types of jobs and describe your own skills and qualities.

 Talking about jobs

When saying what job someone has in French, you do not use an article (even though English uses *a*):

Je voudrais être avocat. *I would like to be a lawyer.*

Mon père est médecin. *My father is a doctor.*

To talk about where someone works, you can use **chez** or à with the name of a company.

Ma mère travaille chez / à Wilsons. *My mother works at Wilsons.*

 Talking about your skills and qualities

Quelles sont vos compétences et vos qualités personnelles?
What are your skills and personal qualities?

Je suis bien organisé(e) / plein(e) d'énergie / enthousiaste / fidèle / travailleur(euse) / honnête.

I am well organised / full of energy / enthusiastic / loyal / hard-working / honest.

J'aime faire partie d'une équipe. *I like to be part of a team.*

Je parle deux langues étrangères. *I speak two foreign languages.*

 Worked example **Grades 4–9**

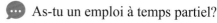 As-tu un emploi à temps partiel?

Depuis six mois, j'ai un emploi à temps partiel dans un supermarché près de chez moi. Je dois travailler à la caisse et aider les clients à trouver des produits dans les rayons. Je travaille le vendredi soir et le samedi. J'aime bien mon petit boulot parce que le travail est varié.

> Use the present tense with **depuis** to say how long you have been doing something.

> This detailed answer says what you do, where and when. It also gives an opinion and a reason.

 Aiming higher

The top answers may include sentences that use the subjunctive:

Il faut **que je finisse / fasse / aie / aille / trouve**.
It is necessary that I finish / do / have / go / find.

Il faut **que je fasse** un travail intéressant.
It is necessary for me to do interesting work.

GRAMMAR LINK PAGE **101**

 Vocabulary

boulot (m) *casual job*

faire quelque chose d'enrichissant *to do something enriching*

entretien (m) *interview*

entreprise (f) *firm / business / enterprise*

espérer *to hope*

gagner *to earn*

métier (m) *job*

recevoir *to receive*

varié *varied*

VOCABULARY LINK PAGE **112**

 Practice **Grades 4–9**

 Lis ce mail de ton ami.

> **Sujet:** Mon travail
>
> Mes copains aiment bien les emplois où on arrive à neuf heures et on repart à cinq heures, mais ça ne me conviendrait pas du tout. En fait, si je devais faire le même travail tous les jours, je m'ennuierais. Quant au salaire, cela n'a aucune importance pour moi car mes besoins ne sont pas grands. Avant tout, je voudrais m'entendre avec mes collègues et éviter un long trajet dans les transports en commun!

Lis les phrases. Mets une croix X dans les **trois** cases correctes.

Exemple	Il n'est pas essentiel de gagner beaucoup d'argent.	X
A	Je cherche un emploi avec des heures régulières.	
B	Je veux avoir des collègues sympas.	
C	Je voudrais des horaires flexibles.	
D	Je voudrais gagner beaucoup d'argent.	
E	Je voudrais travailler près de chez moi.	
F	Je voudrais voyager pour le travail.	
G	Les collègues sont moins importants que le salaire.	

[3 marks]

 Made a start **Feeling confident** **Exam ready**

International events

You need to be able to talk about sporting and music events that can bring the world together.

⑤ Talking about advantages of events ☑

You should be able to express an opinion about big international events and give a reason for it:

- Les événements sportifs sont bons pour la société parce qu'ils unissent les gens. *Sporting events are good for society because they bring people together.*
- Les Jeux Olympiques créent du travail dans la ville hôte et mettent le développement économique en avant. *The Olympic Games create jobs in the host city and promote economic development.*
- Je crois que les rencontres sportives encouragent la pratique du sport. *I believe that sport events encourage people to participate in sport.*

⑤ Vocabulary   A–Z ☑

coupe (f) du monde *World Cup (football)*

développement (m) économique *economic development*

festival (m) (de musique) *(music) festival*

Jeux Olympiques (m pl) *Olympic Games*

fierté (f) nationale *national pride*

rencontre (f) sportive *sports event*

ville (f) hôte *host city*

augmenter *to increase*

créer *to create*

mettre en avant *to promote*

participer *to participate*

Les Jeux Olympiques encouragent la fierté nationale.

Pierre and Adèle both mention negative aspects of big sporting events.

Pierre talks about improved infrastructure (**infrastructure améliorée**) and new metro lines.

Pierre says that movements (**déplacements (m)**) are more difficult.

Farouk mentions that shouting with the crowd (**crier avec la foule**) is exciting (**passionnant**).

⑩ Worked example Grades 4–9 ☑

👓 Read these online comments.

On dit que les événements comme les Jeux Olympiques sont une bonne affaire pour la ville hôte car ils rapportent de l'argent et la ville profite d'une infrastructure améliorée. Cependant, les habitants doivent supporter des années de travaux pour, par exemple, la création de nouvelles lignes de métro. En fait, les déplacements en ville sont plus difficiles pendant les Jeux. **Pierre**

Il est vrai que les grandes compétitions sportives internationales attirent beaucoup de touristes, alors les hôtels augmentent toujours leurs prix pendant ces rencontres! Ce n'est pas juste! À mon avis, il vaut mieux rester chez soi et regarder les compétitions à la télé. **Adèle**

J'adore l'atmosphère des grands événements sportifs. À mon avis, c'est une expérience totalement différente de celle du petit écran. Crier avec la foule, c'est quelque chose de vraiment passionnant. Je n'oublierai jamais la finale de la coupe du monde de foot à laquelle j'ai assisté! **Farouk**

Answer the questions **in English**. You do not need to write in full sentences.

(a) Who has the most positive attitude towards big sporting events? Farouk

(b) What specific lasting benefit for inhabitants of a host city does Pierre mention? improved transport facilities

(c) What does Pierre say about travel during big sporting events? It is more difficult.

(d) Why does Adèle think about the actions of hotels during big sporting events and why? She is critical because they put their prices up.

(e) What is her attitude towards sporting events as a spectator? It's better to watch on TV.

(f) What does Farouk say about spectators at a live event? They are excited and shout.

Il vaut mieux means *it is better.*

㉚ Practice Grades 1–9 ☑

✏ Vous êtes allé(e) à un festival de musique. Écrivez un article pour un magazine pour intéresser les lecteurs.

Vous devez faire référence aux points suivants:

- votre opinion du festival + raison
- l'importance des festivals pour une ville ou une région
- l'impact des festivals sur l'environnement
- vos projets pour assister à un autre événement culturel dans l'avenir.

Justifiez vos idées et vos opinions. Écrivez 130–150 mots environ **en français**.

Campaigns and good causes

You need to be able to talk about campaigns to do with good causes or social issues such as homelessness, poverty and fair trade.

 Le commerce équitable

- Les petits producteurs peuvent obtenir un meilleur prix pour leurs produits. *Small producers can get a better price for their goods.*
- Les employées peuvent travailler dans de bonnes conditions et en sécurité. *Employees can work in good conditions that are safe.*
- Le commerce équitable lutte contre le travail des enfants. *Fair trade fights against child labour.*
- Les producteurs reçoivent de l'argent qu'ils peuvent utiliser pour améliorer les conditions de vie dans leur village. *Producers receive money that they can use to improve conditions in their village.*
- Les ouvriers / enfants ne sont pas exploités. *Workers / children are not exploited.*
- On garantit un salaire minimum. *A minimum wage is guaranteed.*

 Vocabulary

campagne (f) *campaign*
droits (m pl) de l'homme *human rights*
eau (f) douce / potable / salée *fresh / drinking / salt water*
manque (m) de *lack of*
marque (f) *brand*
pauvreté (f) *poverty*
bénéficier *to benefit*
manquer *to lack*
mourir *to die*
respecter *to respect*
sauver *to save*
sensibiliser *to raise awareness*
durable *sustainable*
inacceptable *unacceptable*
mal nourri *malnourished*

Pour sauver la planète, on doit économiser l'eau.

 Worked example **Grades 4–9**

 Lis cet article écrit par un volontaire qui aide les SDF.

> Récemment, j'ai rencontré Paulo qui est venu à Paris sans sa famille pour améliorer sa qualité de vie. Il avait espéré trouver un emploi bien payé, mais il n'a pas eu de chance, bien qu'il ait un diplôme d'ingénieur. Il a gagné un peu d'argent en lavant des voitures mais cela n'était pas suffisant pour payer le loyer.
>
> On penserait que le froid serait le pire aspect de sa situation, mais le soir, il peut aller au centre d'accueil où il peut prendre une douche et où les volontaires lui donnent un repas chaud. Non, le pire, c'est que la vie dans les rues est dangereuse car on risque d'être attaqué par des drogués ou d'être victime d'un accident de la circulation. Il faut absolument aider ces gens.

Rejoindre means to rejoin. Paulo came to Paris **sans** (*without*) his family.

Mets une croix ☒ dans la case correcte.

(a) Paulo est venu à Paris...

A	pour rejoindre sa famille	
B	pour chercher du travail	✗
C	pour obtenir un diplôme	
D	pour s'échapper à la guerre	

(b) Le plus grand problème pour les sans-abri, c'est que dans les rues, on...

A	a froid	
B	n'a rien à manger	
C	est toujours sale	
D	pourrait être blessé ou tué	✗

Sale means dirty; Paulo can shower (**se doucher**) at the refuge centre.

 Practice **Grades 4–5**

Listen to this advertisement from a charitable organisation about a good cause. Answer the questions **in English.**

(a) Who is this advert encouraging listeners to help? Give **two** details.

(b) What is the consequence of the problem mentioned? Give **two** details.

(c) Where is the problem most evident? Give **two** details.

(d) In what way are children particularly affected? Give **two** details.

(e) What can you do personally? Give **two** details.

[10 marks]

  Made a start **Feeling confident** **Exam ready**

Global issues

To talk about global issues, you will need to know vocabulary for natural and man-made disasters.

 Talking about causes and effects

Causes and effects can be expressed by using words such as mener à (*to lead to*), contribuer à (*to contribute to*), à cause de and à la suite de (*because of*).

Dans les pays pauvres, le déboisement tropical par les habitants pour la production de récoltes alimentaires ou l'élevage d'animaux contribue à l'effet de serre et mène au réchauffement de la Terre et à la disparition de plusieurs espèces de plantes et d'animaux.

In poor countries the deforestation of the tropical rain forests by the inhabitants to produce crops or to raise animals contributes to the greenhouse effect and leads to global warming and to the extinction of several animal and plant species.

L'élévation du niveau de la mer est provoquée par le réchauffement de la Terre.

Rising sea levels are caused by global warming.

Beaucoup de gens ont perdu leur maison et tous leurs effets personnels à la suite de l'ouragan qui a ravagé leur pays.

A lot of people have lost their homes and all of their possessions following the hurricane that ravaged their country.

 Worked example | **Grades 4–9**

👓 Lis ce témoinage de Hassan qui parle des problèmes de son pays.

> Les problèmes dans la République du Tchad duraient depuis des années. Au début, il y avait la sécheresse et la terre ne pouvait pas produire à manger. Tout le monde avait faim et je perdais du poids tous les jours. Heureusement, on a reçu de l'aide de la France, ce qui nous a permis de vivre plus facilement. **Hassan**

Mets une croix ✗ dans la case correcte.

Les problèmes dans le pays d'Hassan ont été causés principalement par…

A	le climat	✗
B	un désastre créé par l'homme	
C	la situation politique du pays	
D	le déboisement	

La conséquence de ces problèmes était…

A	la guerre	
B	un tremblement de terre	
C	la famine	✗
D	des inondations	

 Vocabulary A–Z

combustion (f) de combustibles fossiles *the burning of fossil fuels*

déboisement (m) tropical *deforestation of tropical rain forests*

défavorisé *disadvantaged*

désertification (f) *desertification*

disparition (f) des espèces *extinction of species*

effet (m) de serre *greenhouse effect*

éruption (f) volcanique *volcano eruption*

famine (f) *famine*

glissement (m) de terrain *landslide*

guerre (f) *war*

incendie (m) *fire*

inondation (f) *flood*

ouragan (m) *hurricane*

pauvreté (f) *poverty*

réchauffement (m) de la Terre *global warming*

sécheresse (f) *drought*

séisme (m) *earthquake*

service (m) d'urgence *emergency service*

tremblement (m) de terre *earthquake*

VOCABULARY LINK PAGE **111**

 Practice | **Grades 4–9**

🎧 Listen to this discussion programme about environmental and global issues. What does each person mention as the most serious problem? Put a cross ✗ in the **three** correct boxes.

		Yannick	Fatima	Noah	Laure
Example	Pollution	✗			
A	Deforestation				
B	Extinction of species				
C	Global warming				
D	Natural disasters				
E	Population growth				
F	War				
G	Energy sources				

[3 marks]

Try to predict what words you might hear for each problem and jot them down before you listen. For example, natural disaster could be séisme, ouragans, éruption volcanique.

The environment

Talking about environmental issues needs specific vocabulary like 'recycling' and modal verbs like 'we should' and 'we could'.

 Being environmentally friendly

To say what you should, could, or must do, use the verbs **devoir** and **pouvoir** and the following expressions. They are all followed by another verb in the infinitive.

- **Il faut** éteindre les appareils électroniques et la lumière en quittant une pièce.
  It is necessary to / One must switch off appliances and lights when leaving a room.
- **Il est important d'**acheter des produits verts.
  It is important to buy green products.
- **On doit / Nous devons** protéger l'environnement.
  One / We must protect the environment.
- **On devrait / Nous devrions** utiliser du papier recyclé.
  One / we should use recycled paper.
- **On a besoin de** recycler autant que possible.
  We need to recycle as much as possible.

This includes relevant 'environmental' vocabulary, an opinion with a reason, and a perfect tense.

 Vocabulary

arrêter *to stop*
baisser *to lower*
chauffage (m) central *central heating*
centre (m) de recyclage *recycling centre*
déchets (m pl) *rubbish*
détruire *to destroy*
économiser *to save*
emballage (m) *packaging*
éviter *to avoid*
gaspillage (m) *waste*
ordures (f pl) *rubbish*
poubelle (f) *dustbin*
réduire la consommation de *to reduce the consumption of*
sac (m) (en) plastique *plastic bag*
séparer *to separate*
trier *to sort (out) waste*

VOCABULARY LINK PAGE **111**

 Worked example   Grades 1–9

1 Tu aimes recycler? Pourquoi / pourquoi pas?

J'aime bien recycler et je pense que c'est important parce qu'on doit éviter le gaspillage et réduire les ordures ménagères. La semaine dernière, on a porté des boîtes en carton au centre de recyclage. Chez moi, nous compostons toujours les déchets de cuisine.

2 Qu'est-ce que tu as fait récemment pour protéger l'environnement?

Récemment, nous avons baissé le chauffage chez nous et on a tous mis un pull! De cette façon, nous pouvons consommer moins d'énergie. Il est important de protéger notre planète contre les effets du réchauffement de la Terre.

 Aiming higher

Expand on main points expressed in a variety of ways:

Avant, chez nous, on ne faisait rien pour protéger l'environnement, mais mon oncle nous a dit de faire un effort, alors mon père a décidé d'installer des panneaux solaires et de baisser le chauffage central pour ne pas gaspiller d'énergie. À présent, on consomme moins d'électricité, mais il faut qu'on fasse encore plus d'efforts!

This answer uses conjunctions (**mais, alors, pour**) and a variety of tenses to produce a complex sentence.

You don't need to use the subjunctive at GCSE, but if you feel confident about how to use it you could include an example. Useful ones are: **qu'on fasse / qu'on puisse / qu'on aille** (from **faire / pouvoir / aller**).

GRAMMAR LINK PAGE **101**

 **Practice**   Grades 4–9

Listen to this discussion programme about environmental issues. Which issue does each person mention as being of greatest concern to them? Put a cross ✗ in the **three** correct boxes.

		Serge	Ayesha	Paul	Zoë
Example	Food waste	✗			
A	Packaging				
B	Renewable energy sources				
C	Reduce use of the car				
D	Recycling				
E	Saving water				
F	Energy use				

[3 marks]

Pronunciation strategies

Understanding the link between the sound and spelling of a word will help you understand and say French words more accurately. You will gain marks for correct pronunciation in your speaking exam.

(2) General rules

- ☑ The same sound in French may have several different spellings.
- ☑ Many final consonants are silent.
- ☑ There is a liaison (the final consonant is pronounced) when a silent consonant is followed by a vowel.
- ☑ Cognates are invariably pronounced differently from their English equivalent.

(5) Same sound / different spelling

Some vowel sounds in French can be spelled in different ways, but all are pronounced the same:

- aller / allez / allé / nez
- des / j'ai / lait / forêt / dès / craie / palais
- dans / dent / étudiant / vend / grand.

> Remember vowels before **n** and **m** are nasal sounds in French, unless the **n** and **m** are followed by another vowel or are doubled, as in **une, vinaigre** and **pomme**.

(5) Final consonants

As a general rule, the following consonants are **not** pronounced when they are at the end of a word:

- **d**: chaud, froid, nord
- **g**: long, sang
- **m**: parfum, nom
- **n**: vin, fin, juin, selon
- **p**: trop, drap
- **s**: souris, chats, puis, alors, anglais
- **t**: mot, vert
- **x**: heureux, noix, faux, choux
- **z**: chez

> Some common exceptions to this rule are: **sud, mars, huit, oust, sept, strict** and **gaz**.

(10) Making the liaison

You need to pronounce the final consonant when it is followed by a vowel or silent *h*:

- when there is an adjective in front of a masculine singular noun: un grand‿hôtel / un petit‿ami / un mauvais‿exemple
- after determiners: son‿ami / mon‿espagnol / les‿examens / ces‿assiettes
- after monosyllabic prepositions: chez‿eux / aux‿États-unis / en‿Afrique / dans‿un‿instant
- after on, nous, vous, ils and elles: on‿a mangé / nous nous‿amusons / vous‿avez faim / ils‿écrivent des lettres / elles‿arrivent
- after est and ont: le train est‿arrivé / ils‿ont‿une petite maison
- after numbers: trois‿oignons / deux‿oranges.

> Although pronounced when followed by a vowel and also when at the end of a sentence, the letter **x** in **dix** and **six** is not pronounced when followed by a noun beginning with a consonant: **Je voudrais six bananes. / Je serai là dans dix minutes**.

The following consonants **are** usually pronounced when they are at the end of a word:

- **b**: club, flashmob, snob
- **c**: choc, parc
- **f**: neuf, vif, bœuf, chef
- **k**: anorak, folk, rock
- **l**: mal, calcul
- **q**: cinq, coq
- **r**: four, hiver, par

Words that come from other languages invariably have the final consonant pronounced: stop, clown, Islam, amen, autobus, grog, forum.

This also includes words that come from Latin, for example: maximum, minimum, aluminium, aquarium.

> Some common exceptions are: **plomb, estomac, blanc, clef, gentil, fusil**.

(5) Cognates

Most cognates are nearly always pronounced differently. In particular, you should know how to recognise and say words ending in –ion (nation, éducation) and words that begin with im- (impossible, important, impoli) and in- (incapable, incident, inconnu).

(10) Practice

💬 Practise saying the following phrases and then listen to the audio clips to check your pronunciation.

- Ils espèrent trouver la station de métro.
- Nous achetons du riz, du miel, des noix et six bouteilles de vin fin.
- Elles écoutent leur musique sur Internet.

Speaking strategies

In your speaking exam you can use non-verbal strategies, such as facial expressions and gestures, and verbal strategies to keep talking and complete the tasks.

Saying what you want to say

If you don't know or have forgotten the French word for something, here are three strategies that can help:

1 paraphrase: paresseux – *lazy*
C'est quelqu'un qui ne fait pas beaucoup de travail.

2 describe the item: its size, colour, material, shape or position – *a sprout*
C'est un légume vert un peu comme un chou, mais plus petit.

3 refer to the function of an item using words like un objet, un truc or un machin.
C'est un objet qu'on peut utiliser pour couper du bois. This could be accompanied by a non-verbal gesture (couper comme ça) to show whether you mean an axe or a saw.

Filler phrases

Sometimes you may need to give yourself a little time to think as you answer. Filler phrases can be useful as you can be thinking while you say the phrase:

alors *so*

eh bien *well*

c'est-à-dire *that is to say / what I mean*

tu sais / vous savez *you know*

tu vois / vous voyez *you see*

bon *okay*

bon ben *anyway*

euh *uh / um*

bref *in short*

tout simplement *in short*

bien sûr *of course*

Aiming higher

To gain top marks remember to:

- expand on your answer by using adjectives and adverbs to add details
- use a range of tenses. This can be done by making comparisons between different time frames.

Qu'est-ce que tu veux faire après avoir terminé tes études?

Le plus important, à mon avis, c'est de faire quelque chose de gratifiant. Après avoir terminé mes études, j'aimerais faire du bénévolat, peut-être en Chine, puisque c'est un pays qui m'intéresse et me fascine beaucoup. Plus tard, mon rêve serait de travailler dans l'informatique vu que c'est le secteur qui m'attire le plus.

Changing the subject

If you don't automatically have an answer to a question, you should try to say something, even if it isn't strictly true. For example:

Qu'est-ce que tu as fait récemment pour réduire les déchets chez toi?

Don't say Rien.

You could say:

En fait, je n'ai pas fait grand-chose pour réduire les déchets, mais mes parents ont trié les ordures pour les recycler.

Words like **mais**, **cependant** and **pourtant** are useful if you want to steer the conversation in a different direction.

Although these can be helpful phrases, don't overuse them and don't string them together!

Answering questions

You can repeat words and phrases from a question in your answer to give yourself some time to think.

Où es-tu allé(e) pendant les grandes vacances l'année dernière?

L'année dernière, pendant les grandes vacances, je suis allé(e) au pays de Galles...

If you understand the question but are not sure what to say initially, you could use phrases like:

Ça, c'est une question intéressante... *That is an interesting question...*

Laissez-moi réfléchir un moment. *Let me think for a moment.*

Ça dépend... *That depends ...*

Je dirais (que)... *I would say (that) ...*

Laissez-moi réfléchir un moment.

Exam-style practice

Répondez aux questions suivantes.

- Quels sont les effets du réchauffement de la Terre?
- Qu'est-ce qu'on doit faire pour protéger l'environnement?

Asking for clarification strategies

It is useful to know what you can say if you are not sure how to answer a question.

 Exam focus

You may find that you are not sure how to answer a question in your speaking exam. You may not have fully understood the question or you may not have heard what was asked. You will get some credit in the exam if you are able to keep the conversation going by using phrases to ask for clarification or repetition.

 Asking for repetition

There are several ways to ask your teacher to repeat the question:

- Pouvez-vous répéter la question, s'il vous plaît?
- Pourriez-vous répéter la question?
- Tu peux répéter la question, s'il te plaît?
- Vous pouvez parler plus lentement, s'il vous plaît?
- Tu peux parler plus lentement, s'il te plaît?

The conditional **pourriez** is an even more polite way of asking the question.

In the role play scenario, use the **tu** form if your teacher is playing the part of a friend.

Exam focus
Remember to make your voice go up at the end of these sentences to make them into questions.

 Worked example

Look at these three different ways to check the meaning of something.

- Qu'est-ce que tu fais comme activités périscolaires?

Activités périscolaires? Qu'est-ce que ça veut dire?

Pardon, je ne comprends pas le mot « périscolaire ». Qu'est-ce que ça veut dire?

Activités périscolaires? Ce sont les activités qui ont lieu à la fin de la journée scolaire?

Activités périscolaires? What does that mean?
Repeating the word and making it sound like a question is a simple way to communicate that you have not understood it.

I'm sorry, I don't understand the word 'périscolaire'. What does it mean?

Activités périscolaires? Are these after school activities?
Here, you have an idea of what the phrase means, but are just checking.

 Useful phrases

Qu'est-ce que ça veut dire? *What does that mean?*

Je ne comprends pas *I don't understand*

Qu'est-ce que vous voulez dire? *What do you mean?*

Comment dit-on « dégustation » en anglais? *How do you say 'dégustation' in English?*

Je ne sais pas *I don't know*

Comment ça s'écrit? *How do you write that?*

Peux-tu / Pouvez-vous expliquer le mot...? *Can you explain the word...?*

 Aiming higher

If you do need to use one of these strategies, try to use a phrase that demonstrates that you can use a range of tenses.

Je suis désolé(e), je n'ai pas bien compris le mot « dégustation ». Pourrais-tu / Pourriez-vous l'expliquer s'il te / vous plaît?

I am sorry, I haven't understood the word 'dégustation'. Could you explain it please?

This is a good phrase because it also uses an object pronoun.

Pages
24–25,
33–34,
37–39
LINKS

General conversation

In the speaking exam, you choose the first overall theme for the general conversation. You will be allocated a role play and picture stimulus on two of the other four broad themes. You will also be asked questions relating to one of the two remaining themes.

 Worked example

In this example, the student has chosen 'Local area, holiday and travel' as the theme and the second part is based on 'School'.

> If you don't understand the question, ask your teacher: **Les SDF, qu'est-ce que ça veut dire?**

1 Comment est-ce que tu trouves ta ville?

J'aime bien ma ville, car elle n'est ni trop grande ni trop petite, et il n'y a pas trop de circulation comme dans les grandes villes. On peut se déplacer facilement parce que les transports en commun sont excellents. Pour ceux qui aiment la culture, il y a plusieurs musées et un théâtre, mais il n'y a pas de cinéma, ce qui est dommage!

2 Dans beaucoup de grandes villes, on voit souvent des SDF. Qu'est-ce qu'on pourrait faire pour les aider?

À mon avis, la meilleure façon d'aider les SDF est de soutenir les associations caritatives qui travaillent avec eux. On pourrait par exemple aider à préparer des repas pour les SDF ou leur donner des vêtements chauds.

3 Quels sont les avantages de la vie à la campagne?

> You can develop your answer by talking about the disadvantages as well as the advantages of living in the countryside.

Je pense que le plus grand avantage de la vie à la campagne est que l'air est plus frais et qu'il y a moins de pollution. Cependant, les transports en commun sont souvent moins fréquents et on doit aller en ville pour faire des achats.

> Use the same tense as the question in your answer. Here it is the conditional.

4 Comment seraient tes vacances idéales?

Mes vacances idéales seraient au bord de la mer parce que j'aime me détendre et me bronzer. Pourtant, s'il fait mauvais, je trouve intéressant de faire des activités culturelles comme visiter un musée.

5 Qu'est-ce que tu as fait pendant tes vacances l'année dernière?

L'année dernière, je suis allé(e) au pays de Galles où on a fait du camping. Il faisait beau et nous avons pu faire des randonnées presque tous les jours. Un jour, nous sommes montés en haut du Snowdon et nous avons eu une vue magnifique, c'était formidable! Est-ce que vous êtes déjà allé(e) au pays de Galles?

> You must ask a question during the conversation. Remember to use **vous**.

6 Quelles sont tes matières préférées à l'école et pourquoi?

Je trouve les sciences fascinantes, mais ma matière préférée est l'histoire parce que je m'intéresse beaucoup à ce qui s'est passé dans le passé.

> Vary the way you introduce your opinions and use vocabulary. **Établissement** is an alternative for **école** or **collège**.

7 Que penses-tu de l'uniforme scolaire?

Je pense que l'uniforme scolaire est une bonne idée parce qu'on n'a pas besoin de passer du temps le matin à décider ce qu'on veut porter. En plus, ça donne une identité visible à notre établissement. Pourtant, j'ai parfois envie de porter mes propres vêtements comme on le fait en France!

8 Qu'est-ce que tu as fait comme devoirs hier?

> This answer is developed by making reference to differences from France.

Hier, j'ai révisé pour mes examens. J'ai dû relire les notes dans mes cahiers et j'ai fait des exercices de maths. Pour préparer mon examen de français, j'ai enregistré mes réponses à des questions sur mon portable.

9 Quels sont tes projets pour l'année prochaine?

> **Projets** is a clue that you need to use the future tense.

L'année prochaine, je serai en première et j'étudierai les sciences et les maths parce que je veux devenir ingénieur et ces matières sont nécessaires pour obtenir une place à l'université.

 Exam focus

- Use a range of vocabulary and grammatical structures that refer to past, present and future time frames.
- Express opinions and give reasons for them.
- You must also ask a question.

Exam-style practice

Listen to the questions recorded on the audio clip and answer them. The first theme is 'School' and the second is 'Identity and Culture'.

 Made a start   **Feeling confident** 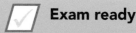 **Exam ready**

Using a picture stimulus

There is a picture-based task in the speaking exam at both tiers, and a photo description task on the writing paper at Foundation tier.

⑤ About the picture-based task

The picture stimulus will be related to one of the five broad overall themes for which you should know the key vocabulary.

The first bullet point in the picture-based task is always la description de la photo and you will be asked Décris-moi la photo. *Describe the photo to me.*

The question and answer section of the task will last for 2 minutes for Foundation tier and 3 minutes for Higher tier.

② Describing the photo

To describe the picture stimulus, think about how you could answer the following questions:

- ☑ Who is in the photo?
- ☑ Where are they?
- ☑ What are they doing?
- ☑ When or what is the time of year / occasion?
- ☑ What is the mood of the photo?
- ☑ Other details, e.g. What is the weather like?

⑩ Worked example

Regarde la photo et prépare des réponses sur les points suivants:

- La description de la photo
- Ton opinion sur les familles nombreuses
- Activités récentes en famille
- Projets pour une réunion familiale
- !

You will be expected to use the past and future tenses in your answer.

Model answer 1

Sur la photo, il y a huit personnes. Ces gens sont probablement membres d'une famille. Ils prennent un selfie et ils sont très heureux. Ils rient. Ils sont à la campagne.

These examples answer the first bullet point.

This answer provides quite a lot of information, but the language is simple and the sentences are short.

Model answer 2

Sur la photo, il y a huit personnes qui sont peut-être membres d'une famille. Elles sont en train de prendre une photo et elles ont l'air très heureuses puisqu'elles rient. Je pense qu'elles font une promenade à la campagne.

Qui is a relative pronoun – use it to join sentences.

Words like peut-être and probablement can be used to make inferences about what is in the photo.

Use connectives like puisque or parce que to introduce a reason for your statement.

⑤ Aiming higher

Replace il y a with a phrase that shows you can manipulate a verb, such as je vois, on voit or on peut voir.

Use peut-être (*perhaps*) to speculate about the photo. It could be a way of introducing another tense.

Ils vont peut-être partager la photo sur des réseaux sociaux.

Perhaps they are going to share the photo on social networks / media.

⑤ Exam-style practice

Regarde la photo et prépare une réponse sur le point suivant:

- La description de la photo

Pages
**15–16,
24–27**
LINKS

Role play (Foundation)

In the role play, at Foundation tier, you will have to complete five tasks, including responding to an unpredictable question and asking a question of your own.

② About the role play

Read the instructions on the card carefully. Make sure you understand what your role in the scenario is and the role that your teacher will play. You will be instructed to use **tu** or **vous**, depending on the context.

During your preparation time, work out what you will say for the four bullet points with information on the card.

Remember you will have to ask a question. It is marked **?**.

There will be an unpredictable question, to which you will have to respond. It is marked **!**. Listen carefully to what you are asked.

The role play will last for approximately 2 minutes.

② Exam focus

- Focus on saying enough to complete the task. There is no need to expand on your answers. You will be awarded up to 10 marks (2 per prompt) for successful communication of the task.
- If you don't understand the unpredictable question (**!**) you can ask your teacher to repeat the question: **Pardon? Vous pouvez répétez la question, s'il vous plaît?**

This tells you whether you should use the **tu** or **vous** form in the role play.

You only need to say one thing you do on the internet. Focus on what you know how to say.

Try to predict what you might be asked for here. If you don't understand, you can ask your teacher to repeat the question. This unpredictable question is: **Quand est-ce que tu utilises Internet?**

You should be ready to ask this question without being prompted. Remember to use the correct form of address (**tu** or **vous**).

Alternative responses:

1. Je fais des recherches pour l'école.
2. À mon avis, Internet est très dangereux.
3. Je vais sur Internet seulement le week-end.
4. On a un cours par semaine (le mardi matin).
5. As-tu un portable? Qu'est-ce que tu as comme portable? Qu'est-ce que tu fais sur ton portable?

⑤ Task instructions

- ☑ **description**: You must describe the item mentioned; this could be size, colour, shape.
- ☑ **une raison**: You must give a reason for your answer – **parce que c'est utile**.
- ☑ **combien de personnes / fois?** *How many people / times?*
- ☑ **où?** *where?* You need to give a place in your answer.
- ☑ **quand?** *when?*
- ☑ **type de** *kind of*. For example, **musique – type de**. Here you will need to talk about a kind of music, but listen carefully to the question you are asked. **Quelle sorte de musique est-ce que tu aimes?** OR **Quelle sorte de musique est-ce que tu n'aimes pas?**
- ☑ **combien de temps / durée**: You must say how long something lasts: **Le festival dure deux jours.**
- ☑ **renseignements** *information*
- ☑ **désiré** – You must say what you want: **vêtement désiré** *desired item of clothing*
- ☑ **prix** *price*

⑤ Worked example

Tu parles de la technologie avec ton ami(e).

1. Internet – une activité
2. Ton opinion d'Internet (**un** détail)
3. **!**
4. L'informatique à l'école – combien de cours par semaine
5. **?** Portable

1. Je fais du shopping en ligne.
2. Je pense qu'Internet est très utile.
3. J'utilise Internet le soir.
4. J'ai un cours d'informatique une fois par semaine.
5. Comment est ton portable?

⑤ Exam-style practice

Vous parlez avec l'employé d'un office de tourisme.

1. Votre nationalité
2. En France – combien de temps
3. **!** (*Comment trouvez-vous la France? Pourquoi?*)
4. Logement – description (**deux** détails)
5. **?** Gare

☑ **Made a start**   ☑ **Feeling confident**   ☑ **Exam ready**

Role play (Higher)

In the role play at Higher tier you will have to complete five tasks.

(2) About the role play

The Higher role play consists of five tasks, including responding to an unpredictable question (marked **!**) and asking two questions yourself (marked **?**).

The unpredictable question will require you to answer using the perfect tense.

Read the instructions on the role play card carefully. Note whether you need to use **tu** or **vous**.

(2) Exam focus

- You will be awarded up to 10 marks (2 per prompt) for successful communication of the task.
- Focus on saying enough to complete the task. There is no need to expand on your answers.
- The role play will last approximately 3 minutes.
- If you don't understand the unpredictable question (**!**) you can ask your teacher to repeat it: Pardon? Vous pouvez répéter la question, s'il vous plaît?

You must address your teacher as **vous** in this task.

(10) Worked example

Vous parlez avec l'employé dans un bureau des objets trouvés.

1. objet perdu – description
2. séjour en France – raison
3. **!**
4. **?** heure d'ouverture demain
5. **?** possibilité de retrouver – opinion

1. J'ai perdu mon porte-monnaie. Il est en cuir marron.
2. Je fais un échange scolaire.
3. Je l'ai perdu dans le bus hier.
4. À quelle heure est-ce que ce bureau est ouvert demain?
5. Est-ce que vous pensez qu'on va retrouver mon porte-monnaie?

Alternative responses
1. J'ai perdu mon portable / appareil photo / sac à dos + different description.
2. Je fais du tourisme, je rends visite à des amis.
3. Je l'ai perdu à la gare routière ce matin.
4. Quand est-ce que le bureau est ouvert demain?
5. Est-ce qu'il sera possible de retrouver mon porte-monnaie, à votre avis?

(5) Task instructions

In addition to the instructions that appear on Foundation role play cards (see page 54), you might see the following on a Higher role play card:

☑ **séjour – durée** *length of stay*

☑ **utilisation – portable / technologie:** You must say how you use your mobile phone / technology.

☑ **? possibilité:** You must ask if something is possible or if you can do something.

☑ **? réparation – coût:** You must ask about the cost of repairs.

☑ **? faire du sport – raison:** You must ask why the other person does sport. Pourquoi est-ce que tu fais du sport?

☑ **? musique classique – opinion:** You must ask the other person's opinion of classical music.

☑ **avantages / inconvénients:** You will have to talk about advantages and disadvantages of something. If the card has **+ raison** on it, you will have to give a reason.

☑ **problème / activité – deux détails:** You will have to say what the problem / activity is and give two pieces of information about it.

☑ **opinion + raison:** You must say what you think about the topic and give a reason.

☑ **utilisation:** You must say something about your use of something.

Use the perfect tense to say what you have lost.

You must give information about why you are in France.

Try to predict what you might be asked for here, given the context and the other tasks. You must use the perfect tense in your answer. The question here could be Où l'avez-vous perdu?.

You must ask a question here. Remember to use the correct form of address (**tu** or **vous**).

(10) Exam-style practice

Tu viens d'arriver chez ton ami(e) français(e).

1. Maison – opinion
2. **!** (*Qu'est-ce que tu as fait pendant le voyage?*)
3. Activités désirées pendant la visite (**deux** détails)
4. **?** dîner – heure
5. **?** possibilité – télévision

Listening strategies

Get to know the strategies that will help you in your listening exam.

 Preparing for your exam

- Learn as much vocabulary as you can for all the topics on the syllabus.
- Listen to as much French as you can. Ask your teacher for suggestions for suitable websites.
- Make sure you understand the link between sound and spelling. Following a transcript as you listen can help. (See page 49.)

 Extra strategies

- If you get stuck with a word, repeat it in your head and try to use your knowledge of phonics to transcribe it. Remember that cognates are nearly always pronounced differently in French.
- Listen out for words that mean the same (or opposite) as a word in the question: monotone = répétitif.
- Focus on the words you do know and try not to be put off by any unknown language. Use familiar words to eliminate options.

 Worked example

Listen to this young woman talking about her future studies and follow the transcript as she speaks.

«J'ai toujours rêvé de devenir médecin, mais on n'est jamais certain d'obtenir une place pour étudier la médecine, alors j'ai décidé de faire autre chose».

Put a cross **✗** in the correct box. The speaker…

A is certain to study medicine ☐

B is not planning to study medicine ✗

C might study medicine ☐

D never wanted to study medicine ☐

alors j'ai décidé de faire autre chose *so I decided to do something else.*

The speaker says **certain**, but uses it with **jamais** *(never)*.

 Before you listen

- Read the questions carefully. Do you need to listen out for a specific detail? Or do you need to draw a conclusion having heard the whole extract?
- Try to predict what you may need to listen out for in order to complete a task. If you are given the following headings to match to news reports, jot down some key words.

  fire (incendie / feu / pompiers / brûler)
  flood (inondation / pluie / tempête / pleuvoir)
  murder (meurtre / tuer / mort / mourir / assassiner)
  robbery (voler / voleur / vol / vole / cambriolage + any item that could be stolen)

- Look at the title as this may help you with key words. You may not know that piste cyclable is a cycle lane, but if you see 'Cycle lanes' as the title of the exercise and you hear the word you should be able to make the connection.

 While listening

- Try to concentrate on just listening when you hear the extract for the first time. If you start to make notes you may miss an important detail.
- Listen for the main points the first time you hear the recording and then for the details the second time.
- If you are listening out for someone's opinion or intentions, keep in mind that little words can change the meaning of a sentence:

  cependant *however*
  pourtant *however*
  mais *but*
  sauf *except*
  alors *so*
  malgré *in spite of*
  d'un autre côté *on the other hand*

- Listen to the whole extract before you draw any conclusions. An important piece of information may come at the end.

 Exam-style practice

Listen to this report about the Olympic Games. Answer the following questions **in English**.

(a) What advantages of being a host country are mentioned in the report (**two** details)? **[2 marks]**

(b) What are the disadvantages (**two** details)? **[2 marks]**

   Made a start Feeling confident 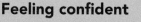 Exam ready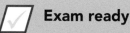

Listening 1

Pages 17–18, 47
LINKS

In the listening paper of your exam, you will need to be able to complete tasks with questions and answers in French.

② Before answering the question(s)

- Read the questions carefully before you listen.
- Try to predict what words you need to listen out for.
- Use the wording of the questions to help you understand what the extract is about.
- Listen to the whole extract before you make any notes and draw conclusions. You could miss an important detail!
- Concentrate on listening for the main details the first time and for the details the second time.

⑮ Worked example

Les fêtes en France

Écoute ce reportage et mets une croix ☒ dans les **trois** cases correctes.

Exemple	À l'origine, la fête des Lumières est une fête religieuse.	☒
A	La première fête des Lumières a eu lieu au seizième siècle.	
B	Uniquement les édifices municipaux sont illuminés pendant la fête des Lumières.	
C	Les habitants de Lyon participent à la fête des Lumières en allumant des chandelles dans leurs maisons.	☒
D	La fête du citron a lieu dans une ville au centre de la France.	
E	Un quart de million de personnes visitent Menton pendant la fête du citron.	☒
F	La fête a lieu dans les rues et les espaces verts de la ville.	☒
G	On peut voir de grandes structures créées avec des fruits de toute sorte de couleurs.	

[3 marks]

You can infer that this festival has its origins in religion from the reference to la Vierge Marie, la mère de Jésus Christ.

The sixteenth century is mentioned in the extract, but this was not when the festival first started.

Uniquement means *only*. The public buildings are not the only things illuminated.

Les habitants de Lyon and les Lyonnais are synonyms. Allumant des chandelles dans leurs maisons means the same as illuminent leurs fenêtres et leurs balcons avec des bougies.

The report says that Menton is *on the coast* (sur la Côte d'Azur).

More than 230 000 people go to the festival.

The report mentions défilés (*parades*); espaces verts can be inferred from the mention of jardins publics.

The report only refers to lemons and oranges, not fruits of all colours.

Exam focus

Remember that you generally will not need to understand the words that appear in the example. Focus on the other vocabulary in the task.

⑩ Exam-style practice

Exemple:

Écoute ce reportage. De quoi s'agit-il?
Mets une croix ☒ dans la case correcte.

A	Inondation	
B	Chute mortelle	☒
C	Incendie catastophique	
D	Manifestation violente	

1 Écoute ce reportage. De quoi s'agit-il?
Mets une croix ☒ dans la case correcte.

A	Violence au collège	
B	Mort d'un prisonnier	
C	Accident de la route	
D	Noyade accidentelle dans une piscine	

[1 mark]

Listening 2

In the listening paper of your exam you will need to be able to complete tasks with written answers in English and answer multiple-response questions in French.

(2) Before answering the questions

Read the questions carefully before you listen. Make sure you understand what kind of information you need to listen out for, and that you select the relevant bits.

You must write down all the information you are asked to give, but you do not need to answer in full sentences as long as your answer is clear.

For gap-fill activities, cross out answers as you use them so that you can see which options you have left.

(10) Worked example

❶ School uniform

Some pupils from a French private school are talking about school uniform. Listen to the recording and answer the following questions **in English**.

(a) What advantage does Florence mention?

don't have to spend time deciding what to wear

(b) What is the problem with the jacket?

too expensive

(c) According to Didier, what happens when pupils wear their uniforms?

They are better behaved.

(d) What does he dislike about his uniform?

He can't express his personality.

❷ L'argent

Gérard parle d'argent. Complète les phrases en choisissant un ou plusieurs mots de la case. Il y a des mots que tu n'utiliseras pas.

thé	en espèce	chocolat chaud
sa carte sans contact	monnaie	cher
pratique	facile	~~café~~

Exemple: Gérard vient de boire un _____café_____.

(a) Gérard paie son café avec

sa carte sans contact _____.

(b) Selon lui, c'est plus *pratique* _____.

(2) Exam focus

You will hear the extract twice and then there will be a pause for you to write down your answer.

Only note down key details while you are listening to the extracts, otherwise you might miss an important piece of information.

Don't worry if there are words you don't understand. Focus on the words you do know.

> *Practical* would also be acceptable.

> *Not elegant* would also be possible here.

(15) Exam-style practice

❶ Le mariage

Claire et Hubert parlent du mariage. Complète les phrases en choisissant un mot ou des mots dans la case. Il y a des mots que tu n'utiliseras pas.

démodé	négative	~~positive~~	jeune	vieux
la société	la famille	les grands-parents		

Exemple: Claire a une opinion ___positive___ du mariage.

(a) Claire ne veut pas se marier trop _____.

(b) Selon Hubert, le mariage est important pour _____.

❷ Holiday problems

Some people are talking about their holiday problems. Listen to the recording and answer the following questions **in English**.

(a) Why was the first speaker disappointed? Give **two** details.

(b) How did they manage to resolve the matter?

(c) What problem did the second speaker have?

(d) How was the problem solved? **[4 marks]**

✓ **Made a start** ✓ **Feeling confident** ✓ **Exam ready**

Reading strategies

Learning strategies that can help you work out the meaning of a text is extremely useful.

Decoding skills

Knowing common patterns between French and English words, as well as the meaning of French prefixes and suffixes, can help you work out the meaning of a text.

English pattern	French pattern	Examples
-c(al)	-que	musique, comique, romantique
-ary	-aire	militaire, grammaire
-y	-ie	comédie, tragédie, géographie
-ory	-oire	histoire, gloire, victoire
-ous	-eux	délicieux, nombreux, nerveux
-ty	-té	liberté, beauté, université
-ive	-if	positif, actif, négatif
-ing	-ant	dégoûtant, charmant
-ly	-ment	rapidement, complètement

Other changes between French and English:

English	French	Examples
s	é or es	espace, éponge, état
s	ô, ê	forêt, hôpital, tempête
dv	v	avantage, aventure
ni	gn	oignon, compagnon
dis	dés	désagréable, désastre

Prefixes and suffixes

Understanding French prefixes and suffixes can help you work out meanings.

re or ré = repeated or again
refaire *to redo / do again*; réouverture *reopening*

in-, im-, ir-, il-, mal-: make opposite meanings, often equivalent to un-, il-, in-, dis- in English.
malhonnête (*dishonest*); illimité (*unlimited*)

Translation into English

- Check you use the correct tense in your translation.
- Don't forget to translate time phrases, adverbs and adjectives.
- Watch out for pronouns like y:
on y voit... *you see... there*.

Strategies for working out meaning

There are bound to be a few words on the reading paper (Paper 3) which you do not know, but you can have strategies for working out the meaning. These include:

- using visual clues, such as images
- using your knowledge of word families to work out the meaning of a word: ami, amical, amicalement – *friend, friendly, in a friendly way*
- looking for cognates and near cognates (words that are either the same or very similar to English or another language that you know)
- using your knowledge of grammar, work out whether the unknown word is a verb, noun or adjective, etc., from its position in a sentence or the endings
- using the context and your knowledge of the French speaking world
- paying attention to high frequency words and what they mean, particularly those that can change the meaning of a sentence: cependant (*however*) or mais (*but*).

False friends

False friends are words that look like an English word but have a completely different meaning, for example:

actuellement *currently*	en fait *actually*
car (m) *coach*	voiture (f) *car*
chance (f) *luck*	occasion (f) *chance*
coin (m) *corner*	pièce (f) de monnaie *coin*
crayon (m) *pencil*	crayon (m) de couleur *crayon*
effectif *real*	efficace *effective*
éventuellement *possibly*	finalement *eventually*
gentil *kind*	doux / douce *gentle*
gros *fat*	dégoûtant *gross (disgusting)*
journée (f) *day*	voyage (m) *journey*
large *wide*	grand *large*
sensible *sensitive*	raisonnable *sensible*
sympathique *nice*	compatissant *sympathetic*

Using context

For unknown words, look at other words nearby to see if there is anything that can help you. Translate the following:

On a transporté le blessé de la scène de l'accident à l'hôpital sur un brancard.

You might not know brancard, but you could use other words as clues: transporté (*transported*), blessé (*injured*) and hôpital (*hospital*), to work out that un brancard is a *stretcher*.

 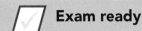

Reading 1

In the reading paper, you will need to complete different tasks with questions and answers in English.

 Exam focus

- Look at the number of marks allocated to each question or question part. This will indicate the amount of information and detail that is required.
- Look at the heading for each task. This will set the context for the extract and reading the question(s) may help you understand words you do not know. Read the whole text through before answering any questions.

Worked example

A life-changing experience

Read this account of a trip to Mali.

> J'ai toujours voulu voyager et j'avais aussi envie d'échapper à la vie quotidienne en France. Quand la chance de vivre pendant trois semaines avec les nomades dans le désert du Mali s'est présentée, j'ai tout de suite sauté sur l'occasion. C'était la première fois que je partais si loin toute seule. Une fois arrivée à Bamako, la capitale, le dépaysement était immédiatement évident, je n'oublierai jamais les odeurs et les couleurs. Le deuxième jour, je suis partie dans le désert au nord du pays pour rejoindre la famille nomade. J'ai tout de suite remarqué l'immensité du désert où il n'y avait rien ni personne.
>
> C'est dans le désert, chez cette famille, que j'ai appris à communiquer sans mots en faisant des gestes, des grimaces et des sourires, puisque la famille ne parlait pas français et que moi, je ne parlais ni arabe ni leur langue natale. J'allais tous les jours chercher de l'eau avec eux, car il leur manquait l'eau courante. On nourrissait les chèvres et on faisait du pain. En plus, j'ai eu des expériences uniques comme une improvisation musicale et un mariage nomade.
>
> Cette expérience m'a aidée à changer mon quotidien et à apprécier ce qui est important dans la vie. **Sandrine**

Use the cognates and the context in this paragraph to help you work out any words you don't know.

Manquait means lacked and will appear in a range of contexts. Make sure you know common words like this.

Use the context of having to fetch water to work out that eau (f) courante means running water.

Put a cross **✗** in the correct box.

(a) When Sandrine had the chance to go to Mali, she…

A	hesitated	
B	acted very quickly	✗
C	thought about it for three weeks	
D	talked to her family	

(b) She noticed the differences between France and Mali…

A	straight away	✗
B	in the north of Morocco	
C	gradually	
D	at the end of her stay	

(c) During her stay she…

A	spoke French and Arabic	
B	didn't need to speak to communicate with the family	✗
C	used a mix of French and the local language	
D	learned the local language	

The key phrase is tout de suite (immediately).

She describes the change of scene as being immédiatement évident.

She learned to communicate sans mots (without words).

 Exam-style practice

Read the account of the trip to Mali. Answer the following questions **in English**.

(a) What was the one thing that she had to do every day and why? **[2 marks]**

(b) What unique experiences did she have? Give **two** details. **[2 marks]**

(c) In what way did the experience change Sandrine? **[1 mark]**

 Made a start **Feeling confident** **Exam ready**

Reading 2

Pages 19, 23 LINKS

In the reading paper of your exam, you will need to be able to complete different tasks with questions and answers in French.

② Before answering

Look at the heading and any introductory text. This will set the context for the extract and reading the question(s) may help you understand words in the text you do not know. Make sure you read the whole text through before answering any questions.

Exam focus

At Foundation tier, there will only be multiple-response type questions in French. At Higher tier, you will have to write short answers in French.

⑮ Worked example

La télé et les habitudes

Lis les commentaires dans un forum sur la télévision.

> Chez nous, la télévision reste allumée toute la journée, même si personne ne la regarde. Pour moi, la télé, c'est un bruit de fond, mais pour ma grand-mère qui passe des heures entières toute seule, le petit écran est son fidèle compagnon. **Manon (17 ans)**

The television is described as a companion for Manon's grandmother.

> Dès que je rentre chez moi, j'allume la télé et le week-end, je m'assieds devant l'écran et je regarde de nouveaux films que je ne veux pas manquer. Parfois, je suis tellement absorbée par le petit écran que je n'arrive pas à faire mes tâches ménagères. **Agnès (24 ans)**

Qui est la personne correcte? Choisis entre **Manon** et **Agnès**.

(a) ___Agnès___ est accro à la télé.

(b) Chez ___Manon___, la télé est constamment allumée.

(c) ___Agnès___ néglige parfois des choses qu'elle devrait faire.

(d) La télé est importante pour quelqu'un que ___Manon___ connais.

accro means *addicted to* or *hooked on*. Manon describes TV as **bruit de fond** (*background noise*), whereas Agnès gets really absorbed in what she watches.

Néglige means *neglect*. Agnès says she sometimes doesn't get her housework (**tâches ménagères**) done.

Constamment (*constantly*) has the same meaning as **toute la journée** (*all day*).

⑩ Exam-style practice

Les Misérables de Victor Hugo

Lis cet extrait.

> Vers le milieu de la nuit, Jean Valjean s'est réveillé. Il était d'une pauvre famille de paysans du nord de la France. Dans son enfance, il n'avait pas appris à lire. (...) Sa mère s'appelait Jeanne Mathieu; son père Jean Valjean ou Vlajean, (...) contraction de Voilà Jean. Jean Valjean était d'un caractère pensif sans être triste. (...) Il avait perdu en très bas âge son père et sa mère. Sa mère était morte d'une fièvre de lait mal soignée.

Réponds aux questions **en français**. Il n'est pas nécessaire d'écrire des phrases complètes.

(a) D'où vient Valjean?

(b) Qu'est-ce que Valjean ne pouvait pas faire quand il était jeune?

(c) Quelle est l'origine du nom de Valjean?

(d) Pourquoi la vie était-elle peut-être difficile pour Valjean quand il était jeune? **[4 marks]**

Reading 3

In the reading paper of your exam, you will need to be able to read information and find opinions or draw conclusions from it.

 Exam focus

- Start by looking at the title for each extract. This gives you the context of the text and you can start to predict what words you might see.
- Read through the text carefully first, focusing on what you know. Don't worry too much about words you don't know, they may not be important. Try to understand the overall of the gist of the text and some of the main ideas.
- Read the questions carefully before you read the text for a second time. Make sure you understand what the question is asking you to do. Answer in English where it tells you to, and in French when this is required.
- Sometimes, the words in the questions may help you understand a word you didn't know in the text.
- Answer the questions you are most sure of first. You don't have to answer them in order.

Worked example

Family life

Read this extract from a news article.

mercredi **LA VOIX** **le 5 juin 2017**

Selon une étude récente en France, un enfant sur dix vit dans une famille recomposée, c'est-à-dire dans une famille où les enfants ne sont pas tous ceux du couple actuel. Le plus souvent, c'est un enfant qui vit avec sa mère et un beau-père. En plus, le nombre de familles monoparentales a augmenté.

> If you don't recognise **recomposée**, you will be expected to work it out from the context and apply your knowledge of how prefixes **re-** (again) and cognates work.

> Look at the questions to help you work out the meaning of **monoparentales** if you don't know it.

> It may help to start by eliminating the statements that you think are false.

> Read the statements carefully, paying close attention to negatives and words like *both* and *only*.

Which statements are **true**? Put a cross | ✗ | in the **three** correct boxes.

A	It is common for children in France to live with their father and his partner.	
B	A child in France will often live with their mother and stepfather.	✗
C	One in ten children in France do not live with both of their biological parents.	✗
D	Only one in ten children in France lives with their biological parents.	
E	The number of single parent families has decreased.	
F	There are now more single parent families than before.	✗

 Exam-style practice

School life

Read this comment from an online forum.

> À mon avis, deux mois, c'est trop long. On oublie la majorité de ce qu'on a appris pendant l'année et on ne voit pas ses copains pendant plusieurs semaines.

What aspect of school is being discussed? ← You need to read the information and draw a conclusion.

[1 mark]

Made a start   Feeling confident   Exam ready

Reading 4

In the reading paper of your exam, you may come across longer texts or literary texts that contain unfamiliar vocabulary.

⑤ About longer texts

You will not be expected to understand every word of a longer text. Read the text first to get the overall gist and then the questions to find out what information you need to extract. This may also help you to understand any language that is not clear to you on first reading. Don't waste time trying to work out the meaning of unnecessary details. You may need to infer to answer a question. You may also have to make deductions by looking at the clues and working out an answer.

⑮ Worked example

Souvenirs by Guy de Maupassant

Read this extract.

> Oh! Comme je suis surtout traversée par des souvenirs brusques de mes promenades de jeune fille. Là, sur mon fauteuil, devant mon feu, j'ai retrouvé étrangement, l'autre soir, un coucher de soleil que j'ai vu, étant bien jeune, sur une plage de Bretagne. Je l'avais oublié, certes, depuis longtemps, et il m'est revenu tout à coup, sans raison, ou peut-être parce qu'une lueur de tisons rouges aura réveillé dans ma mémoire la vision de cette lueur géante qui embrasait l'horizon ce soir-là! Je me suis tout rappelé: le paysage, ma robe, et même des détails de rien du tout, un petit bobo que j'avais au doigt depuis quelques jours, et cela si vivement, que j'ai cru en souffrir encore. J'ai senti l'odeur salée, humide et fraîche des sables mouillés (…), et je me suis mise à respirer à longs traits l'air marin qui me soufflait dans la figure. Oui, vraiment, j'ai eu seize ans pendant quelques minutes.

The title tells you the story is about memories.

The ending on the past participle (**traversée**) is a clue that the narrator is female.

Feu is a key word. If you don't know it, the options in Question 3 may help you work it out.

re (*again*) + **trouvé** = *found again* = *remembered*.

Use word patterns to work out the meaning of **étrangement**: **é** at the start of a word = **s** in English, **-ment** = *ly* → *strangely*.

This is a description of the fire, linking the red of the fire and the memory of a sunset (**coucher de soleil**).

The writer says **jeune fille**, but this is an older person looking back.

Put a cross ☒ in the correct box.

❶ At the time of writing this extract the narrator is …

A	a young girl	
B	an old woman	✘
C	an old man	
D	a young boy	

❷ The memory relates to an experience…

A	to do with fire	
B	by the sea	✘
C	in an armchair	
D	in the countryside	

The word *sea* (**mer**) is not used, but implied through language such as **plage** (*beach*), **l'air marin** (*marine air*) and **sables** (*sands*).

⑤ Exam-style practice

Answer these questions about the text from *Souvenirs*. Put a cross ☒ in the correct box.

❶ The narrator's memory of the event uses their...

A	senses of sight and smell	
B	senses of touch and sound	
C	senses of sound and smell	
D	sound and sight	

[1 mark]

❷ The narrator's memory of the experience comes on...

A	suddenly and is brief	
B	gradually but lasts a long time	
C	suddenly and lasts a long time	
D	gradually and is brief	

[1 mark]

 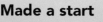

Translation into English

At the end of the reading paper, you will have a short passage to translate into English.

② Translation into English

At Foundation level, the passage will consist of about 35 words, and at Higher level about 50 words.

There will be references to a variety of tenses (past, present and future) in both passages.

At Higher level you can expect a wider range of vocabulary and grammatical structures to feature in the passage.

⑤ Translating idioms

Some words and phrases are expressed differently in French and English. Watch out for the following when you have to translate them:

- expressions with avoir:
  J'ai quinze ans *I am 15* (**not** *I have 15 years*); avoir froid / chaud / peur / de la chance *to be cold / hot / afraid / lucky* (**not** *to have cold / hot / afraid / luck*); il y a *there is / are*

- weather expressions:
  Il y a du vent / du soleil. *It is windy / sunny.* Il y a de l'orage. *It is stormy.*

- de to show possession: le copain de ma sœur *my sister's friend* (**not** *the friend of my sister*)

- articles used in French, but not in English and vice versa:
  J'adore le cyclisme. *I love cycling.* Il est professeur. *He's a teacher.*

- chez *at someone's house*: chez moi *at my home*

- à, de and en can all have different meanings depending on the context in which they are used.

- depuis used in the present tense can mean *have done / been doing* something since a specific date or for a length of time. J'apprends le français depuis cinq ans. *I have been learning French for five years.*

- venir de used in the present tense means 'to have just done something'. Il vient de téléphoner. *He has just rung.*

- watch out for false friends. (See reading strategies, page 59)

⑩ Worked example

Translate this passage **into English**.

> Dans mon collège, il y a une bibliothèque et une salle d'informatique. Hier, en cours d'informatique, j'ai travaillé sur ordinateur. Quelquefois, j'utilise mon portable pour acheter quelque chose. Le week-end prochain, je vais acheter un nouveau pantalon.

In my school, there is a library and an IT room. I worked on the computer in the IT lesson yesterday. Sometimes I use my mobile phone to buy something. Next weekend, I am going to buy a new pair of trousers.

This is *secondary school*, not college.

Salle d'informatique is literally *room of IT*, but make sure that what you write sounds natural in English.

Pour does **not** mean *for* here – it means *to* in the sense of *in order to*.

French sometimes uses an article where it is left out in English.

Trousers is a singular noun in French, unlike English.

⑩ Exam-style practice

① Translate the following sentences **into English**.

(a) Avec une télécommande, on peut changer d'émission de télévision sans quitter sa chaise ou le canapé. **[2 marks]**

(b) Je suis allé à la pharmacie avec l'ordonnance que le médecin m'avait donnée pour obtenir des médicaments. **[2 marks]**

② You read the following review for a hotel on a website. Your friend asks you to translate it **into English**.

> Je viens de passer une semaine dans cet établissement au bord de la mer. On l'a récemment remis à neuf avec de nouveaux meubles partout. Au rez-de-chaussée, il y a une belle salle à manger où on sert le dîner chaque soir. Ce que j'ai aimé le plus, c'était la piscine chauffée. J'aimerais bien y retourner l'année prochaine.

Writing strategies

Checking your work and making sure you have completed all aspects of the task is key to success in written tasks.

 Checking for communication

Check your work for communication and make sure that you have:

- addressed all elements of the task
- used the correct number of words.

 Checking for quality of language

Aim to include a wide variety of vocabulary and structures in your written work. This includes a variety of:

- tenses – past (imperfect, perfect and pluperfect); present; future and conditional
- time phrases: il y a un mois / dans l'avenir / maintenant
- opinions: je pense que / à mon avis
- justification and reasons for opinions: parce que / car / à cause de
- connectives: et, mais, pourtant
- comparatives and superlatives: plus / moins que
- negatives: ne jamais / plus / rien

 Writing checklist

☑ **Different ways of saying things**
Be flexible in your thinking. If you are not sure whether you have expressed an idea correctly, try to go about it another way. For example, you could express *I visited my friends* as Je suis allé(e) voir mes ami(e)s, J'ai rendu visite à mes ami(e)s or J'ai vu mes ami(e)s.

☑ **Be consistent**
When writing an email or letter, stick to either tu or vous form all the way through. Check verb endings as well as the possessives ton/ta/tes and votre/vos.

☑ **Improving your work**
Look for ways to improve your work by adding some interesting adjectives and adverbs or by varying the way you express your ideas. For example, you could express disliking something as Je n'aime pas du tout (la natation), Je déteste (la natation) or (La natation) ne me plaît pas.

☑ **Know your problem areas**
You will probably be aware of the kinds of mistakes you make when you are writing in French. If you know that you often leave off accents or have difficulty with verb endings, give these extra attention in your exam.

☑ **Time management**
Manage your time so that you have a few minutes to check your work once you have finished writing it.

 Checking for accuracy

Once you have completed a written task, check it carefully for spelling and grammatical accuracy. Look out for the following:

Adjectives
- Do they agree? Les fleurs sont jolies; des problèmes énormes
- Are they in the correct position? Il a les cheveux gris; une bonne raison

Verbs
- Have you got the correct ending for the subject of the verb? Est-ce que tu manges...? Mon ami et moi allons...
- Is the verb reflexive or irregular, or does it have spelling changes? Je me lève...; Les filles vont...; nous mangeons
- Have you used the correct tense? Le week-end prochain, je ferai une randonnée. (future); Hier soir, nous avons vu nos amis (perfect tense for a single action in the past); Pendant l'été, je voyais mes amis tous les jours (imperfect tense, for a repeated action over time); Quand j'étais jeune, je lisais beaucoup (imperfect tense for description and for when something used to happen)
- Does the past participle need to agree? Elles sont allées; Paul et Marc sont arrivés.

Gender
- Have you used the correct gender for nouns, pronouns and possessives? J'ai deux frères, ils s'appellent...; Ma maison est grande et elle est entourée d'arbres.

Spellings
- Are accents used correctly and plurals of nouns formed correctly? des chevaux (sing. = cheval); des gâteaux délicieux.
- Do you need capital letters? le mardi; en mai.

 Exam-style practice

Ton ami français veut savoir comment tu fêtes ton anniversaire. Écris-lui un mail. Tu dois faire référence aux points suivants:

- ton anniversaire – fêté comment
- dates importantes dans ta famille
- les relations familiales
- projets – week-end prochain.

Écris 80–90 mots environ **en français**.

Try out the strategies on this page while you practise.

 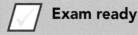

Translation into French (Foundation)

As part of the writing paper, you will have short sentences to translate into French.

At Foundation tier, the translation will consist of five different, short sentences. You will be expected to get the key messages across and to show that you know how to accurately apply the grammar and structures appropriate to Foundation level. In particular, you should pay attention to:

- verb forms: do you need the 'I', 'he, she, it' or some other form of the verb?
- verb tense: do you need to use the present tense or the future? The perfect or imperfect?
- adjective agreements: is the adjective describing a singular or plural noun? Is it masculine or feminine?

Ma famille
Traduis les phrases suivantes **en français**.

1 My sister is small.

2 My brother doesn't like playing football.

3 On Saturdays, I go shopping with my cousin.

4 My family go to the park next to the cinema.

5 Yesterday, I watched television with my parents and my brother.

1 Ma sœur est petite.

2 Mon frère n'aime pas jouer au foot.

3 Le samedi, je vais faire des courses / du shopping / des achats avec mon cousin / ma cousine.

4 Ma famille va au parc à côté du cinéma.

5 Hier, j'ai regardé la télévision avec mes parents et mon frère.

Remember to use the verb **avoir** when you say how old someone is.

Use the correct word for *library* in French. **Librairie** means *bookshop* and is a 'false friend'.

Think: do you need **avoir** or **être** to make the perfect tense of the verb **aller**?

There is more than one way of saying *people*. It doesn't matter which you use.

You could be asked to translate sentences that contain:

- a verb that refers to someone else, e.g. a friend
- references to simple opinions such as likes or dislikes and negatives
- different verbs in each sentence, and at least one sentence in a tense other than the present
- common idioms, time phrases and high frequency language, e.g. **il y a** *there is / are*
- references to time and place
- vocabulary covering more than one context.

The possessive adjective **ma** and adjective **petite** must agree with **sœur**.

Ne ... pas must go round the verb. The verb **aimer** (to like) is followed by the infinitive. You need the correct form of **à** to go with school: **au collège / à l'école**.

Days of the week are spelled with a lower case letter. Use the definite article + day of the week to convey the idea that something happens regularly.

Cinéma is masculine, so **de** (à côté de) changes to **du**.

Make sure you use the correct part of the verb **avoir** and that you have the correct past participle. The possessive adjective (*my*) must agree with parents (plural) and brother (singular).

Ma famille
Traduis les phrases suivantes **en français**.

1 My brother is 13 years old. **[2 marks]**

2 My mum goes to the library opposite the supermarket. **[2 marks]**

3 Last week I went to the theatre with my family. **[3 marks]**

4 There are four people in my family. **[2 marks]**

5 My sister plays the piano in the evening. **[3 marks]**

Do you need **à** or **de** when you talk about playing a musical instrument?

Translation into French (Higher)

As part of the writing paper, you will have a short passage to translate into French.

About the translation task

At Higher tier the translation will consist of a passage of at least 50 words. It is likely to consist of the following features:

- a mix of subject and vocabulary areas
- higher level grammar structures and vocabulary.

You will be assessed both for your ability to convey the message and for the accuracy of the grammar and spelling.

Exam focus

The passage that you will have to translate is likely to include:

- verbs that refer to someone other than yourself
- references to opinions such as likes or dislikes with reasons
- a variety of verbs (regular and irregular) and tenses: present, perfect, imperfect, future and conditional
- references to time, place and comparisons.

Worked example

Traduis le passage suivant **en français**:

Last week I went to a restaurant in town to celebrate my father's birthday. My mother had chicken and we drank mineral water. I like cooking at home and sometimes I prepare dinner on Saturdays. Next week I will go to a classical music concert with my friends. If I had the choice we would go and see a film in the cinema.

La semaine dernière, je suis allé(e) dans un restaurant en ville pour fêter l'anniversaire de mon père. Ma mère a pris du poulet et nous avons bu de l'eau minérale. J'aime faire la cuisine à la maison et quelquefois, je prépare le dîner le samedi soir. La semaine prochaine, j'irai à un concert de musique classique avec mes copains. Si j'avais le choix, on irait voir un film au cinéma.

You must make the noun and adjective agree.

Remember to use **de** (of my father) when you have to translate 'apostrophe s' showing possession.

The verb **aimer** is followed by an infinitive.

You need the future tense here. **Aller** is irregular in the future.

Use **de** here – a concert of classical music.

You need to use the imperfect and the conditional in this sentence.

Célébrer could also be used, instead of **fêter**.

You could use **mangé** instead of **pris**.

Exam focus

Remember to check your translation carefully.

- Word order – Are the adjectives and pronouns in the correct position?
- Have all the necessary agreements been made: gender (masculine / feminine) and singular / plural?
- Verbs – Have you used the correct tense and have you conjugated the verb correctly?
- Spelling – Have you spelled words correctly?

Exam-style practice

1 Les vacances d'été
Traduis le passage suivant **en français**:

In the summer, I went on holiday with my family to the south of Spain. The hotel was quite small and my room was dirty. My parents like Spanish food but I prefer spicier dishes. Next week it is my brother's birthday. I will buy him some white socks and a book. **[12 marks]**

2 Les échanges
Traduis le passage suivant **en français**:

In February, I went on a school trip to France. The journey was too long and I was seasick. In the future I would prefer to travel by plane. I stayed with a nice family who lived in the town centre. Next year my French friend will come to my house and we will go sightseeing. **[12 marks]**

Writing (Foundation)

In the writing paper of your exam at Foundation tier, you will need to complete different tasks involving writing in French.

 About Task 1

You must write 20–30 words in French, describing the picture and giving your opinion about the topic of the picture. You will be assessed both for communication and content, and for linguistic knowledge and accuracy. Focus on using words and language you know. You could:

- set the scene
- say what one or more people are doing
- use an adjective to say what something is like
- add a further piece of information e.g. the weather, mood or further description.

 About Tasks 2 and 3

In both Task 2 and Task 3 you have to write about all four bullet points. You will be assessed for communication and content, and for linguistic knowledge and accuracy.

In Task 2 you will need to write 40–50 words in French and you must use the formal (**vous**) form.

In Task 3 you will need to write 80–90 words in French and you will have a choice of questions. You should use the informal (**tu**) form.

 Worked example

1 Mes vacances

Tu es avec ta famille. Tu postes cette photo sur un réseau social pour tes amis.

Écris une description de la photo et exprime ton opinion sur les vacances.

Écris 20–30 mots environ **en français**.

Me voici en vacances avec ma famille. Nous sommes à la plage et il fait très beau et chaud. À mon avis, les vacances sont importantes parce qu'on peut oublier le travail.

Here you could also write **au bord de la mer**.

2 Mon boulot à la colonie

Vous allez travailler dans une colonie de vacances. Écrivez un mail au directeur avec les informations suivantes:

- arrivée – date et heure
- moyen de transport
- travail désiré
- sports que vous aimez

Il faut écrire en phrases complètes. Écrivez 40–50 mots environ **en français**.

Monsieur / Madame,

J'arrive à votre colonie de vacances le dix juillet à quinze heures. Je vais voyager en train. Pendant mon séjour chez vous, je voudrais aider avec les activités sportives. Mon sport préféré est le basket mais j'aime aussi la natation.

Cordialement

This first sentence sets the scene. You could also write: **Je suis en vacances avec ma famille.**

You could use another weather expression here: **Il y a du soleil.**

You could say **parce qu'on peut se détendre.**

 Exam-style practice

Une carte postale

Tu passes tes vacances en France. Écris une carte postale à ton ami(e) français(e). Tu dois faire référence aux points suivants:

- où tu es et activités récentes
- différences entre la France et la Grande-Bretagne
- projets pour les vacances l'année prochaine
- l'importance des vacances.

Écris 80–90 mots environ **en français**.   **[20 marks]**

You will need the perfect tense here.

You must use descriptive language with adjectives here.

This will require the future tense.

You must give your opinion.

Pages
10, 39
LINKS

Writing (Higher)

In the writing paper of your exam at Higher tier, you will need to complete different tasks involving writing in French.

② About the longer writing task

The task will consist of four bullet points that you must cover in 130–150 words. You must use the formal (vous) register and justify your ideas and opinions. You will also be assessed on your ability to interest or convince the reader. Try to include all of the following in your writing: adjectives (and intensifiers); a variety of verbs and tenses; opinions (with reasons); conjunctions and connectives; adverbs; details and originality (something a bit different).

Make sure you answer in the correct tense for the bullet point – past, present or future. If you wish, you can incorporate other verb tenses where appropriate, to show off the range of language you are confident with.

⑤ Aiming higher

- Don't use the same words or phrases more than once. Use synonyms and antonyms: ennuyeux = monotone, répétitif / intéressant, passionnant.
- Justify your opinions using different phrases: parce que / car *because*; pour + infinitive *(in order) to*; afin de + infinitive *in order to*; alors, par contre, mais, puisque.
- Include higher level language and structures: pluperfect tense, perfect infinitive (après avoir / être + past participle).
- Use the conditional to write about what you would or could do in the future.

⑩ Worked example

Les échanges scolaires

Un magazine français cherche des articles sur les échanges scolaires. Écrivez un article pour intéresser les lecteurs. Vous devez faire référence aux points suivants:

- le contact avec votre correspondant avant l'échange
- l'activité la plus intéressante
- pourquoi les échanges sont importants
- une autre visite scolaire que vous allez faire.

L'année dernière, j'ai passé une semaine en France en échange scolaire. Avant d'y aller, j'avais envoyé des mails à mon correspondant pour faire sa connaissance. Lui et sa famille étaient très gentils et on s'est bien entendus pendant mon séjour. Un jour, nous avons fait une excursion en car à un vieux château dans la région. J'ai trouvé le paysage très beau et l'histoire du château était tout à fait fascinante. Les autres jours, je suis allé au collège avec mon correspondant.

On s'est bien entendus is an example of a reflexive verb in the perfect tense.

You have to write about your experience on an exchange and give your opinion about the importance of exchanges. Make something up if you have to!

À mon avis, l'échange m'a permis de me familiariser avec un nouveau pays et une nouvelle culture. C'était une expérience que je n'oublierai jamais. J'ai remarqué que les repas sont plus importants pour les Français que pour nous, puisqu'il faut beaucoup de temps pour les préparer, et qu'ensuite, on passe beaucoup de temps à table. Les choses les plus importantes sont qu'on améliore son français et qu'on communique avec d'autres personnes. Cette année, j'ai l'intention de participer à l'échange en Espagne.

You can introduce the pluperfect tense (j'avais envoyé) with avant de (before + ing).

Try to include a comparative or superlative.

② Checking your work

Remember to check your work for the following:

- spellings, accents and capital letters (for proper nouns – a person's name, towns and countries) are used correctly
- gender (masculine or feminine) and adjective agreements, including position
- verbs: tenses and formation; correct auxiliary (avoir or être) in the perfect tense.

See page 65 for more on writing strategies.

⑳ Exam-style practice

L'amitié

Un magazine français en ligne organise un concours pour un article au sujet de 'l'amitié' pour un prix de 100 euros.

Écrivez un article pour persuader les organisateurs du concours. Vous devez faire référence aux points suivants:

- l'importance d'avoir de bons amis
- ce que vous avez fait pour être un(e) bon(ne) ami(e)
- pourquoi vous avez aidé votre ami(e)
- ce que vous ferez avec les 100 euros du prix.

Justifiez vos idées et vos opinions. Écrivez 130–150 mots environ **en français**. **[28 marks]**

Articles

Articles are the little words that mean *the* (le, la, l', les) and *a, an* or *some* (un, une, des).

② About articles

In French, the article changes depending on whether the noun it goes with is masculine, feminine or plural.

	masc	fem	plural
definite article (*the*)	le / l'	la / l'	les
indefinite article (*a / an / some*)	un	une	des

L' is used in front of a vowel or a silent 'h': l'arbre, l'homme.

② Using the indefinite article

Un and une are used more or less in the same way as you would use *a* in English.

They are left out when saying someone's job or profession:

Il est professeur. *He is a teacher.*

Ma mère est médecin. *My mother is a doctor.*

⑤ Using the definite article

The definite article is used to refer to something specific.

Le château est très grand. *The castle is very big.*

In French the definite article (le, la, l', les) is used with some nouns where it is left out in English, such as:

- school subjects: On doit étudier les maths et l'anglais.
- languages: Le chinois est une langue difficile. ◄
- parts of the body: Il a les yeux bleus et les cheveux blonds.

  Il s'est cassé la jambe.
- likes and dislikes: J'aime les pommes, mais je déteste les bananes.
- countries: La France est plus grande que la Suisse.
- abstract nouns and generalisations: La gastronomie française est très connue.
- with quantities when referring to the price: quatre euros le litre.
- time phrases: le week-end dernier; le samedi (meaning *every Saturday*).

> **!** Exceptions are with **parler** and **en**: **je parle français**; **Comment dit-on ... en français?**

On prend le petit déjeuner à sept heures.

⑮ Practice

1 Complete the following with the correct form of the article.

(a) J'apprends _____ portugais.

(b) Qu'est-ce qu'il fait _____ soir?

(c) Je me suis cassé _____ bras.

(d) _____ Allemagne a une frontière avec _____ Pays-Bas.

(e) Les oranges sont deux euros _____ kilo.

(f) _____ année prochaine, je vais visiter _____ Italie.

(g) J'aime regarder _____ tennis à _____ télé.

(h) _____ poste se trouve entre _____ banque et _____ hôtel de ville.

(i) J'adore _____ cuisine française.

(j) _____ racisme est un problème dans quelques pays.

2 Traduis les phrases suivantes en français.

(a) He has grey hair and green eyes.

(b) She is a nurse and she works in a hospital.

(c) There are some shops in the village.

(d) We eat breakfast in the kitchen.

(e) I visited Spain last summer.

 Made a start **Feeling confident** **Exam ready**

Prepositions

Prepositions are short words like *in*, *on*, *at* and *with*. They provide important information in a sentence.

 About prepositions

Prepositions usually go in front of a noun or pronoun and tell you about how, where, when or for whom something is.

dans *in*
devant *in front of*
derrière *behind*
entre *between*
contre *against*

sur *on / on top of*
sous *under*
à travers *across / through*
vers *towards*
chez *at someone's house, shop or business*

Je regarde la télé **dans** le salon. *I watch TV **in** the living room.*

chez le boucher *at the butcher's*

Other common prepositions:

avec *with*
malgré *in spite of*
parmi *among*
sans *without*

sauf *except*
selon *according to*
pour *for*

 The preposition *en*

En is used without an article, directly in front of a noun and has a different meaning depending on its use.

* with feminine countries, continents and regions it means *to* or *in*:
  Je vais en France. *I am going to France.*
  J'habite en Angleterre. *I live in England.*

* with means of transport it means *by*:
  en avion (*by plane*); en voiture (*by car*); en train (*by train*); en vélo (*by bike*).

  > You can also say **par le train** and **à vélo**.

* with languages to say *in*:
  Comment dit-on ... en anglais? *How do you say ... in English?*

* with months and seasons to say *in*:
  en juillet (*in July*), en été / automne / hiver (*in summer / autumn / winter*)

  > *In spring* is **au** printemps.

* to describe what something is made out of:
  un porte-monnaie en cuir *a leather purse*; une écharpe en soie / coton / laine *a silk / cotton / woollen scarf*; une bague en argent / or *a silver / gold ring*

* to form the present participle (see page 99) and a lot of common expressions:
  en bas *downstairs*; en haut *upstairs*; en bonne santé *in good health*; en fait *in fact*; en tout cas *in any case*; en même temps *at the same time*; en plein air *in the fresh air*; en vacances *on holiday*; en route pour *on the way to*.

 Expressions of time

The following prepositions tell you when something happens.

avant le dîner ***before*** *dinner*

après les cours ***after*** *lessons*

vers six heures ***at about*** *(towards) six o'clock*

Nous avons cours **jusqu'à** quatre heures. *We have lessons **until** four o'clock.*

Le train part **dans** dix minutes. *The train leaves **in** ten minutes.*

pendant la journée ***during*** *the day*

J'ai fait mes devoirs **pendant** trois heures. *I did my homework **for** three hours.*

J'irai en France **pour** une semaine. *I will go to France **for** a week.*

> **Pour** can only be used to translate *for*, when referring to a specific length of time in the future. **Pendant** can be used to translate *for* when talking about a specific length of time in the past, present or future. If an action started in the past and is still going on, then use **depuis** with the present tense (e.g. **je joue du piano depuis dix ans** *I have been playing the piano for ten years*).

Some time expressions that have a preposition in English do not need one in French:

le week-end *at the weekend*

le dimanche *on Sundays (every Sunday)*

le matin *in the morning*

 Practice

✏ Translate the following prepositional phrases into French.

(a) *towards* the station
(b) *against* England
(c) *in spite of* the rain
(d) *among* my friends
(e) *for* my birthday
(f) *at* my house
(g) *without* milk
(h) *except* Tuesdays
(i) *according to* a survey

 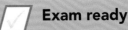

The preposition à

The preposition à often means *to* or *at*, but has other meanings too so is a very useful little word.

 About the preposition à

Take care when à is followed by le or les. À combines with these articles to form **au** and **aux**.

le	la	l'	les
au	à la	à l'	aux

Some common uses of à:

- with towns to mean *to* or *in*:
  Je vais **à** Paris. *I am going to Paris.*
  Mon frère habite **à** Nice. *My brother lives in Nice.*

- with places to mean *to* or *at*:
  Je vais **au** parc. *I am going to the park.*
  On se retrouve **au** cinéma?
  Shall we meet up at the cinema?
  Cet après-midi, on va **aux** Champs-Élysées.
  We are going to the Champs-Élysées this afternoon.

- with masculine or plural countries to mean *to* and *in*:
  Je suis allé **au** Japon. *I've been to Japan.*
  Ma sœur habite **aux** Pays-Bas. *My sister lives in the Netherlands / Holland.*

Remember that feminine countries take **en**:
L'année prochaine, je vais en Allemagne.
Next year, I'm going to Germany.
La Grande Muraille est en Chine. *The Great Wall is in China.*

J'ai mal **à la** tête.

 More uses of à

- To give the flavour or style of something: une crêpe au chocolat *a pancake with chocolate*; une glace à la vanille *a vanilla ice cream*.

- To mean *with* when describing someone or something: le garçon **aux** cheveux roux *the boy with red hair*.

- To mean *on*: au rez-de-chaussée *on the ground floor*; à cheval *on horseback*; à pied *on foot*; à la télé *on television*.

- With time phrases and occasions: à dix heures *at ten o'clock*; au printemps *in spring*.

For the other seasons use **en** to mean *in*: **en été** / **en automne** / **en hiver**.

- To indicate distance and direction: à cent cinquante mètres d'ici *150 metres from here*; Prenez la deuxième rue à droite. *Take the second road on the right.*

- With the verb jouer + sport: jouer au tennis / football; jouer aux échecs *to play tennis / football / chess*.

Remember that **jouer** + *de* is used when talking about playing an instrument.

- With avoir mal à + part of the body, meaning *to hurt*: Elle a mal au dos. *Her back hurts / she has backache.*

- To show possession (with emphatic pronouns): C'est à qui? *Whose is this?* C'est à moi. *It's mine.*

- After some verbs, to link them to another verb: s'amuser à, apprendre à, commencer à, s'intéresser à, ressembler à.
  Il commence à pleuvoir. *It's starting to rain.*
  Je m'intéresse aux sports nautiques. *I'm interested in water sports.*

- Other common expressions: à mon avis *in my opinion*; à vélo *by bike*; peu à peu *little by little*.

 Practice

1 Fill in the gaps with **au, à la, à l'** or **aux.**
- **(a)** Comment vas-tu _____ collège?
- **(b)** J'irai _____ États-Unis pendant les vacances.
- **(c)** Pour aller _____ hôpital, s'il vous plaît?
- **(d)** Je vous attends _____ gare.
- **(e)** J'ai fait du ski _____ Canada.

2 Translate the following into English.
- **(a)** Je voudrais un sandwich au jambon.
- **(b)** C'est la fille aux yeux bleus.
- **(c)** Mon appartement est au troisième étage.
- **(d)** J'avais mal à l'estomac.
- **(e)** Ils sont en train de jouer au volley.

3 Translate the following into French.
- **(a)** I have earache.
- **(b)** How much is the coffee ice cream?
- **(c)** They are playing cards.
- **(d)** I love onion soup.

  Made a start 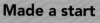 **Feeling confident** **Exam ready**

Partitives and preposition *de*

The word *de* means *some* or *any*, and it is also a preposition meaning *from* or *of*.

⑤ Forms of the partitive

The partitive article *de* combines with definite articles (le, la, l', les).

	partitive
masculine singular *de + le*	du
feminine singular *de + la*	de la
before a vowel / silent 'h' singular *de + l'*	de l'
plural *de + les*	des

Use it to refer to an unknown quantity of something. In English, you can sometimes leave out *some* or *any*, but you can't in French.

Je voudrais **du** pain et **des** tomates. *I'd like some bread and tomatoes.*

Avez-vous **du** beurre? *Have you got any butter?*

Est-ce que vous vendez **de** l'eau minérale? *Do you sell (any) mineral water?*

⑤ Using *de* or *d'* on its own

Use *de / d'* for the following:

• after a negative:

Il n'a pas mangé **de** fromage. *He didn't eat any cheese.*

Je n'ai pas **d'**argent. *I haven't got any money.*

Les végétariens ne mangent pas **de** viande. *Vegetarians don't eat meat.*

Il n'y avait pas **de** pêches au marché. *There weren't any peaches in the market.*

• after an expression of quantity:

Il y a beaucoup **d'**arbres et **de** fleurs. *There are a lot of trees and flowers.*

un kilo **de** pommes de terre *a kilo of potatoes*

• When a plural adjective comes in front of a noun:

Elle a **de** grandes oreilles. *She has big ears.*

Il y a **de** jolies fleurs. *There are some pretty flowers.*

① Showing possession with *de*

The preposition *de* is also used to indicate ownership.

le copain de Paul *Paul's friend*

⑤ Prepositions + *de* 〔A–Z〕

Several preposition phrases contain *de*:

autour de *around*	à droite de *to the right of*
au bord de *at the side / edge of*	en face de *opposite*
au bout de *at the end of*	au fond de *at the back of*
à cause de *because of*	à gauche de *to the left of*
à côté de *next to*	au lieu de *instead of*
en dehors de *outside*	loin de *far from*
au-dessous de *below*	au milieu de *in the middle of*
au-dessus de *above*	près de *near to*

La gare est loin du centre-ville. *The station is far from the town centre.*

L'hôtel est en face de la poste et à côté du musée. *The hotel is opposite the post office and next to the museum.*

② Verbs followed by *de*

A number of common verbs are followed by *de* to link them to another verb.

avoir envie de *to feel like*

avoir besoin de *to need*

choisir de *to choose to*

décider de *to decide to*

essayer de *to try to*

finir de *to finish*

penser de *to think of / about* ◄

refuser de *to refuse*

J'ai décidé / choisi d'étudier l'histoire. *I've decided / chosen to study history.*

> ! This means *to think of / about* in the sense of an opinion:
>
> **Que penses-tu de ce livre?** *What do you think of / about this book?*
>
> *To think of / about* in the sense of 'something on your mind' is **penser à**, so be careful:
>
> **J'ai pensé à toi!** *I thought of / about you!*

⑩ Practice

✎ Traduis les phrases suivantes en français.

(a) I have bought some milk, some meat and some eggs.

(b) He hasn't got any fish.

(c) My sister's boyfriend is quite tall.

(d) The park is next to the castle.

(e) I tried to do my homework.

Nouns

Nouns are words that name people, places, things and abstract concepts.

② About nouns

Nouns are words that you can usually put *a* or *the* in front of. In French, all nouns have a gender: either masculine (m) or feminine (f). The gender of a noun is always listed in a dictionary, but when you learn nouns you should learn their gender too.

② Masculine nouns

The following are always masculine:

- days, months and seasons: le lundi, le mois, le printemps
- languages: le français, le portugais
- weights and measures: un kilo, un litre, un kilomètre
- male people and members of the family: le professeur, le grand-père, le frère
- nouns formed from infinitives: le devoir.

Masculine noun endings

The following endings are generally masculine:

ending	example
-age, -ège	le fromage, le village, le collège
-eau, -ou	le bateau, le gâteau, le bijou, le genou
-ier	le quartier
-eur	un ascenseur, le moniteur
-ment	un appartement, le monument
-isme	le tourisme, le cyclisme, le rascisme
-phone, -scope	le téléphone, le microscope

Exceptions are **la peau** and **l'eau**.

Exceptions are **la page, la plage, la cage** and **l'image**.

⑤ Plurals of nouns

Most nouns form the plural by adding -s: un arbre, des arbres. Nouns that end in -s, -x, or -z do not change: une souris / des souris; la voix / des voix; le nez / les nez.

Words with the following endings make the plural as follows:

- -al changes to -aux: un animal, des animaux
- -eau changes to -eaux: un chapeau, des chapeaux

A few nouns have an irregular plural form:

un œil → des yeux; monsieur → messieurs; madame → mesdames; mademoiselle → mesdemoiselles.

② Feminine nouns

The following are always feminine:

- most shops: la boulangerie, la pharmacie (not le supermarché)
- continents: l'Asie, l'Europe
- most countries: la France, la Belgique, la Suisse

Exceptions include **le Canada, les États-Unis**.

- female people and family members: la directrice, la tante, la sœur, la mère
- most rivers: la Seine, la Loire, but not le Rhône or le Rhin.

Feminine noun endings

The following endings are generally feminine:

ending	example
-tion, -aison	la nation, la combinaison
-ette, -esse	la chaussette, la toilette
-ence, -ance, -ense, -anse	la patience, l'enfance, la défense, la danse
-ité	la cité, une université, une activité
-ure	la nature, la culture
-ode, -ade, -ude	la méthode, la limonade, l'attitude

② Masculine and feminine jobs

Many jobs and occupations have different endings depending on whether they refer to a man or a woman.

VOCABULARY LINK
PAGE **112**

change	masculine	feminine
add -e	avocat	avocate
-ier → -ière	fermier	fermière
-ien → -ienne	musicien	musicienne
-eur → -euse	vendeur	vendeuse
-er → -ère	boulanger	boulangère
-teur → -trice	acteur	actrice

⑤ Practice

✏ What is the gender of each of the following nouns?

(a) mercredi   **(e)** rire

(b) pharmacienne   **(f)** serveuse

(c) révolution   **(g)** nourriture

(d) chinois   **(h)** chou

 Made a start   Feeling confident   Exam ready

Adjectives

You need to take care with agreement and position of adjectives in French.

(5) Adjective agreement

In French, adjectives must agree with the gender (masculine or feminine) and number (singular or plural) of the noun that they describe. Most adjectives add an -e in the feminine form, and add an -s in the plural.

m sing	un chat noir	*a black cat*
f sing	une table noire	*a black table*
m pl	des chats noirs	*black cats*
f pl	des tables noires	*black tables*

If the adjective already ends in -e it does not add another, so the masculine and feminine forms are the same.

un problème grave *a serious problem*
une maladie grave *a serious illness*

If the adjective already ends in -s, the masculine singular and masculine plural are the same:

un lapin gris *a grey rabbit*; des lapins gris *grey rabbits*

(5) Irregular adjectives

The following adjectives are irregular and have a different masculine singular form used in front of a vowel or silent 'h'.

	beautiful	**old**	**new**
masc sing	beau	vieux	nouveau
masc + vowel	bel	vieil	nouvel
fem sing	belle	vieille	nouvelle
masc pl	beaux	vieux	nouveaux
fem pl	belles	vieilles	nouvelles

un vieil homme, le Nouvel An, un bel arbre

(5) Position of adjectives

Most adjectives in French go after the noun they describe, unlike in English. This always happens with adjectives relating to colour, shape or nationality:

la maison blanche *the white house*; la langue française *the French language*; une table ronde *a round table*.

The following adjectives go in front of the noun:

beau; bon; grand; gros; haut; jeune; joli; long; mauvais; nouveau; petit; premier; vieux.

e.g. une grande maison *a big house*

Some adjectives change their meaning depending on whether they go before or after the noun.

une chambre propre *a clean room*
ma propre chambre *my own room*

Other adjectives like this are: ancien *former / ancient*, même *same / very* or *exact* and seul *only / lonely*.

(5) Spelling changes in adjectives

Some adjectives double the final consonant and add an -e for the feminine form: bon / bonne; gros / grosse.

Adjectives ending in –al change to –aux in the masculine plural: un journal national / des journaux nationaux.

Adjectives with the following endings have a different form in the feminine form:

masc ending	fem ending	example
-er / ier	-ère	cher / chère; premier / première
-x	-se	heureux / heureuse
-et	-ète or -ette	inquiet / inquiète; cadet / cadette
-aux	-ausse	faux / fausse
-ien	-ienne	ancien / ancienne
-f	-ve	actif / active; neuf / neuve
-c	-che	blanc / blanche

Other irregular feminine forms: frais → fraîche; favori → favorite; long → longue.

> Masculine adjectives that end in **-x** do not change in the plural: **un sport dangereux / des sports dangereux**. **Sec** changes to **sèche**.

(5) Invariable adjectives

A small number of adjectives do not change their ending: cool, chic, extra, marron, orange.

la musique cool; des lunettes de soleil cool

Il a les cheveux marron et porte des baskets orange.

Combination colours of two words are also invariable.

une jupe bleu marine *a navy blue skirt*

des chaussettes vert foncé *dark green socks*

(5) Practice

✎ Translate the following sentences into French.

(a) a good question
(b) a small garden
(c) a jealous friend (female)
(d) a light grey shirt
(e) an old object

Comparatives and superlatives

Comparatives compare two things, saying that one is more or less ... (adjective) than the other.

 Using *plus* and *moins*

In English, some comparatives end in -er (*faster, easier*): in French, use plus + adjective + que.

> Remember that the adjective must agree with the subject. **!**

Le train est **plus cher que** le bus. *The train is more expensive than the bus.*

L'Angleterre est **plus grande que** le pays de Galles. *England is bigger than Wales.*

Les exercices de français sont **plus faciles que** les devoirs d'anglais. *French exercises are easier than English homework.*

Use moins + adjective + que to say *less... than...*

L'escalade est **moins dangereuse que** le parapente. *Climbing is less dangerous than hang-gliding.*

Mon frère est **moins patient que** moi. *My brother is less patient than me.*

 Using *aussi ... que*

Use aussi + adjective + que to say *as ... as.*

Elle est **aussi grande que** sa sœur. *She is as tall as her sister.*

Use pas aussi + adjective + que to say *not as ... as.*

L'espagnol n'est **pas aussi difficile que** le chinois. *Spanish is not as difficult as Chinese.*

 Irregular comparatives

As in English, bon *good* and mauvais *bad* have irregular comparative forms.

	bon	**mauvais**
masc sing	meilleur	pire
fem sing	meilleure	pire
masc pl	meilleurs	pires
fem pl	meilleures	pires
English	better	worse

Ce film est **meilleur que** l'autre film. *This film is better than the other film.*

Les émissions de télé-réalité sont **pires que** les émissions de sport. *Reality TV programmes are worse than sports programmes.*

Les légumes sont **meilleurs** pour la santé que les gâteaux. *Vegetables are better for your health than cakes.*

 The superlative

In English, the superlative is often recognisable by the ending -est (*biggest / fastest / smallest*).

In French, use le / la / les + plus / moins + adjective. The adjective must agree with the noun it is describing.

l'animal **le plus dangereux** *the most dangerous animal*

l'étudiant **le moins sportif** *the least sporty student*

les films **les plus longs** *the longest films*

Adjectives that go in front of the noun also go in front when used in the superlative form.

Elle est **la plus belle** fille. *She is the most beautiful girl.*

Le Mont Blanc est **la plus haute** montagne d'Europe. *Mont Blanc is the highest mountain **in** Europe.*

To say *the best* use: le meilleur / la meilleure / les meilleur(e)s. To say *the worst* use: le / la pire / les pires. They all go in front of the noun. **le meilleur** acteur *the best actor;* **le pire** film *the worst film*

 Practice

🖉 Traduis les phrases suivantes en français.

(a) Horror films are more exciting than romantic films.

(b) Soap operas are more entertaining than the news.

(c) Sports programmes are as interesting as documentaries.

(d) *Amélie* is the funniest film.

(e) That is the most boring TV programme.

(f) Adele is the best singer.

(g) He is the worst actor.

(h) He chose the most expensive main course.

(i) I bought the least expensive souvenir.

(j) They are the most uncomfortable seats.

Possessive and demonstrative adjectives

Possessive and demonstrative adjectives in a sentence indicate ownership or reference to a specific thing.

 Possessive adjectives

Possessive adjectives are words like *my*, *your* and *his*. They go in front of a noun to indicate to whom or what something belongs.

	masculine	feminine	plural
my	mon	ma	mes
your (sing)	ton	ta	tes
his / her / its	son	sa	ses
our	notre	notre	nos
your	votre	votre	vos
their	leur	leur	leurs

Possessive adjectives agree with the noun that follows them, not with the owner.

Je joue au tennis avec **mon** frère. (frère = m sing)
I play tennis with my brother.

Je joue au tennis avec **ma** sœur. (sœur = f sing)
I play tennis with my sister.

Je joue au tennis avec **mes** frères. (frères = m pl)
I play tennis with my brothers.

Je joue au tennis avec **mes** sœurs. (sœurs = f pl)
I play tennis with my sisters.

The possessive adjective of **on** is notre / nos.
On s'est promenés avec **notre** chien.

Mon, **ton** and **son** are used in front of a feminine noun that begins with a vowel or silent 'h'.

Mon émission préférée est *EastEnders*. (émission = f sing). *My favourite TV programme is EastEnders.*

Il va au cinéma avec **son** amie. (amie = f sing)
He is going to the cinema with his (female) friend.

Son, **sa** and **ses** can mean either *his*, *her* or *its* depending on the context of the sentence.

Robert et **son** frère *Robert and his brother*

Anne et **son** frère *Anne and her brother*

le chat et **ses** petits *the cat and its little ones*

 Possessives and parts of the body

Use the definite article rather than a possessive adjective when you are referring to parts of the body.

Je me lave les mains. *I wash my hands.*

Ils se brossent les dents. *They brush their teeth.*

Elle s'est coupé le doigt. *She cut her finger.*

Il s'est cassé la jambe. *He broke his leg.*

 Demonstrative adjectives

Demonstrative adjectives are the words for *this*, *that*, *these* and *those*. The adjective changes its ending to agree with the noun it goes with.

	sing this / that	plural these / those
masc	ce / cet	ces
fem	cette	ces

There are two forms of the masculine singular adjective. **Cet** is used in front of a vowel or silent 'h'.

ce fromage *this / that cheese*; **cet** œuf *this / that egg*; **cette** assiette *this / that plate*; **ces** plats *these / those dishes*; **ces** glaces *these / those ice creams*

You can distinguish between *this* and *that* by adding **–ci** or **–là** after the noun.

ce restaurant**-ci** *this restaurant*; **ces** magasins**-ci** *these shops*; **ce** café**-là** *that café*; **ces** pommes**-là** *those apples*

 Using demonstrative adjectives

When listing things, repeat the demonstrative adjective before each noun:

cet anorak, **cette** chemise, **ces** chaussures
this anorak, this shirt, these shoes

You can use demonstrative adjectives in front of adjectives and numbers.

cette belle robe *this beautiful dress*

ce joli tee-shirt *this pretty T-shirt*

ces chaussures noires *these black shoes*

ces trois personnes *these three people*

Remember to use **rendre visite à** *to visit* a person.
Visiter means *to visit* a place.

 Practice

✏ Translate the following sentences into French.

(a) My father lost his mobile phone in that shop.

(b) We visited our cousins.

(c) His parents and their friends stayed in that house.

(d) My friend (m) bought that souvenir for his sister.

Indefinite and interrogative adjectives

These adjectives are used to say *all*, *every* and *each*, and quel allows you to ask questions with *which* or *what*.

 Using *tout*

Tout can be used as an adjective to mean *all*, *the whole* or *every*. It has to agree with the noun that follows.

masculine singular	feminine singular	masculine plural	feminine plural
tout	toute	tous	toutes

tout le temps *all the time / the whole time*
toute la journée *all day*
tous les mercredis *every Wednesday*
toutes les chansons *all the songs*

 Using *chaque* and *quelques*

Chaque means *each* or *every* and is only used with singular nouns. It does not change.

chaque samedi *every Saturday*
chaque personne *each person*

Quelques means *some* or *a few*. It is only used with plural nouns.

il y a quelques mois *a few months ago*

 Interrogative adjectives

Interrogative adjectives are the words for *which* or *what*. The adjective agrees with the noun it goes with.

masculine singular	masculine plural
quel	quels

feminine singular	feminine plural
quelle	quelles

Quel temps fait-il? *What is the weather like?*
Quelle heure est-il? *What time is it?*
Vous désirez quelles chaussures? *Which shoes do you want?*
Vous prenez quel dessert? *Which dessert are you having?*

Sometimes quel is not next to the noun it goes with, but it still agrees with it.

Quelle est la date de ton anniversaire? *What is the date of your birthday?*
Quel est ton sport préféré? *What is your favourite sport?*
Quelles sont les meilleures émissions à la télé? *What are the best TV programmes?*

> **Quel / quelle** and a noun can also make an exclamation:
> **Quel dommage!** *What a pity!*

 **Practice**

1 Fill in the gaps in the following phrases with the correct form of *tout*. What does each phrase mean?

(a) _____ les jours
(b) _____ les stations
(c) _____ la classe
(d) _____ le fromage
(e) _____ la famille

2 Translate the following phrases into French.

(a) every morning
(b) each student
(c) a few people
(d) a few words
(e) some time

3 Fill in the gaps with the correct form of *quel / quelle / quels / quelles*. What does each sentence mean?

(a) _____ boisson prends-tu?
(b) _____ taille voulez-vous?
(c) _____ sport aimes-tu?
(d) _____ genre de musique n'aimes-tu pas?
(e) _____ sont tes matières préférées?
(f) _____ est ton passe-temps préféré?
(g) Tu aimes _____ sorte de films?
(h) _____ sont les meilleurs feuilletons?
(i) _____ chance!

 Made a start 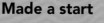 **Feeling confident** **Exam ready**

Adverbs

Adverbs are used to describe actions and to add meaning to a verb or an adjective.

 Formation of adverbs

Adverbs tell you where, when or how an action is being done or taking place. They usually follow the verb.

Many adverbs in French are formed by adding -ment to the feminine singular form of the adjective. This is the equivalent of the -ly ending in English.

adjective masc sing	adjective fem sing	adverb
heureux	heureuse	heureusement
immédiat	immédiate	immédiatement
franc	franche	franchement
doux	douce	doucement

If the adjective ends in a vowel just add –ment.

facile → facilement *easily*

vrai → vraiment *really*

absolu → absolument *absolutely*

Some adverbs add an accent: énormément *enormously*; précisément *precisely*.

Adjectives that end in –ant or –ent change to –amment or –emment (an exception is lentement = *slowly*).

courant → couramment *fluently*

évident → évidemment *evidently*

récent → récemment *recently*

A few adverbs are irregular:

gentil → gentiment *gently*; bref → brièvement *briefly*.

 Adverbs of time and place

déjà *already*

de nouveau *again*

en retard *late*

tout de suite *immediately*

en bas / haut *downstairs / upstairs*

là-bas *over there*

partout *everywhere*

Je viendrai tout de suite. *I will come immediately.*

Mon frère est là-bas. *My brother is over there.*

 Frequency adverbs

Frequency adverbs tell you how often an action takes place. Common frequency adverbs are:

de temps en temps *from time to time*

d'habitude *usually*

jamais *never*

normalement *normally*

quelquefois *sometimes*

rarement *rarely*

souvent *often*

toujours *always*

Nous allons souvent au cinéma le week-end. *We often go to the cinema at the weekend.*

 Comparatives and superlatives

Adverbs form the comparative in the same way as adjectives, using plus ... que, moins ... que, aussi ... que and pas si ... que.

Ma grand-mère marche plus lentement que mon grand-père. *My grandmother walks more slowly than my grandfather.*

Mon frère travaille moins sérieusement que moi. *My brother works less seriously than me.*

The superlative is formed by using le plus or le moins + adverb

L'espagnol est la langue que je parle le plus couramment. *Spanish is the language I speak the most fluently.*

C'est le vin anglais qui coûte le moins cher. *English wine costs the least.*

VOCABULARY LINK PAGE **110**

Irregular comparatives and superlatives

bien *well*	mieux *better*	le mieux *best*
mal *badly*	plus mal *worse*	le plus mal *the worst*
beaucoup *a lot*	plus *more*	le plus *the most*
peu *little*	moins *less*	le moins *the least*

Ma sœur parle mieux français que mon frère. *My sister speaks French better than my brother.*

 Practice

🖉 Translate the following sentences into French.

(a) I usually leave the house early.

(b) Sometimes we go to the café.

(c) I play the piano better than my brother.

(d) He speaks more softly than me.

(e) Unfortunately the weather was bad.

Quantifiers and intensifiers

Quantifiers and intensifiers are words that can be used to add emphasis or meaning.

Intensifiers

Intensifiers are used with adverbs and adjectives to add emphasis and meaning. Common intensifiers include:

assez *quite*
aussi *as*
de moins en moins *less and less*
de plus en plus *more and more*
pas du tout *not at all*
plutôt *rather*
presque *almost*
si *so*
tout à fait *utterly*
très *very*
trop *too*
un peu *a little*

Il n'est pas riche du tout. *He is not at all rich.*
Je devais parler de plus en plus lentement. *I had to speak more and more slowly.*
Les billets étaient trop chers. *The tickets were too expensive.*

Adverbs of quantity

The following adverbs all refer to quantity. They are always followed by de + noun without an article:

beaucoup de *a lot of*
assez de *enough*
combien de *how many*
moins de *less / fewer*
pas mal de *quite a bit / lots of*
plein de *lots of / full of*
plus de *more*
tant de *so much / many*
trop de *too much*

Encore (*more*), la moitié (*half*), and la plupart (*most*) are followed by du / de la / de l' / des + noun.

Voulez-vous encore du pain?
Do you want some more bread?
La plupart des professeurs sont sympas.
Most teachers are nice.
la moitié du groupe *half the group*

Vocabulary

Adverbs as intensifiers
Many adverbs that end in –ment can be used as intensifiers.

absolument *absolutely*
complètement *completely*
énormément *enormously*
extrêmement *extremely*
incroyablement *incredibly*
relativement *relatively*
strictement *strictly*
tellement *so*
vraiment *really*

Aiming higher

Using a wide variety of intensifiers adds originality to your answers, and is a feature of the best answers.
C'est complètement stupide! *It's completely stupid!*
Ce n'est pas absolument nécessaire! *It's not absolutely necessary!*

Expressions of quantity

Expressions of quantity are followed by de + noun without an article. Common expressions of quantity are:

un kilo de pommes *a kilo of apples*
une bouteille d'eau *a bottle of water*
un paquet de biscuits *a packet of biscuits*
une boîte de tomates *a tin of tomatoes*
un morceau de fromage *a piece of cheese*
une tranche de pain *a slice of bread*

Practice

Translate the following sentences into French.
(a) There are a lot of trees in the garden.
(b) I ate too many cakes.
(c) You see so many homeless people on the streets.
(d) After a few days I had seen enough sights.
(e) My parents are so annoying.

Subject and object pronouns

Pronouns are words like *she*, *they*, *it*, *him* and *them* and can be used in place of a noun or someone's name.

 ## Subject pronouns

Subject pronouns replace nouns that are doing an action: they are the subject of the verb. Elle can replace ma sœur in the phrase Ma sœur aime les bananes. → Elle aime les bananes. (*She likes bananas.*)

singular		plural	
je / j'	*I*	nous	*we*
tu	*you*	vous	*you*
il	*he / it*	ils	*they*
elle	*she / it*	elles	*they*
on	*one, we, you, they*		

- On can be used to refer to no one in particular, like *they*, *you* or *one* in English. It can also mean *we*: Qu'est-ce qu'on fait ce soir? *What are we doing this evening*?
- You need to know the gender of the word that the pronoun is replacing. As well as being used for people, il is used for masculine nouns and elle for feminine nouns: le livre est → il est; la table est → elle est.

 ## Object pronouns

Direct object pronouns replace nouns in a sentence when that noun is the object of a verb: I am reading a book → I am reading **it**; We are visiting our grandparents → We are visiting **them**.

singular		plural	
me	*me*	nous	*us*
te	*you*	vous	*you*
le	*him / it*	les	*them*
la	*her / it*		

- In French, the object pronoun goes in front of the verb: Ça m'énerve! *That annoys me!*

- In a negative sentence, ne goes in front of the pronoun, and the pas after the verb: Je ne l'achète pas.
- When there are two verbs in a sentence, the pronoun goes in front of the second verb in the infinitive: Je vais le faire. *I am going to do* **it**.
- In the perfect tense, the pronoun goes in front of the part of avoir and the past participle agrees with the pronoun:
  Je l'ai achetée (la pomme). *I bought* **it.**
  Je l'ai vu (le film). *I saw* **it**.

 ## Indirect object pronouns

Indirect object pronouns are used when you want to say *to me*, *to him / her*, etc. They are used with many verbs followed by à, e.g. donner à, dire à, parler à, offrir à, envoyer à, écrire à, demander à and répondre à.

	indirect object pronoun
(to) me	me
(to) you (sing)	te
(to) him / her / it	lui
(to) us	nous
(to) you (pl)	vous
(to) them	leur

 ## Aiming higher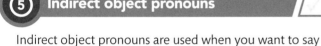

When there is both a direct and indirect object pronoun in a sentence, the pronouns go in front of the verb in the following order: me, te, nous, vous le, la, les, lui, leur.

Il envoie le message à sa sœur. → Il le lui envoie. *He sends it to her.*

Je montre mes photos à mes copains. → Je les leur montre. *I show them to them.*

Il me le donne. *He is giving it to me.*

Using indefinite pronouns such as quelqu'un (*someone*) or chacun (*each one*) is also a feature of top grade answers.

 ## Practice

✏️ Replace the underlined words with a pronoun.

(a) Mes parents donnent un vélo à mon frère.

(b) Le professeur a parlé aux élèves.

(c) Ma sœur est en train de lire le livre.

(d) Mon frère et moi voulons voir le film.

(e) J'ai acheté les billets.

Stressed and possessive pronouns

Stressed pronouns are words like moi meaning *me*, and lui meaning *him*. They are also known as emphatic or disjunctive pronouns.

Stressed pronouns

singular		plural	
moi	*I / me*	nous	*we / us*
toi	*you*	vous	*you*
lui	*he / him*	eux	*they / them* (m)
elle	*she / her*	elles	*they / them* (f)
soi	*oneself*		

Stressed pronouns and prepositions

Stressed pronouns are often used after prepositions like these:

avec *with*
de *from / of*
sans *without*
pour *for*
selon *according to*
chez *at home*
pas *not*

C'est pour toi. *It's for you;* selon lui *according to him*

Using stressed pronouns

Stressed pronouns can be used in the following ways:

☑ to add emphasis to the subject pronoun:
Moi, je vais le faire. Lui, il a peur. *I am going to do it.* **He** *is afraid.*

☑ at the end of a sentence:
Tu aimes les escargots, toi? *Do* **you** *like snails?*
Je ne sais pas, moi. **I** *don't know.*

☑ after the verb 'to be':
C'est lui / elle. *It's* **him / her**.

☑ to show possession:
Ce vélo est à lui. *This bike is* **his.**
C'est à moi. *It's* **mine.**

☑ in comparisons:
Mon frère est plus grand que moi. *My brother is bigger than* **me.**

Possessive pronouns

Possessive pronouns in English are words like *mine, yours, his* and *theirs*. In French, they have to agree with the noun they replace. You need to be able to recognise these pronouns at Higher level.

	masculine singular	feminine singular	masculine plural	feminine plural
mine	le mien	la mienne	les miens	les miennes
yours (sing / familiar)	le tien	la tienne	les tiens	les tiennes
his, hers, its	le sien	la sienne	les siens	les siennes
ours	le nôtre	la nôtre	les nôtres	les nôtres
yours (plural / formal)	le vôtre	la vôtre	les vôtres	les vôtres
theirs	le leur	la leur	les leurs	les leurs

Aiming higher

Use of possessive pronouns is a feature of top grade answers.

Voici mes chaussures. Où sont les tiennes?
Here are my shoes. Where are yours? (feminine plural to match les chaussures)

Ma sœur est plus grande que la sienne.
My sister is taller than his / hers. (feminine singular to match ma sœur)

It should be clear from the context of a text whether la sienne means *his* or *hers*.

Practice

👓 Translate the following sentences into English.

(a) Mes notes sont meilleures que les tiennes.

(b) Nos vacances étaient formidables. Comment étaient les vôtres?

(c) Tu as ton portable? Je ne trouve pas le mien.

(d) Il n'a pas de casquette? Il peut emprunter la mienne.

 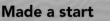

Relative and demonstrative pronouns

Relative pronouns, qui, que and dont, are used to link two parts of a sentence.

(10) Relative pronouns

Relative pronouns are words like *who, that, which, where* and *whose* and are used to link two parts of a sentence.

Qui means *who* when referring to a person or *which*, when referring to a thing or a place. It is normally followed by a verb, and is the **subject** of that verb.

Qui cannot be shortened to qu'.

L'homme **qui** porte un pull lit le journal. *The man **who** is wearing a jumper is reading the newspaper.*

Que means *whom, that* or *which*. It is the **object** of the verb that follows it and it can be shortened to qu' if it comes before a vowel.

Le manteau **que** je porte est très à la mode. *The coat **that** I am wearing is very fashionable.*

Les pommes **qu'**on a achetées étaient très bonnes. *The apples **that** we bought were very good.*

> In the perfect tense the past participle (in this example, **achetées**) must agree with the noun to which **que** or **qu'** refers: **pommes** = feminine plural.

> **Ce qui** means *which* if it refers back to an idea and not a specific noun and is the subject in a sentence:
> **Il a oublié d'acheter du lait, ce qui l'a énervé.** *He forgot to buy milk, **which** annoyed him.*
> **Ce que** follows the same rules as **ce qui** but as the object of a sentence.
> **Elle a laissé son portable dans le train, ce qu'elle a regretté plus tard.** *She left her mobile on the train, **which** she regretted later.*

Dont can have various meanings: *whose, of which / whom* and *about which / whom*.

La femme **dont** le mari est mort vient nous voir. *The woman **whose** husband died is coming to see us.*

It is often used with verbs followed by de.
Le livre **dont** j'ai besoin n'est pas disponible. *The book I need is not available.* (avoir besoin de)

(2) Using *où*

Où links two parts of a sentence when referring to a place or a time. It means *where*, or may be omitted in English.

Le magasin **où** j'ai trouvé mon tee-shirt... *The shop where I found my T-shirt...*

Le jour **où** nous sommes arrivés... *The day we arrived...*

(5) Demonstrative pronouns

Demonstrative pronouns are used when you want to say *the one* or *the ones*. The pronoun agrees with the noun to which it is referring.

	masc	**fem**	**English**
singular	celui	celle	*this / that / the one*
plural	ceux	celles	*these / those ones*

On a vu beaucoup de pulls au marché. **Celui** que j'ai acheté n'était pas cher. *We saw lots of jumpers in the market. **The one** I bought wasn't expensive.*

Quelles pommes voulez-vous? **Celles** qui sont moins chères. *Which apples do you want? **The ones** that are less expensive.*

(2) This one / that one

Add -ci (*this / these*) or -là (*that / those*) to be more specific.
Je voudrais celui-ci (m sing). *I would like this one.*
Ceux-là sont très bons (m pl). *Those are very good.*

> **Ceci** means *this*, and **cela** (**ça** for short) means *that*, when referring to something general or unspecified, e.g.
> **Ça (Cela) m'étonne**. *That surprises me.*
> **Ceci est difficile**. *This is difficult.*

(2) Showing possession

Celui, celle, ceux and celles can be used with de to show something belonging to someone / something.

Mes notes sont meilleures que **celles** de mon frère. *My marks are better than those of my brother.*

Les fromages français ont un meilleur goût que **ceux** d'Espagne. *French cheeses taste better than Spanish ones.*

(5) Practice

👓 Translate the following sentences into English.
(a) Le magasin qui se trouve à côté du musée est fermé.
(b) L'homme que j'ai vu portait un pull noir.
(c) Les enfants dont je m'occupe sont mignons.

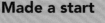 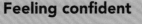

Pronouns y and en

Y means *there* and en means *some* or *any*. They are two common pronouns that go in front of the verb.

About the pronoun *en*

En means *some* or *any* and replaces nouns preceded by du, de la, de l' and des.

Est-ce qu'il y a **du** pain? *Is there* **any** *bread?*

Oui, il y **en** a. *Yes, there is* **some**.

Non, il n'y **en** a pas. *No, there isn't* **any**.

En and expressions of quantity

En means *of it* or *of them* when referring to expressions of quantity, often in response to combien?

Combien de pommes de terre as-tu acheté? *How many potatoes did you buy?*
J'**en** ai acheté un kilo. *I bought a kilo (of them).*

Vous avez de l'argent? *Do you have any money?*

Oui, mais je n'**en** ai pas assez. *Yes, but I don't have enough (of it).*

Oui, j'**en** ai beaucoup. *Yes, I have a lot (of it).*

En and verbs followed by *de*

En is used to replace phrases introduced by de. This occurs with verbs that use de to link to an infinitive or to a noun.

avoir envie de:
Vous avez envie de venir? Oui, j'**en** ai envie. *Do you want to come? Yes, I want to.*

être capable de:
Est-ce que tu es capable d'effectuer cette tâche? Non, je n'**en** suis pas capable. *Are you capable of doing this task? No, I am not capable* **of it**.

En can be used with the following common verbs:

rentrer de *to return from / be back from*; se souvenir de *to remember*; arriver de *to arrive*

Il est rentré du collège. → Il **en** est rentré. *He's back from school.* → *He's back from it.*

Je me souviens de mon anniversaire.
→ Je m'**en** souviens. *I remember my birthday.* →
I remember **it**.

> When **y** and **en** appear together, **y** always goes before **en**.

About the pronoun y

Y replaces a phrase referring to a place (à or en + place) and means *there* or *here* depending on the context.

We went **to the cinema.** → *We went* **there.**

It goes in front of the verb, regardless of the tense.
Je vais au cinéma. → J'**y** vais.

With the immediate future tense it goes in front of the infinitive.

On va aller au cinéma. → On va **y** aller.

Y and verbs followed by *à*

Y is used to replace phrases introduced by à (referring to something, rather than someone). This occurs with verbs that use à to link to an infinitive or to a noun.

réussir à: Tu a réussi à répondre aux questions? *Did you manage to answer the questions?*
-Oui, j'**y** ai réussi. *Yes I managed.*

répondre à: Est-ce que tu as répondu à son mail? *Did you reply to his email?*

-Oui, j'**y** ai répondu. *Yes, I replied* **to it**.

-Non, je n'**y** ai pas répondu. *No, I haven't replied* **to it.**

Vocabulary

Common expressions with *en*

Je n'**en** sais rien. *I don't know anything (about it).*

J'**en** ai marre. *I'm fed up (with it).*

J'**en** ai assez. *I've had enough (of it).*

Il n'**y en** a plus. *There isn't / aren't any left.*

Common expressions with *y*

il **y** a *there is / there* **are**: Il **y** a un château et un parc. *There is a castle and a park.*

il **y** a + time phrase *ago*: il **y** a une semaine *a week ago*

Ça **y** est! *That's it!*

y compris *including*

Il **y** a trente personnes dans la salle de classe, **y** compris le professeur. *There are thirty people in the classroom, including the teacher.*

Practice

Traduis les phrases suivantes en français.

(a) Do you want some more salad?

(b) Yes, I want some.

(c) No, I don't want any.

(d) Do you need any money?

(e) Yes, I need some.

(f) He's back from the concert. → He's back from it.

(g) I went to France.

(h) I went there.

(i) Are you thinking of coming?

(j) Yes, I am thinking about it.

Made a start   Feeling confident   Exam ready

Conjunctions and connectives

Conjunctions and connectives are words that link ideas together in a sentence or paragraph.

⑤ Coordinating conjunctions

Coordinating conjunctions are words that link together words or phrases of equal importance in a sentence. Common coordinating conjunctions are: **et** (*and*), **mais** (*but*), **ou** (*or*), **car** (*because*) and **donc** (*so / therefore*).

Il y a trop d'ordures **car** on ne recycle pas assez.
There is too much rubbish because we don't recycle enough.

Je ne me suis pas levé de bonne heure, **donc** j'ai raté le bus.
I didn't get up early, so I missed the bus.

Ce jour-là, il pleuvait **et** il y avait du vent. *On that day, it was raining and it was windy.*

Je voudrais sortir ce soir **mais** mes parents ne me le permettent pas. *I would like to go out this evening, but my parents won't allow it.*

On va aller au parc d'attractions **ou** à la fête foraine.
We are going to go to the theme park or to the funfair.

⑤ Time connectives

Connectives link ideas across two separate sentences or paragraphs. Use the following to describe a sequence of events across a period of time.

d'abord *first of all*

lorsque / quand *when*

ensuite / puis *then*

après que *after*

aussitôt que / dès que *as soon as*

tandis que / pendant que *while / whereas*

enfin / à la fin *finally / in the end*

avant de + infinitive *before (doing) something*

Quand nous sommes arrivés, nous avons fait la connaissance de nos partenaires. ***When*** *we arrived we got to know our partners.*

J'ai mis la table **pendant que** ma mère préparait le dîner. *I laid the table **while** my mother was preparing dinner.*

② Presenting an argument A–Z

Use the following connectives to look at different sides of an argument, or at the advantages and disadvantages of something:

à part *apart from*

cependant *however*

d'un côté *on the one hand*

d'un autre côté *on the other hand*

évidemment *evidently / obviously*

par contre *on the other hand*

c'est-à-dire *that is to say*

même si *even if*

pourtant *however*

par exemple *for example*

sans doute *without doubt / probably*

sinon *otherwise*

y compris *including*

② Reasons and consequences A–Z

Use the following connectives when you want to give a reason for something or to justify an opinion.

ainsi *so / therefore*

alors *so / therefore / then*

car *because / for*

donc *so / therefore*

puisque *since*

à cause de *because of*

lorsque *when*

par conséquent *as a result*

parce que *because*

si *if*

sinon *otherwise*

afin de + infinitive *in order to*

sans + infinitive *without + –ing, e.g. doing*

comme *as / like*

⑤ Exam focus

Pay attention to conjunctions in reading and listening texts, especially words like **mais**, **pourtant**, **cependant** and **par contre**. They can change the meaning of a sentence.

On dit que les films de guerre sont trop violents, **pourtant**, je ne suis pas d'accord car on pourrait dire que les films d'horreur sont pires.

*It is said that war films are too violent, **however** I disagree, because you could say that horror films are worse.*

This indicates that the speaker is about to disagree with the statement just made.

⑩ Practice

✏ Traduis les phrases suivantes en français.

(a) I hate living in town because there is too much pollution.

(b) We must stop the deforestation of our forests, otherwise we'll see more floods.

(c) You see a lot of homeless people on the streets because of the problems of unemployment and poverty.

(d) I think one should buy green products whereas my parents think that we must use less energy.

The present tense

Use this page to revise how to form and use the present tense.

⑤ About the present tense

Use the present tense to describe what is happening now or what usually happens. In English, there are two forms of the present tense: *I play* and *I am playing*.
In French however, you use je joue for both.

It can sometimes be used with a future sense:
Je vais à Paris demain. *I am going to Paris tomorrow.*

Remember, in negative statements you do not need an extra verb for *do*:

I don't play. Je ne joue pas.

② The present tense + *depuis*

When the present tense is used with depuis (*for / since*) it expresses how long something has been done for.
Je joue du violon depuis l'âge de sept ans.
I have been playing the violin since the age of seven.

> Verbs in the -er group make up about 80% of all French verbs. When new verbs are created from English words, they are -er verbs: for example, on social media you have tchatter, liker, bloguer.

⑩ Verb patterns

When you look up a verb in the dictionary it is listed in the infinitive form, for example, **to** eat, **to** start, **to** sell. Most verbs belong to one of three groups of regular verbs: -er, -ir or -re. In the present tense, these have the same endings depending on their group. Look at these examples of regular verbs for jouer *(to play)*, finir *(to finish)* and descendre *(to go down)*. Faire *(to make / do)*, venir *(to come)* and boire *(to drink)* are examples of irregular verbs.

	-er e.g. jouer	-ir e.g. finir	-re e.g. descendre
je	joue	finis	descends
tu	joues	finis	descends
il / elle / on	joue	finit	descend
nous	jouons	finissons	descendons
vous	jouez	finissez	descendez
ils / elles	jouent	finissent	descendent

	faire to make / do	venir to come	boire to drink
je	fais	viens	bois
tu	fais	viens	bois
il / elle / on	fait	vient	boit
nous	faisons	venons	buvons
vous	faites	venez	buvez
ils / elles	font	viennent	boivent

⑤ -er verbs with spelling changes

Some -er verbs make slight changes to their stem in the singular and third person plural of the present tense.
Look out for other verbs that follow the same patterns as the examples.

	add grave accent	double consonant	y → i
infinitive	acheter	jeter	nettoyer
je / j'	achète	jette	nettoie
tu	achètes	jettes	nettoies
il / elle / on	achète	jette	nettoie
nous	achetons	jetons	nettoyons
vous	achetez	jetez	nettoyez
ils / elles	achètent	jettent	nettoient

> **manger** and **commencer** make slight changes in the **nous** form:
> **nous mangeons** (add **e** before **-ons**)
> **nous commençons** (add cedilla to **c**)

② The verb *faire*

The verb faire is used in a lot of common expressions.
faire des bêtises *to do something stupid*
faire la fête *to party*
faire les bagages *to pack*
faire la grève *to go on strike*
faire jour / nuit *to be daytime / night-time*
ça ne fait rien *that doesn't matter*

⑩ Practice

✎ Traduis les phrases suivantes en français.

(a) I send text messages to my friends every day.

(b) We are reading some poems in class at the moment.

(c) We are going to the cinema today.

(d) I don't know him well.

(e) I have been learning French for five years.

Made a start **Feeling confident** **Exam ready**

Key verbs

Revise how to form and use the verbs avoir and être, and modal verbs.

⑤ Auxiliary verbs

Avoir and être are auxiliary verbs. They are used in the formation of past tenses of all other verbs. The present tense of these two verbs is used to form the perfect tense, and their imperfect tense is used to form the pluperfect.

The verb *avoir*

The verb avoir means *to have*. It is used in a lot of common expressions as well as in the formation of the perfect and pluperfect tenses.

	present	imperfect
j'	ai *have*	avais *had*
tu	as *have*	avais *had*
il / elle / on	a *has*	avait *had*
nous	avons *have*	avions *had*
vous	avez *have*	aviez *had*
ils / elles	ont *have*	avaient *had*

The verb *être*

The verb être means *to be*. It is used to form the perfect and pluperfect tense of reflexive verbs and certain other verbs.

	present	imperfect
je / j'	suis *am*	étais *was*
tu	es *are*	étais *were*
il / elle / on	est *is*	était *was*
nous	sommes *are*	étions *were*
vous	êtes *are*	étiez *were*
ils / elles	sont *are*	étaient *were*

⑩ Modal verbs and the verb *aller*

Vouloir, devoir and pouvoir are modal verbs. They are followed by another verb in the infinitive. Aller is used to form the immediate future tense (see page 91).

	vouloir *to want*	pouvoir *to be able / can*	devoir *to have to / must*	aller *to go*
je	veux	peux	dois	vais
tu	veux	peux	dois	vas
il / elle / on	veut	peut	doit	va
nous	voulons	pouvons	devons	allons
vous	voulez	pouvez	devez	allez
ils / elles	veulent	peuvent	doivent	vont

Nous **voulons aller** à Londres ce week-end. We **want to go** to London this weekend.

Je ne **peux** pas parler couramment. I **can't speak** fluently.

On **doit faire** des efforts pour avoir de bonnes notes. You **have to make** an effort to get good marks.

Pendant les vacances scolaires, je **vais faire** du bénévolat. During the school holidays I **am going to do** some volunteering.

On **voulait aller** au cinéma. We **wanted to go** to the cinema.

Je **devais aider** mes parents. I **had to help** my parents.

Nous **devrions recycler** les sacs en plastique. We **ought to recycle** plastic bags.

Je ne **pouvais** pas finir l'exercice. I **couldn't (wasn't able to) finish** the exercise.

Pourrais-tu m'aider? **Could** you (**would** you **be able to**) **help** me?

⑤ Modal verbs in other tenses

je voudrais *I would like to / I'd like to* (conditional)
je voulais *I wanted to* (imperfect)
je devrais *I ought to / I should* (conditional)
je devais *I had to* (imperfect)
je pourrais *I could / I would be able to* (conditional)
je pouvais *I could / I was able to* (imperfect)

⑩ Practice

❶ Translate the following common expressions using *avoir* into English.

(a) J'ai envie de sortir.

(b) Est-ce que tu as faim?

(c) On avait besoin d'aide.

(d) Ils ont soif.

(e) Nous n'avons pas eu de chance.

(f) Vous avez raison.

(g) Elle a peur des serpents.

❷ Translate the following common expressions using *être* into English.

(a) Elle est en train de faire la cuisine.

(b) Il est enrhumé depuis trois jours.

(c) On était obligé de partir avant la fin du concert.

(d) Je ne suis pas d'accord avec toi.

(e) Nous sommes sur le point de partir.

(f) Je suis de retour.

The perfect tense

The perfect tense is a past tense used for describing completed actions and is made up of two parts.

 About the perfect tense

The perfect tense is made up of two parts: auxiliary verb (present tense of avoir or être) + past participle.

Hier soir, j'**ai regardé** la télévision, mes parents **ont écouté** de la musique et mon frère **a lu** son livre.

Yesterday evening I **watched** TV, my parents **listened** to music and my brother **read** his book.

Regular verbs form the past participle in the following ways:

- er verbs: remove the r from the infinitive and add an acute accent to the e: jouer → joué
- ir verbs: remove the r from the infinitive: finir → fini
- re verbs: remove the re from the infinitive, add u to the stem: vendre → vendu

The perfect tense can be translated in a number of different ways: j'ai joué = I played, I have played, I did play.
Most verbs form the perfect tense with avoir. Reflexive verbs and some other verbs form the perfect tense with être.

 The perfect tense formed with *être*

Past participles formed with être agree with the subject.

je suis allé(e)	I went
tu es allé(e)	you went
il est allé	he went
elle est allée	she went
on est allé(e/s)	we went
nous sommes allé(e)s	we went
vous êtes allé(e/s)	you went (formal / pl)
ils sont allés	they went (m or mixed)
elles sont allées	they went (only f)

Verbs that take être: **MRS DR VANDERTRAMP**

verb	past participle
monter to go up	monté
rester to stay	resté
sortir to go out	sorti
descendre to go down	descendu
retourner to return	retourné
venir to come	venu
aller to go	allé
naître to be born	né
devenir to become	devenu
entrer to enter	entré
revenir to come back	revenu
tomber to fall	tombé
rentrer to return	rentré
arriver to arrive	arrivé
mourir to die	mort
partir to leave	parti

Ma sœur est allée à Paris avec ses copines. Elles sont parties de bonne heure et elles y sont arrivées à midi.
My sister went to Paris with her friends. They left early and arrived there at midday.

Common irregular verbs

All these verbs form the perfect tense with the present tense of avoir.

avoir to have	eu
boire to drink	bu
connaître to know	connu
croire to believe	cru
devoir to have to	dû
dire to say	dit
écrire to write	écrit
être to be	été
faire to do / make	fait
lire to read	lu
mettre to put	mis
ouvrir to open	ouvert
pouvoir to be able to	pu
prendre to take	pris
recevoir to receive	reçu
savoir to know (a fact)	su
voir to see	vu
vouloir to want	voulu

Remember to make the past participle *opened* agree with the direct object *presents*.

 Practice

✏ Traduis le passage suivant en français:

Yesterday I celebrated my birthday. My parents gave me a lot of presents that I opened in the morning. In the evening we had a party and a lot of my friends came. We drank cola and afterwards we danced. What did you do last weekend?

 Made a start **Feeling confident** 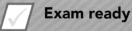 **Exam ready**

The imperfect tense

Revise how to form and use the imperfect tense.

(5) About the imperfect tense

The imperfect tense is used to say:
- what things were like in the past:
  Il faisait chaud. *It was hot.*
  Le voyage était affreux. *The journey was awful.*
  Il y avait du monde. *There were a lot of people.*
- what used to happen:
  J'habitais à Lille *I lived / used to live in Lille.*
- what happened habitually or frequently:
  On rendait souvent visite à mes grands-parents.
  We often visited my grandparents.
- what someone was doing when an action was interrupted:
  Je regardais la télévision quand le téléphone a sonné.
  I was watching television when the phone rang.

(2) Making suggestions

The imperfect tense can be used to make suggestions.
Si on allait au théâtre? *How about going to the theatre?*
Si on faisait une excursion? *Shall we go on an outing?*
Si on mangeait au restaurant? *How about eating in a restaurant?*

(2) Venir + de

The imperfect tense of venir + de + infinitive is used to say something *had just* happened.
Il venait de finir son dîner quand quelqu'un a frappé à la porte. *He had just finished his dinner when someone knocked on the door.*

(10) Forming the imperfect tense

To form the imperfect tense, take the –ons ending off the nous form of the present tense and add the imperfect endings shown in the table. The one exception to this rule is the verb être which simply adds the endings to the stem ét-.

	jouer *to play* (nous jouons)	finir *to finish* (nous finissons)	descendre *to go down* (nous descendons)
je	jouais	finissais	descendais
tu	jouais	finissais	descendais
il / elle / on	jouait	finissait	descendait
nous	jouions	finissions	descendions
vous	jouiez	finissiez	descendiez
ils / elles	jouaient	finissaient	descendaient

être	*to be*
j'étais	*I was*
tu étais	*you were*
il / elle / on était	*he / she was*
nous étions	*we were*
vous étiez	*you were*
ils / elles étaient	*they were*

(2) Si + imperfect

The imperfect is often combined with the conditional in sentences to say what you *would* do. See page 93.
Si j'étais riche, j'achèterais une belle maison.
If I were rich I would buy a nice house.
Si j'avais du temps, j'irais le voir.
If I had time I would go and see him.

(2) Aiming higher (↑)

Use depuis followed by a verb in the imperfect tense to express for how long something *had been* done.
J'habitais à Londres depuis trois ans.
I had been living in London for three years.
J'habitais à Londres depuis septembre.
I had been living in London since September.

(5) Practice

✎ Traduis les phrases suivantes en français.
(a) I was doing my homework when my mother asked me to go downstairs.
(b) I was in the middle of reading my book when someone knocked on the door.
(c) We were crossing the road when the accident happened.
(d) We had just arrived when it started to rain.

The pluperfect tense

The pluperfect tense is used to talk about events that happened further back in the past than those described using the perfect tense.

 About the pluperfect tense

Use the pluperfect tense to say what you had done or what had happened.

Mes parents se fâchaient parce que je n'avais pas fait mes devoirs. *My parents were getting angry because I **hadn't done** my homework.*

Je n'étais jamais allé en France avant cette visite-là. *I **had** never **been** to France before that visit.*

 Regular verbs

The pluperfect tense is formed in a similar way to the perfect tense, but instead uses the imperfect tense of avoir or être before the past participle.

auxiliary	-er	-ir	-re
j'avais	joué	fini	vendu
tu avais	joué	fini	vendu
il / elle / on avait	joué	fini	vendu
nous avions	joué	fini	vendu
vous aviez	joué	fini	vendu
ils / elles avaient	joué	fini	vendu

J'avais fini mon dîner. *I **had finished** my dinner.*
Il avait vendu la maison. *He **had sold** the house.*
Elle avait mangé une glace. *She **had eaten** an ice cream.*

 Verbs with être

Verbs that form the perfect tense using a present tense être auxiliary use an imperfect être auxiliary in the pluperfect tense. The verb and the subject have to agree.

j'étais allé(e)	I had been / gone
tu étais allé(e)	you had been / gone
il était allé	he had been / gone
elle était allée	she had been / gone
on était allé(e/s)	we had been / gone
nous étions allé(e)s	we had been / gone
vous étiez allé(e/s)	you had been / gone (formal / pl)
ils étaient allés	they had been / gone (m or mixed)
elles étaient allées	they had been / gone (only f)

Nous n'étions jamais allées à Paris. *We (f) had never been to Paris.*

 Reported speech

Use the pluperfect tense to report speech.

Elle a dit qu'elle s'était bien amusée. *She said she had had a good time.*

Il a dit que son équipe n'avait pas gagné le match. *He said that his team hadn't won the match.*

Il a dit qu'il avait perdu son portable. *He said he had lost his mobile phone.*

Irregular verbs

For the past participles of irregular verbs see page 88, *The perfect tense.*

J'avais pris le train. *I had taken the train.*
Il avait mis son manteau. *He had put on his coat.*
Nous avions bu du thé. *We had drunk some tea.*
Ils avaient fait une erreur. *They had made a mistake.*
J'avais déjà lu ce livre. *I had already read that book.*
Elle lui avait écrit une lettre. *She had written a letter to him / her.*
On avait ouvert la fenêtre. *We had opened the window.*
Est-ce que tu l'avais vu auparavant? *Had you seen it / him before?*

 Aiming higher

Sentences that contain examples of the pluperfect tense are characteristic of the top grade answers at Higher level.

J'ai eu de bonnes notes parce que j'avais travaillé dur. *I got good marks because I had worked hard.*

 Practice

👓 Translate the following sentences into English.
(a) Mon frère était allé au café pour retrouver ses copains mais personne n'est venu.
(b) J'avais choisi mon repas avant d'aller au restaurant.
(c) Je n'avais jamais vu cette personne auparavant.
(d) Quand je suis arrivé au marché, j'ai remarqué que j'avais oublié mon porte-monnaie.
(e) Nous étions partis de bonne heure mais nous sommes arrivés tard à notre hôtel.

  Made a start 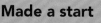 **Feeling confident** **Exam ready**

The immediate future tense

The immediate future tense is used to say what is going to happen, and is formed using the verb aller.

⑤ About the immediate future tense

Use the immediate future tense to talk about events that will happen soon. It is the equivalent of the English *going to...* and is formed by using the present tense of the verb aller + the infinitive. It can also be used to talk about future plans.

Je **vais lire** ce livre. I'**m going to read** this book.

Qu'est-ce que tu **vas faire**? What **are** you **going to do**?

On **va manger** en ville. We **are going to eat** in town.

Nous **allons louer** des vélos. We **are going to hire** some bikes.

Est-ce que vous **allez voir** ce film? **Are** you **going to see** this film?

Ils **vont regarder** la télé. They **are going to watch** television.

⑤ Other future expressions

You can use:

- the present tense with a future time phrase:

  Il **part dans deux heures**. *He is leaving in two hours.*

  Mes parents **rentrent tard ce soir**. *My parents are coming home late this evening.*

- **être sur le point de** *to be on the point of / about to do something*

  Nous **sommes sur le point de** partir. *We are about to leave.*

⑤ Aiming higher ⬆

If you use a reflexive verb in the immediate future, you need to make the reflexive pronoun agree with the subject.

Je **vais me** lever de bonne heure.

I am going to get up early.

Est-ce que **tu** vas **t'**habiller avant de prendre le petit déjeuner?

Are you going to get dressed before having breakfast?

Il **va s'**échauffer avant de faire de l'exercice.
He's going to warm up before exercising.

Nous **allons nous** / On **va se** balader dans le parc cet après-midi. *We are going to go for a stroll in the park this afternoon.*

Est-ce que **vous** allez **vous** reposer?
Are you going to have a rest?

Ils **vont se** détendre en écoutant de la musique.
They are going to relax by listening to music.

② Future time phrases A–Z

après-demain *the day after tomorrow*

bientôt *soon*

ce soir *tonight / this evening*

dans l'avenir *in the future*

dans deux jours *in two days*

demain *tomorrow*

demain matin *tomorrow morning*

l'été prochain *next summer*

la semaine prochaine *next week*

le mois prochain *next month*

le week-end prochain *next weekend*

l'année prochaine *next year*

lundi prochain *next Monday*

pendant les vacances *during the holidays*

plus tard *later*

VOCABULARY LINK
PAGE 102

Il va pleuvoir.

⑤ Practice

✏ Traduis les phrases suivantes en français.

(a) We are going to visit a museum during the exchange.

(b) They are going to see a film this evening.

(c) It is going to be windy.

(d) I hope it is going to snow soon.

(e) France is going to win the match.

The future tense

The future tense is used to say what will happen in the future.

 Forming the future tense

For verbs ending in -er and -ir, you add the future endings to the infinitive.

person	ending
je / j'	-ai
tu	-as
il / elle / on	-a
nous	-ons
vous	-ez
ils / elles	-ont

-er verbs that add an accent or double a consonant in the present tense make similar changes to their stem in the future tense.

J'appellerai mon copain. *I will call my friend.*

Elle achètera des provisions. *She will buy food.*

Some -er verbs with y in their stem change to i.

nettoyer (*to clean*), employer (*to employ*), essuyer (*to wipe*).

Nous nettoierons la cuisine. *We will clean the kitchen.*

 Verbs ending in -re

Verbs that end in -re drop the e at the end of the infinitive before adding the endings.

Je prendrai la soupe à l'oignon. *I'll have the onion soup.*

Est-ce que tu boiras de l'eau? *Will you drink water?*

Il ne dira rien. *He won't say anything.*

Nous écrirons des lettres. *We'll write some letters.*

Est-ce que vous mettrez vos baskets? *Will you be wearing your trainers?*

Ils vivront en France. *They will live in France.*

 Future tense with *si* and *quand*

Use the future tense in sentences where the other half is si + present tense.

S'il fait beau demain, on fera un pique-nique.

If it is fine tomorrow, we will have a picnic.

Si j'ai de la chance, je gagnerai à la loterie.

If I'm lucky, I will win the lottery.

Use the future tense after quand if the verb describes what will happen in the future. Take care with this as it's different from what happens in English.

Quand j'aurai trente ans, je me marierai.

When I am thirty I will get married.

 Common irregular future forms

A number of common verbs use an irregular stem, to which the future tense endings are added.

aller *to go*	ir-	pouvoir *to be able to*	pourr-
avoir *to have*	aur-	recevoir *to receive*	recevr-
courir *to run*	courr-	savoir *to know*	saur-
devoir *to have to*	devr-	venir *to come*	viendr-
envoyer *to send*	enverr-	voir *to see*	verr-
être *to be*	ser-	vouloir *to want*	voudr-
faire *to do*	fer-		

devenir (*to become*), tenir (*to hold*) and revenir (*to come back*) follow this pattern.

mourir (*to die*) follows this pattern.

Impersonal verbs such as pleuvoir (*to rain*), falloir (*to be necessary*) and valoir (*to be worth*) are all irregular.

il faudra *it will be necessary*; il pleuvra *it will rain*; il vaudra *it will be worth*

 Aiming higher

The best answers will include a variety of verbs in a range of tenses. Include examples of the future tense, especially irregular verbs.

À la fin de ma scolarité, je prendrai une année sabbatique et j'irai à l'étranger pour faire du bénévolat.

At the end of my schooling, I will take a gap year and I will go abroad to volunteer.

 Practice

Traduis les phrases suivantes en français.

(a) I will see him tomorrow.

(b) We will have to take the bus.

(c) She will be twenty years old.

(d) Will you (sing inf) go cycling tomorrow?

(e) How will he be coming?

(f) We will go to the theatre.

(g) He won't buy anything.

(h) What will you (pl) eat?

(i) When will you (sing inf) go out?

(j) I won't have a starter.

The conditional

The conditional is used to say what would or could happen.

 Forming the conditional

The conditional is formed in a similar way to the future tense. The conditional endings are the same as the imperfect endings and are added to the infinitive of -er and -ir verbs.

person	ending
je / j'	-ais
tu	-ais
il / elle / on	-ait
nous	-ions
vous	-iez
ils / elles	-aient

jouer → je jouer**ais** *I would play*

finir → je finir**ais** *I would finish*

For -re verbs, take off the final **e** of the infinitive and add the conditional endings.

vendre → je vendr**ais** *I would sell*

 Using the conditional with *si*

If a **si** clause uses the imperfect, the second part of the sentence should be in the conditional. (This follows the same pattern as in English.)

- Si mes parents ne se fâchaient pas, je **serais** plus heureux.
  If my parents didn't get angry, I would be happier.
- S'il avait de l'argent, il **achèterait** un nouveau portable.
  If he had the money, he would buy a new mobile phone.
- Si j'étais riche, j'**aurais** une belle maison.
  If I were rich, I would have a nice house.
- Si on recyclait plus, il y **aurait** moins de gaspillage.
  If we recycled more, there would be less waste.
- Si nous allions en France, nous **pourrions** perfectionner notre français.
  If we went to France, we could improve our French.
- Si j'avais le choix, j'**habiterais** dans un pays chaud.
  If I had the choice, I would live in a warm country.

 Irregular verbs in the conditional

Verbs that have irregular stems in the future tense (see page 92) use the same stem to form the conditional.

aller *to go*	ir-
avoir *to have*	aur-
courir *to run*	courr-
devoir *to have to*	devr-
envoyer *to send*	enverr-
être *to be*	ser-
faire *to do*	fer-
pouvoir *to be able*	pourr-
recevoir *to receive*	recevr-
savoir *to know*	saur-
venir *to come*	viendr-
voir *to see*	verr-
vouloir *to want*	voudr-

j'aurais *I would have*
je serais *I would be*

 Polite requests and statements

Using the conditional form makes requests sound even more polite.

Pourriez-vous m'aider?
Could you help me?

Pourriez-vous répéter la question, s'il vous plaît?
Could you repeat the question?

Est-ce qu'**il serait possible de** venir demain?
Would it be possible to come tomorrow?

Est-ce que je **pourrais** vous poser une question?
Could I ask you a question?

Je **voudrais** savoir si... *I would like to know if...*

J'**aimerais** mieux partir demain.
I would prefer to leave tomorrow.

 Practice

Traduis les phrases suivantes en français.

(a) If he was rich he wouldn't work.

(b) I would prefer to go to Spain.

(c) If I went to Paris I could go up the Eiffel Tower.

(d) If my mobile phone no longer worked I would buy a new one.

(e) If I had no money I would find a job.

Use la tour Eiffel.

Use the verb fonctionner.

Use en in front of the verb *to buy*.

 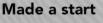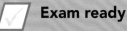

Negative forms

Revise how to make a sentence negative, using ne ... pas and other negative expressions with verbs.

(5) Formation of the negative

The negative is made up of two parts: **ne** and **pas**, which you put either side of the verb.

Je **ne** joue **pas** au tennis. *I don't play tennis.*

ne shortens to **n'** in front of a vowel or silent *h*.

Ils **n'**aiment **pas** les films de guerre. *They don't like war films.*

Elle **n'**habite **pas** au centre-ville. *She doesn't live in the town centre.*

(2) Pas / plus + de

After **pas** or **plus**, just use **de** or **d'** instead of **du, de la, de l'** and **des**.

Je **n'**ai **pas** **de** frères. *I don't have any brothers.*

On **n'**a **pas** **d'**argent. *We don't have any money.*

(2) Word order with pronouns

Je **ne** l'aime **pas**. *I don't like it.*

Il **n'**en mange **pas**. *He doesn't eat any of it.*

Le prof **ne** leur donne **pas** de devoirs. *The teacher doesn't give them any homework.*

(2) Word order in the perfect tense

In the perfect tense, **ne** and **pas** go around the auxiliary être / avoir verb.

Je **n'**ai **pas** fait mes devoirs. *I haven't done my homework.*

Ils **ne** sont **pas** allés au cinéma. *They didn't go to the cinema.*

(2) Word order with two verbs

When two verbs are used together, the **ne** and **pas** go around the first verb, not around the infinitive.

Je **ne** vais **pas** voir ce film. *I am not going to see this film.*

Ils **ne** veulent **pas** aider à la maison. *They don't want to help at home.*

To contradict a negative statement or question you use **si**, meaning *yes*.

Il n'y a plus de lait. *There's no more milk.*

-Si, il y en a. *Yes, there is some.*

Tu n'aimes pas les bananes? *You don't like bananas?*

-Si, je les aime. *Yes, I do like them.*

(2) Other negative forms

ne ... **plus** *no longer / not any more*

ne ... **jamais** *never / not ever*

ne ... **rien** *nothing / not anything*

ne ... **personne** *no one / not anyone*

ne ... **que** *only / nothing but*

ne ... **ni ... ni ...** *neither ... nor*

ne ... **guère** *hardly / scarcely*

ne ... **nulle part** *nowhere*

ne ... **pas encore** *not yet*

These work in the same way as ne ... pas.

Il **ne** travaille **plus**. *He doesn't work anymore.*

VOCABULARY LINK
PAGE
105

Personne and **que** are slightly different from other negatives, in that they go after the complete verb in the perfect tense, rather than just after the auxiliary.

Je **n'**ai vu **personne** ce soir. *I didn't see anyone this evening.*

On **n'**a acheté **que** deux pizzas. *We only bought two pizzas.*

(2) Negative imperatives

With imperatives, put **ne** and **pas** (or other negation) around the verb.

Ne cours **pas**! *Don't run!*

Ne fumez **pas**! *Don't smoke!*

Ne soyez **jamais** impoli(s)! *Never be rude!*

(5) Negative questions

In questions where the subject and verb are inverted (Veux-tu...?), put **ne** and **pas** round the whole structure.

Ne veux-tu **pas** sortir ce soir? *Don't you want to go out this evening?*

N'aimes-tu **pas** cette musique? *Don't you like this music?*

N'a-t-il **pas** de portable? *Hasn't he got a mobile phone?*

(10) Practice

✏ Traduis les phrases suivantes en français.

(a) There is no butter left.

(b) I have never been to France.

(c) We didn't go to the cinema.

(d) We are not going there.

(e) He didn't talk to anyone.

Reflexive verbs

Reflexive verbs have an extra pronoun between the subject and verb.

About reflexive verbs

Reflexive verbs are listed with se in front of them in the dictionary: se lever *to get up*; se dépêcher *to hurry*.

The reflexive pronoun changes depending on who or what the subject is and always comes immediately before the verb. The verb endings are as they would normally be.

Negative form of reflexive verbs

To make a reflexive verb negative, the ne goes in front of the reflexive pronoun.

Elle ne s'est pas dépêchée. *She didn't hurry.*

Je ne me couche pas de bonne heure. *I don't go to bed early.*

The present tense of reflexive verbs

Many reflexive verbs are –er verbs with regular endings.

se réveiller	*to wake up*
je me réveille	*I wake up*
tu te réveilles	*you wake up*
il / elle / on se réveille	*he / she / it / one wakes up*
nous nous réveillons	*we wake up*
vous vous réveillez	*you wake up*
ils / elles se réveillent	*they wake up*

me, **te** and **se** become **m'**, **t'** and **s'** in front of a vowel or a silent 'h': **je m'appelle, tu t'ennuies, il s'habille**.

Reflexive verbs used in the infinitive

The reflexive pronoun changes to agree with the subject when a reflexive verb is used in the infinitive, after verbs such as vouloir, devoir, pouvoir and aller.

Je vais me coucher de bonne heure.
I am going to go to bed early.

Voulez-vous vous asseoir là-bas?
Do you want to sit down over there?

Se and **nous** can sometimes mean *each other*, for example:

On doit se revoir bientôt.
We must see each other again soon.

Perfect tense of reflexive verbs

Reflexive verbs form the perfect tense with the verb être. The past participle must agree with the subject.

je me suis réveillé(e)	*I woke up*	nous nous sommes réveillé(e)s	*we woke up*
tu t'es réveillé(e)	*you woke up*	vous vous êtes réveillé(e/s)	*you woke up*
il s'est réveillé	*he woke up*	ils se sont réveillés	*they woke up (m / mixed)*
elle s'est réveillée	*she woke up*	elles se sont réveillées	*they woke up (f)*
on s'est réveillé(e/s)	*one / we / you woke up*		

Reflexive verbs and parts of the body

Reflexive verbs are often used with parts of the body.

se brosser les dents *to brush one's teeth*
se laver les mains *to wash one's hands*

When a reflexive verb is used with a part of the body in the perfect tense, the past participle does not agree.

Elle s'est coupé le doigt. *She cut her finger.*

Reflexive verbs and the imperative

In the imperative, the pronoun follows the verb.
Te changes to toi.

Lève-toi, levez-vous! *Get up!*
Levons-nous. *Let's get up.*
Assieds-toi, asseyez-vous! *Sit down!*
Asseyons-nous. *Let's sit down.*

Practice

Translate the following sentences into French.

(a) I don't get up early.
(b) They never argue.
(c) They washed their hands.
(d) We want to have a good time.

The imperative

You can use the imperative form of a verb to give instructions, orders and advice or to make a request.

 Forming the imperative

There are three forms of the imperative, used for addressing *you* (familiar), *you* (polite) and *us*. These are simply the **tu**, **nous** and **vous** forms of the present tense of the verb, but without the pronoun.

(For **-er** verbs, drop the **-s** in the **tu** form, except when followed by **y** or **en**.)

	travailler *to work*	choisir *to choose*	attendre *to wait*
tu	travaille	choisis	attends
nous	travaillons	choisissons	attendons
vous	travaillez	choisissez	attendez

Travaillez plus dur. *Work harder.*

Choisis ton entrée. *Choose your starter.*

Attendons le bus là-bas. *Let's wait for the bus over there.*

Manges-en! *Eat some!*

Faites vos devoirs. *Do your homework.*

> The verb **aller** drops the **-s** in the **tu** form except when followed by **y**.
> **Va chez le médecin.** *Go to the doctor.*
> **Vas-y.** *Go (on).*

> The verb **ouvrir,** which takes **-er** endings in the present tense, drops the **-s** in the **tu** form.
> **Ouvre la porte!** *Open the door!*

 Irregular imperatives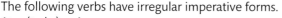

The following verbs have irregular imperative forms.
être (*to be*): sois, soyons, soyez
avoir (*to have*): aie, ayons, ayez
savoir (*to know*): sache, sachons, sachez
vouloir (*to want*): veuille, veuillons, veuillez

 Reflexive verbs and imperatives

Réveille-toi! *Wake up!*

Réveillez-vous! *Wake up!*

Réveillons-nous à sept heures. *Let's wake up at seven o'clock.*

In a negative sentence, the reflexive pronoun comes before the imperative.

Ne t'inquiète pas! *Don't worry!*

Ne vous inquiétez pas! *Don't worry!*

Ne nous inquiétons pas! *Let's not worry!*

 Using the imperative

The imperative is often used in the following contexts:
- advice for a healthy lifestyle
- school rules
- instructions for how to do something: a recipe or an exercise
- giving directions
- rubrics on the exam paper.

 Negative imperatives

Put **ne** and **pas** (or other negation) around the verb.

N'aie pas peur. *Don't be afraid.*

Ne soyez jamais impolis. *Never be rude.*

Ne mangez pas trop de frites. *Don't eat too many chips.*

 Practice

1 Your friend has left some directions for you in a voicemail. Listen to the instructions and complete the following sentences using phrases from the box. There will be some phrases you don't need.

> continue straight ahead   cross the square
> cross the bridge   go as far as the traffic lights
> go towards the river   go up to the crossroads
> turn left   turn right

(a) On leaving the station you must _____.

(b) At the traffic lights _____.

(c) After 200 metres _____.

(d) At the end of the rue Victor Hugo _____.

2 Traduis les phrases suivantes en français.

(a) Pour une vie saine...

(b) ... buvez huit verres d'eau par jour.

(c) ... mangez au moins cinq portions de fruits et de légumes par jour.

(d) ... ne fumez pas.

(e) ... évitez les aliments riches en matières grasses.

(f) ... faites de l'exercice régulièrement.

(g) ... ne restez pas assis trop longtemps.

  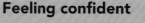

Impersonal verbs

Impersonal verbs are used to make general statements. They are only used in the il form of the verb.

Il y a

- **Il y a** means *there is* or *there are*.
  Il y a des magasins près de chez moi. *There are some shops near my home.*
- **Il y avait** means *there was* or *there were* (imperfect).
  Il y avait du brouillard. *It was foggy.*
  Il y avait une trentaine d'invités. *There were about thirty guests.*
- **Il y aura** means *there will be* (future).
  Il y aura du monde. *There will be a lot of people.*

  il y a + period of time = *ago*
  il y a un an = *a year ago*

Weather expressions

Il fait is used for a lot of common weather phrases.
Il fait beau / mauvais. *It is fine / bad weather.*
Il faisait chaud / froid. *It was hot / cold.*
Il fera beau. *It will be nice weather.*

 VOCABULARY LINK PAGE **102**

present	imperfect	future
il pleut	il pleuvait	il pleuvra
it's raining	*it was raining*	*it will rain*
il neige	il neigeait	il neigera
it's snowing	*it was snowing*	*it will snow*
il gèle	il gelait	il gèlera
it's freezing	*it was freezing*	*it will be freezing*

Other impersonal verbs

il reste *there is / are ... left*
Il reste des places. *There are some seats left.*
il manque *it is missing / lacking*
Il manque du pain. *The bread is missing / There is no bread left.*
Il manque du personnel. *There is a lack of staff.*
il vaut mieux *it's better / it would be better / best*
Il vaut mieux venir maintenant. *It's best to come now.*

Il faut

Il faut comes from the verb **falloir** *(to be necessary)*.
Use it as an alternative to **devoir**. It can be followed by an infinitive or by **que** + subjunctive (see page 101).

It can be translated in different ways, depending on the context.

Il faut partir de bonne heure. *You / we have to leave early.*

You might see it used in other tenses, such as imperfect (**il fallait**) and future (**il faudra**).

Il faudra trouver un emplacement. *We will have to find a camping spot.*

Impersonal phrases with *être*

Il est facile de trouver de l'information. *It's easy to find some information.*

Il est difficile de comprendre ce texte. *It is difficult to understand this text.*

Il est possible de trouver des solutions. *It's possible to find some solutions.*

Il est défendu / interdit de fumer. *It is forbidden to smoke.*

> Use **C'est...** if you are using an adjective only:
> **C'est facile.** *It's easy.*
> **C'est incroyable.** *It's incredible.*

Aiming higher

Use impersonal verbs to expand and develop your answers.

il s'agit de *it's about / it's a question of*
Il s'agit d'un garçon et d'une fille... *It's about a boy and a girl...*
il suffit de *it's enough to / you just have to*
Il suffit d'acheter un billet. *You just need to buy a ticket.*
Il semble qu'il va arriver en retard. *It seems that he is going to arrive late.*

Practice

1 Traduis les phrases suivantes en français.
 (a) There is some money left.
(b) It was windy.
(c) There is a lack of information.
(d) It was about a true story.

2 Translate the following sentences into English.
 (a) À cause de la grève, il fallait aller au collège à pied.
(b) Il suffit de parler avec lui.
(c) Il est interdit de marcher sur la pelouse.

The infinitive

The infinitive is the form of the verb you will find first in the dictionary.

② About the infinitive

In English, the infinitive has *to* in front of the verb: *to do; to eat.* In French, the infinitive form of the verb ends in -er, -ir or -re: jouer, choisir, attendre.

The infinitive is used after a number of common verbs such as: aimer, adorer, détester and préférer.
With these verbs, the infinitive is often translated into English by *-ing*: J'aime jouer du piano. *I like playing the piano.*

⑤ Verbs followed by the infinitive

Common verbs that are followed by another verb in the infinitive (without de or à) are:

- **Modal verbs**: vouloir, pouvoir and devoir
  Peux-tu venir ce soir? *Can you come this evening?*
  Je veux voir ce film. *I want to see this film.*
  Nous devons porter un uniforme. *We have to wear a uniform.*
- **Aller** to form the immediate future tense:
  Je vais étudier le français. *I am going to study French.*
- Verbs such as aimer, détester, espérer, préférer and savoir.
  J'espère prendre une année sabbatique. *I hope to take a gap year.*

⑤ Aiming higher

Include verbs that are followed by the preposition à + infinitive of another verb.

s'amuser à *to enjoy oneself (doing)*; apprendre à *to learn*;

commencer à *to begin*; continuer à *to continue*;

hésiter à *to hesitate*; inviter à *to invite*;

se mettre à *to start*

Il a commencé à pleuvoir. *It started to rain.*

J'ai appris à faire du ski. *I learnt how to ski.*

Include verbs that are followed by the preposition de + infinitive of another verb.

décider de *to decide*; essayer de *to try*;

oublier de *to forget*; refuser de *to refuse*;

s'arrêter de *to stop*

Il a oublié d'acheter le pain. *He forgot to buy the bread.*

> venir de + infinitive means *to have just done something.*
> Je viens de visiter la France. *I have just visited France.*

⑤ Prepositions + infinitive

Use the infinitive after the following prepositions: pour (*for*), sans (*without*), au lieu de (*instead of*) and avant de (*before*).

Je prends le petit déjeuner avant d'aller au collège.
I have breakfast before going to school.

J'ai lu mon livre au lieu de regarder la télé.
I read my book instead of watching television.

Je vais en ville pour acheter des provisions.
I am going to town to buy some food.

⑤ Perfect infinitive

The perfect infinitive is avoir or être + the past participle of the verb: avoir mangé; être arrivé(e/s).

It is often used after après to mean *after having done something.*

Après avoir fait mes devoirs, j'ai regardé la télé.
After having done my homework, I watched TV.

Après être rentrées chez elles, les filles ont bu un chocolat chaud.
After having returned home, the girls drank a hot chocolate.

> The past participle rentrées has to agree with the subject to which it refers.

⑩ Practice

① Traduis les phrases suivantes en français.
✏ **(a)** He hates doing his homework.
(b) She loves listening to music.
(c) I tried to learn the new words.
(d) I can (know how to) swim.

② Translate the following sentences into English.
👓 **(a)** On nous a invités à participer à un sondage.
(b) Après avoir mangé, on est allés au cinéma.
(c) Ils ont décidé de partir de bonne heure.
(d) Il est parti sans dire un mot.

The present participle

The present participle ends in **-ant** in French and is the equivalent of *-ing* in English.

About the present participle

The present participle is used to show that two things are happening at the same time and can be translated by *while -**ing*** something.

Il a fait ses devoirs **en écoutant** de la musique.
*He did his homework **while listening** to music.*

Elle a parlé avec ses copines **en attendant** le car de ramassage scolaire.
*She talked to her friends **while waiting for** the school bus.*

Formation of the present participle

The present participle is formed by removing the **-ons** ending from the **nous** form of the present tense, and adding **-ant**.

nous écrivons → écrivant

nous choisissons → choisissant

The present participle follows **en**:

en écrivant; en choisissant

The following verbs have irregular present participles:

être → étant

avoir → ayant

savoir → sachant.

Aiming higher

Using the present participle to convey the idea of *while* or *on doing* something is a feature of higher level answers.

Elle avait perdu son portable en faisant de la voile.
She lost her mobile phone while sailing.

Il a fait du repassage en regardant la télévision.
He did the ironing while watching TV.

En faisant ses devoirs de français, elle a appris tout son vocabulaire.
While doing her French homework, she learnt all her vocabulary.

En rentrant du collège, il a allumé la télévision.
On returning home from school, he switched on the TV.

By –ing…

Nicole a amélioré son français…
Nicole improved her French…

… en apprenant beaucoup de mots.
… by learning a lot of words.

… en écoutant des podcasts.
… by listening to podcasts.

… en faisant des exercices de grammaire.
… by doing grammar exercises.

… en lisant des textes en ligne.
… by reading texts on line.

As a noun

The present participle is sometimes used as a noun. In this case it has masculine and feminine forms and the noun rarely contains *–ing*.

un étudiant / une étudiante *student*

un participant / une participante *participant*

un enseignant / une enseignante *teacher*

un assistant / une assistante *assistant*

As an adjective

The present participle can often be used as an adjective. It has to agree with the noun or pronoun it corresponds with.

une ville charmante *a charming town*

une histoire fascinante *a fascinating story*

des voitures polluantes *polluting cars*

un sport fatigant *a tiring sport*

Practice

👓 Translate the following sentences into English.

(a) Ayant peur de la violence, elle n'est pas allée voir ce film de guerre.

(b) En épargnant son argent de poche, il a pu acheter un nouveau vélo.

(c) Il s'est trouvé en difficulté en nageant.

(d) Je me suis coupé le doigt en préparant le dîner.

(e) En entendant le bruit, nous nous sommes réveillés.

 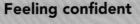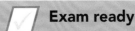

The passive voice

The passive form is when the subject has something done to it, rather than actively doing whatever is expressed in the verb.

 About the passive

In a passive sentence, the subject is not doing the action, but having something done to it.

The boy broke the window. (active)

The window was broken by the boy. (passive)

The passive is formed by using an être auxiliary (tense dependent on context) + past participle. The past participle has to agree with the subject.

La fenêtre a été cassée par le garçon.

This agrees with **fenêtre** (feminine singular).

Le dîner est servi.

 Forming the passive

The passive can have different tenses, by using different tenses of the verb être.

Present: Les bouteilles sont recyclées. *The bottles **are** recycled.*

Perfect: Les bouteilles ont été recyclées. *The bottles **were** recycled.*

Pluperfect: Les bouteilles avaient été recyclées. *The bottles **had been** recycled.*

Future: Les bouteilles seront recyclées. *The bottles **will be** recycled.*

 Use of the passive

The passive is often used to describe processes.

Les plantes sont cultivées dans des pays tropicaux. *The plants are cultivated in tropical countries.*

Les grains de café sont cueillis par des ouvriers. *The coffee beans are picked by the workers.*

Ils sont transportés en bateau vers les pays européens. *They are transported by boat to European countries.*

Le café est mis en paquet dans des usines, et il est vendu partout. *The coffee is packaged in factories and is sold all over.*

 Avoiding the passive

It is often more natural in French to use other constructions and avoid the passive. The sentence can use **on** instead (note that the English translation might still use a passive form if appropriate).

On a construit l'église au douzième siècle. *The church was built in the twelfth century.*

On a réduit les prix. *Prices have been reduced.*

On a organisé des excursions. *Outings were organised. / They organised outings.*

On m'a invité au mariage. *I was invited to the wedding.*

A verb can sometimes be made reflexive to avoid the passive.

Comment ça s'écrit? *How is that written?*

 Aiming higher

Although you are not expected to be able to use the passive at GCSE level, if you feel confident you could include an example, such as: Il a été invité. (*He was invited*). You are expected to recognise the use of the passive at Higher level in your French GCSE.

 Practice

 Translate the following sentences into English.

(a) Le château a été construit au seizième siècle.

(b) La rue est bloquée par un arbre.

(c) Les bâtiments ont été détruits par le tremblement de terre.

(d) Les voleurs ont été arrêtés.

(e) Les prix seront réduits.

The subjunctive mood

The subjunctive mood is a form of the verb that is used in certain circumstances, such as expressing uncertainty.

 ## About the subjunctive

The subjunctive mood has four different tenses: present, imperfect, perfect and pluperfect. However, at Higher level GCSE you will only be expected to recognise some common expressions in the present tense form.

The subjunctive is usually introduced by a verb that expresses an opinion, attitude or emotion, followed by que.

Je veux qu'il vienne à ma fête. *I want him to come to my party.*

Je suis désolé que tu sois malade. *I am sorry that you are ill.*

It is also used after expressions such as:

* il faut que *it is necessary that*
* bien que *although*
* quoique *although*
* pour que *so that*
* afin que *so that*
* jusqu'à ce que *until.*

 ## Using the subjunctive

Use the subjunctive after the following:

vouloir: **Il veut que** je parte maintenant.
He wants me to leave now.

préférer: **Je préfère qu'**elle s'en aille maintenant.
I'd prefer that she go away now. / I'd prefer her to go away now.

croire + negative: **Je ne crois pas que** vous ayez raison.
I don't think that you are right.

regretter: **Je regrette qu'**ils soient en retard.
I regret that they are late.

Il est important que vous compreniez.
It's important that you understand.

Il faut qu'on boive de l'eau.
We must drink some water.

 ## Common irregular forms

faire → **Il faut que** je le **fasse**. *I must do it.*

pouvoir → **Il est important que** tu **puisses** venir.
It's important that you are able to come.

savoir → **Je veux que** tu **saches** la vérité.
I want you to know the truth.

The verbs être, avoir and aller are also irregular:

être: sois, sois, soit, soyons, soyez, soient

avoir: aie, aies, aie, ayons, ayez, aient

aller: aille, ailles, aille, allions, alliez, aillent.

Liberté • Égalité • Fraternité

RÉPUBLIQUE FRANÇAISE

Vive la France!

Vive la France! is a patriotic expression that uses the subjunctive of vivre. It means *Long live France!* People say it at sporting events, national holidays and political rallies. You might also hear Vive la liberté! (*Long live liberty!*), Vive l'égalité! (*Long live equality!*) and Vive la fraternité! (*Long live fraternity!*)

 ## Formation of present subjunctive

As a general rule the present subjunctive is formed by removing the -ent ending from the ils / elles form of the present tense and adding the subjunctive endings: -e, -es, -e, -ions, -iez, -ent .

	ils jouent	ils finissent	ils vendent
je	joue	finisse	vende
tu	joues	finisses	vendes
il / elle / on	joue	finisse	vende
nous	jouions	finissions	vendions
vous	jouiez	finissiez	vendiez
ils / elles	jouent	finissent	vendent

* The nous and vous forms are the same as the imperfect tense.
* For –er verbs, the singular and ils / elles forms are the same as the present tense.
* For –ir and –re verbs, the ils / elles form is the same as the present tense.

 ## Practice

👓 Translate the following sentences into English.

(a) Je préfère y aller à pied, bien que j'aie une voiture.

(b) Je lui ai envoyé un mail afin qu'il sache l'heure du rendez-vous.

(c) Je resterai près du téléphone jusqu'à ce qu'il revienne.

(d) Bien qu'il soit riche, il n'est pas généreux.

General vocabulary

Here is some of the vocabulary that you will need for this Revision Guide and for your exam. Higher-tier vocabulary is marked *. You can find the full list of vocabulary on the Edexcel website: qualifications.pearson.com/en/qualifications/edexcel-gcses/french-2016.html

Time expressions

à la fois	at the same time
à l'avenir	in future
à l'heure	on time
an (m)	year
année (f)	year
après	after
après-demain	the day after tomorrow
après-midi	afternoon
aujourd'hui	today
auparavant	formerly, in the past
avant	before
avant-hier	the day before yesterday
bientôt	soon
d'abord	at first, firstly
d'habitude	usually
de bonne heure	early
début (m)	start
demain	tomorrow
dernier / dernière	last
de temps en temps	from time to time
déjà	already
de nouveau	again
en attendant	whilst waiting (for), meanwhile
en avance	in advance
en ce moment	at the moment
en retard	late
en même temps	at the same time
encore une fois	once more, again
enfin	at last, finally
environ	about, approximately
fin (f)	end
hier	yesterday
il y a	ago
jour (m)	day
journée (f)	day
lendemain (m)	the next day
longtemps	a long time
maintenant	now
matin (m)	morning
mois (m)	month
normalement	normally
nuit (f)	night
parfois	sometimes
passé (m)	past
pendant	during
plus tard	later
presque	almost, nearly

prochain	next
quelquefois	sometimes
rarement	rarely
récemment	recently
semaine (f)	week
seulement	only
siècle (m)	century
soir (m)	evening
soudain	suddenly
souvent	often
suivant	following
tard	late
tôt	early
toujours	always, still
tous les jours	every day
tout à coup	suddenly, all of a sudden
tout de suite	immediately
vite	quickly

Seasons

printemps (m)	spring
été (m)	summer
automne (m)	autumn
hiver (m)	winter

Weather

averse (f)	shower
briller	to shine
brouillard (m)	fog
brume (f)	mist
chaleur (f)	heat
ciel (m)	sky
climat (m)	climate
couvert	overcast
doux	mild
éclair (m)	lightning
*éclaircie (f)	bright spell
ensoleillé	sunny
faire beau	to be fine (weather)
faire mauvais	to be bad (weather)
geler	to freeze
glace (f)	ice
humide	humid, wet
météo (f)	weather forecast
mouillé	wet
neiger	to snow
nuage (m)	cloud
nuageux	cloudy
ombre (f)	shade, shadow

orage (m)	storm
*orageux	stormy
pleuvoir	to rain
pluie (f)	rain
sec / sèche	dry
tempête (f)	storm
temps (m)	weather
tonnerre (m)	thunder
tremper	to soak
vent (m)	wind

Greetings and exclamations

à bientôt	see you soon
à demain	see you tomorrow
à tout à l'heure	see you soon / later
allô	hello (on phone)
amitiés	best wishes
au secours	help
bien sûr	of course, certainly
bienvenue	welcome
bon anniversaire	happy birthday
bon appétit	enjoy your meal
bon voyage	have a good trip
bonne année	Happy New Year
bonne chance	good luck
bonne idée	good idea
bonne nuit	good night
bonnes vacances	have a good holiday
bonsoir	good evening
d'accord	ok
de rien	don't mention it
désolé(e)	sorry
excusez-moi	excuse me
félicitations	congratulations
joyeux Noël	Merry Christmas
meilleurs vœux	best wishes
pardon	excuse me, sorry
quel dommage	what a pity
salut	hi
santé	cheers
s'il te / vous plaît	please

Expressing opinions

absolument	absolutely
avis (m)	opinion
à mon avis	in my opinion
bien entendu	of course
bien sûr	of course
ça dépend	that depends
ça m'énerve	it gets on my nerves

 Made a start   **Feeling confident**   ☑ **Exam ready**

ça me fait rire	it makes me laugh
ça me plaît	I like it
ça m'est égal	it's all the same to me
ça ne me dit rien	it means nothing to me, I don't fancy that, I don't feel like it
ça suffit	that's enough
certainement	certainly
comme ci comme ça	so-so
croire	to believe
désirer	to want
détester	to hate
dire	to say
en général	in general
espérer	to hope
évidemment	obviously
franchement	frankly
généralement	generally
(s')intéresser à	to be interested in
marre (en avoir)	(to be) fed up
(moi) non plus	me neither, nor do I
penser	to think
peut-être	perhaps
préférer	to prefer
promettre	to promise
sembler	to seem
supporter	to put up with
vouloir	to wish, want
vraiment	really, truly

Opinions: adjectives

affreux	awful
agréable	pleasant
amusant	funny
barbant	boring
casse-pieds	annoying
cher	dear, expensive
chouette	great
compliqué	complicated
content	happy
désagréable	unpleasant
drôle	funny
embêtant	annoying
enchanté	delighted
ennuyeux	boring
étonné	astonished, amazed
facile	easy
faible	weak
formidable	great
génial	great

grave	serious
habile	clever
injuste	unfair
intéressant	interesting
inutile	useless
incroyable	incredible
inquiet / inquiète	worried
marrant	funny
mauvais	bad
merveilleux / merveilleuse	marvellous
mignon / mignonne	cute
moche	ugly
nouveau	new
nul	rubbish
parfait	perfect
passionnant	exciting
pratique	practical
ridicule	ridiculous
rigolo	funny
sage	well-behaved
sensass	sensational
utile	useful

Questions

à quelle heure?	at what time?
ça s'écrit comment?	how is that written?
c'est combien?	how much is it?
c'est quelle date?	what is the date?
c'est quel jour?	what day is it?
de quelle couleur?	what colour?
d'où?	from where?
où?	where?
pour combien de temps?	for how long?
pourquoi?	why?
quand?	when?
que?	what?
que veut dire...?	what does...mean?
quel / quelle?	which?
quelle heure est-il?	what time is it?
qu'est-ce que?	what?
qu'est-ce qui?	what?
qu'est-ce que c'est?	what is it?
qui?	who?
quoi?	what?

Conjunctions and connectives

à cause de	because of
à part	apart from
ainsi	so, therefore

alors	so, therefore, then
aussi	also
car	because
cependant	however
c'est-à-dire	that is to say, ie
comme	as, like
d'un côté, d'un autre côté	on the one hand, on the other hand
donc	so, therefore
ensuite	next
mais	but
même si	even if
ou	or
par contre	on the other hand
par exemple	for example
pendant que	while
pourtant	however
puis	then
puisque	seeing that, since
quand	when
sans doute	undoubtedly, without doubt, probably
si	if
y compris	including

Location and distance

à droite	on / to the right
à gauche	on / to the left
banlieue (f)	suburb
centre-ville (m)	town centre
campagne (f)	countryside
chez	at the house of
de chaque côté	from each side
de l'autre côté	from the other side
en bas	down(stairs)
en haut	up(stairs)
est (m)	east
ici	here
là	there
là-bas	over there
loin de	far from
nord (m)	north
nulle part	nowhere
ouest (m)	west
par	by
partout	everywhere
quelque part	somewhere
situé(e)	situated
sud (m)	south
tout droit	straight ahead
tout près	very near
toutes directions	all directions
ville (f)	town

Made a start   Feeling confident   Exam ready

Colours

blanc / blanche	white
bleu	blue
brun	brown (of hair)
châtain	light brown (of hair)
clair	light
foncé	dark
gris	grey
marron	brown
noir	black
noisette	hazel
violet	purple
rose	pink
rouge	red
roux	ginger
vert	green

Weights and measures

assez	enough, quite
bas	low
boîte (f)	box, tin, can
bouteille (f)	bottle
court	short
demi (m)	half
encore de	more
étroit	narrow
haut	high
large	wide
moitié (f)	half
morceau (m)	piece
nombre (m)	number
paquet (m)	packet
pas mal de	lots of
peser	to weigh
peu	little
un peu de	a little
plein de	full of, lots of
plus de	more
pointure (f)	size (for shoes)
suffisamment	sufficiently
taille (f)	size (for clothes)
tranche (f)	slice
trop	too (much)

Shape

carré	square
rond	round

Access

complet / complète	full
entrée (f)	entry, entrance
libre	free, vacant, unoccupied
fermer	to close
interdit	forbidden, not allowed
occupé	taken, occupied, engaged
ouvert	open
ouvrir	to open
sortie (f)	exit

Correctness

avoir raison	to be right
avoir tort	to be wrong
corriger	to correct
erreur (f)	error, mistake
faute (f)	fault, mistake
faux / fausse	false
il (me) faut	you (I) must
juste	correct
obligatoire	compulsory
parfait	perfect
sûr	certain, sure
se tromper	to make a mistake
vrai	true

Materials

argent (m)	silver
béton (m)	concrete
bois (m)	wood
cuir (m)	leather
fer (m)	iron
laine (f)	wool
or (m)	gold
*soie (f)	silk
verre (m)	glass

Comparatives and superlatives

plus / moins	more / less
plus que / moins que	more than / less than
bon / meilleur / le meilleur	good / better / best
mauvais / pire / le pire	bad / worse / worst
bien / mieux / le mieux	well / better / best
mal / plus mal / le plus mal	badly / worse / worst
beaucoup / plus / le plus	lots / more / the most
peu / moins / le moins	few, little / less / the least

General verbs

accepter	to accept
accompagner	to accompany
adorer	to love
*s'adresser à	to apply at / speak to
aimer	to like
ajouter	to add
s'amuser	to enjoy oneself
annuler	to cancel
appeler	to call
s'appeler	to be called
arriver	to arrive
s'asseoir	to sit down
attendre	to wait (for)
atterrir	to land
avoir	to have
bavarder	to chat
casser	to break
changer	to change
charger	to load, charge
coller	to stick
connaître	to know (be familiar with)
conseiller	to advise
contacter	to contact
copier	to copy
se débrouiller	to get by, to cope
décider	to decide
décrire	to describe
se dépêcher	to hurry
déranger	to disturb
descendre	to go down
se déshabiller	to get undressed
désirer	to want, desire
détester	to hate
dire	to say, tell
donner	to give
donner sur	to overlook
durer	to last
s'échapper	to escape
écouter	to listen
écrire	to write
emprunter	to borrow
s'endormir	to fall asleep
entendre	to hear
en train de (faire...)	(to be) doing
entrer	to enter, go in
s'ennuyer	to be bored
être	to be
expliquer	to explain
se fâcher	to get angry

 Made a start   **Feeling confident**   **Exam ready**

faire la connaissance de quelqu'un	to get to know someone
fermer	to close, switch off
finir	to finish, end
frapper	to knock, hit
gérer	to manage (business)
s'habiller	to get dressed
habiter	to live
(s')habituer à	to get used to
informer	to inform
introduire	to introduce
inviter	to invite
lever	to lift
manger	to eat
*manquer	to miss, lack
marcher	to walk
mériter	to deserve
monter	to climb, go up
monter dans	to get on, in
montrer	to show
noter	to note
s'occuper de	to look after
offrir	to give (presents)
organiser	to organise
ouvrir	to open
paraître	to seem
pardonner	to forgive
parler	to speak
passer	to pass (by)
perdre	to lose
plaire	to please
pleurer	to cry
poser	to put down
poser une question	to ask a question
pousser	to push
pouvoir	to be able
préférer	to prefer
présenter	to present
*se présenter	to introduce / present oneself
prêter	to lend
prévenir	to warn
se promener	to go for a walk
quitter	to leave (a place)
raconter	to tell
se rappeler	to remember

rater	to miss (bus), fail
rechercher / faire des recherches	to research
recommander	to recommend
regretter	to regret, be sorry
rembourser	to refund
remettre	to put back
remplacer	to replace
rendre visite à	to visit (a person)
rentrer	to return
renverser	to knock over
réparer	to repair
répondre	to answer, reply
*ressembler à	to look like, resemble
réviser	to revise
rire	to laugh
rouler	to go along (in a car)
sauter	to jump
sembler	to seem
servir	to serve
se servir de	to use
signer	to sign
signifier	to mean
sonner	to ring
souhaiter	to wish
sourire	to smile
se souvenir de	to remember
stationner	to park
sur le point de (être)	(to be) about to
se taire	to be quiet
taper	to type
téléphoner	to phone
tenir	to hold
se terminer	to end
tirer	to pull
tomber	to fall
toucher	to touch
tourner	to turn
*traduire	to translate
*traverser	to cross, go across
se trouver	to be located
venir	to come
vérifier	to check
visiter	to visit (a place)
vivre	to live
vouloir	to want

Negatives

ne ... jamais	never
ne ... pas	not
ne ... personne	nobody, no-one
ne ... plus	no more, no longer
ne ... que	only, nothing but
ne ... rien	nothing
ni ... ni	neither ... nor
pas encore	not yet

Prepositions

à	to, at
à côté de	next to
à travers	across, through
au bord de	at the side / edge of
au bout de	at the end of (ie length, rather than time)
au-dessous de	beneath, below
au-dessus de	above, over
au fond de	at the back of, at the bottom of
au lieu de	instead of
au milieu de	in the middle of
autour de	around
contre	against
de	of, from
depuis	since, for
derrière	behind
devant	in front of
en	in, within (time)
en dehors de	outside (of)
en face de	opposite
entre	between
*jusqu'à	up to, until, as far as
malgré	despite, in spite of
parmi	amongst
pour	for, in order to
près de	near
sans	without
selon	according to
sous	under
sur	on
vers	towards

Lifestyle

Describing appearance

barbe (f)	beard
beau / bel / belle	beautiful
bouclé	curly
*bouton (m)	spot, pimple
cheveux (m pl)	hair
court	short
frisé	curly
gros / grosse	fat
jeune	young
joli	pretty
laid	ugly
long / longue	long
lunettes (f pl)	glasses
maigre	skinny, thin
mince	slim, thin
mi-long	medium length
moyen / moyenne	medium, average
ondulé	wavy
raide	straight
de taille moyenne	medium height
vieux / vieil / vieille	old
yeux (m pl)	eyes

Describing personality

aimable	kind
aîné	elder
s'appeler	to be called
avoir ... ans	to be ... years old
bavard	chatty, talkative
bête	stupid, silly
célèbre	famous
*compréhensif / compréhensive	understanding
confiance (f)	trust
de mauvaise humeur	in a bad mood
égoïste	selfish
esprit (m)	mind
étonnant	amazing
étrange	strange
fâché	angry
fier / fière	proud
*fou / folle	mad, crazy
gêner	to annoy
*généreux / généreuse	generous
gentil / gentille	kind, nice
heureux / heureuse	happy
*jaloux / jalouse	jealous
marre (en avoir)	(to be) fed up
méchant	naughty

mépriser	to despise
se mettre en colère	to get angry
paresseux / paresseuse	lazy
pénible	annoying
sens de l'humour (m)	sense of humour
sportif / sportive	sporty
sympa	kind, nice
timide	shy
tranquille	quiet, calm
travailleur / travailleuse	hard-working
triste	sad
vif / vive	lively

Relationships

amour (m)	love
bague (f)	ring
beau-père (m)	stepfather
belle-mère (f)	stepmother
*célibataire	single
connaître	to know (a person)
copain (m) / copine (f)	friend, mate
demi-frère (m)	half-brother
demi-sœur (f)	half-sister
se disputer	to argue
ensemble	together
s'entendre (avec)	to get on (with)
épouser	to marry
se faire des amis	to make friends
femme (f)	wife, woman
fiançailles (f pl)	engagement
fille (f)	daughter, girl
fils (m)	son
gâter	to spoil
grand-mère (f)	grandmother
grand-père (m)	grandfather
grands-parents (m pl)	grandparents
jumeau (m) / jumelle (f)	twin
jeunesse (f)	youth
mari (m)	husband
se marier	to get married, marry
mort	dead
mourir	to die
naissance (f)	birth
naître	to be born
né(e) le...	born on the...
neveu (m)	nephew
*noces (f pl)	wedding

nom (m)	name
partager	to share
partenaire (m/f)	partner
petit ami (m)	boyfriend
petite amie (f)	girlfriend
petite-fille (f)	granddaughter
petit-fils (m)	grandson
prénom (m)	first name
*rapports (m pl)	relationships
se rendre compte	to realise
séparé	separated
(se) séparer	to separate
sortir	to go out
tante (f)	aunt
unique	only

Healthy living

aller bien	to be well
aller mieux	to be better
avoir sommeil	to be sleepy
bonheur (m)	happiness
cancer (m) (du poumon)	(lung) cancer
crise cardiaque (f)	heart attack
dégoûtant	disgusting
*déprimé	depressed
désintoxiquer	to detox
se détendre	to relax
dormir	to sleep
douleur (f)	pain
en bonne forme	fit
en bonne santé	in good health
s'entraîner	to train
épuiser	to exhaust
*équilibré	balanced
essoufflé	breathless
faible	weak
se faire mal	to hurt oneself
faire un régime	to be on a diet
fatigué	tired
foie (m)	liver
forme (f)	fitness
fort	strong
fumer	to smoke
garder	to look after
gras	fatty
hors d'haleine	out of breath
habitude (f)	habit
laver	to wash
(se) laver	to get washed
lentement	slowly
malade	ill, sick

 Made a start   Feeling confident ✓ Exam ready

maladie (f)	illness	voix (f)	voice	égalité (f)	equality
malsain	unhealthy	vomir	to be sick	s'enivrer	to get drunk
matières (f pl) grasses	fats			enquête (f)	enquiry
médecin (m)	doctor			entraînement (m)	training

Social issues

accro	addicted
agir (il s'agit de)	to act (it's a question of)
alcool (m)	alcohol
alcoolique	alcoholic
(s')arrêter	to stop
association (f) caritative	charity
avertir	to warn
cacher	to hide
combattre	to combat
conseil (m)	advice
consommation (f)	consumption, usage
coupable	guilty
dette (f)	debt
devenir	to become
drogue (f)	drug
se droguer	to take drugs
eau potable (f)	drinking water

médicament (m)	medicine
musculation (f)	weight training
obésité (f)	obesity
odeur (f)	smell
peau (f)	skin
pressé	in a hurry, rushed, squeezed
se relaxer	to relax
quotidien(ne)	daily
respirer	to breathe
sain	healthy
santé (f)	health
(se) sentir	to feel
soigner	to care for
soin (m)	care
sommeil (m)	sleep
tabac (m)	tobacco
tousser	to cough
valoir mieux	to be better, preferable

égalité (f)	equality
s'enivrer	to get drunk
enquête (f)	enquiry
entraînement (m)	training
*espace (m) vert	green area
éviter	to avoid
ivre	drunk
*mannequin (m)	model
mener	to lead
personnes (f pl) défavorisées	disadvantaged people
renoncer	to give up
réussir	to succeed
sida (m)	AIDS
suivre	to follow
surveiller	to watch
tabagisme (m)	addiction to smoking
tatouage (m)	tattooing
tenter	to attempt
toxicomane (m/f)	drug addict
travail (m) bénévole	voluntary work
tuer	to kill
vide	empty

Leisure and the media

Free time

s'abonner	to subscribe
actualités (f pl)	news
ado (m/f)	adolescent
argent (m)	money
chorale (f)	choir
club des jeunes (m)	youth club
commencer	to start
coûter	to cost
débuter	to begin
distractions (f pl)	things to do
échecs (m pl)	chess
essayer	to try
fan de	a fan of
s'intéresser à	to be interested in
lieu (m) (*avoir lieu)	place (to take place)
passe-temps (m)	hobby
passer du temps	to spend time
payer	to pay (for)
pêche (f)	fishing, peach
prendre	to take
randonnée (f)	walk, hike
rencontrer	to meet

se reposer	to rest
temps (m) libre	free time
vouloir	to wish, want

Music, cinema and television

billet (m)	ticket
chanter	to sing
chanteur (m) / chanteuse (f)	singer
chanson (f)	song
effets (m pl) spéciaux	special effects
espèce (f)	type, kind
dessin (m) animé	cartoon
feuilleton (m)	soap opera
film (m) de guerre	war film
*film (m) policier	detective film
jeu (m) télévisé	game show
publicité (f)	adverts
séance (f)	performance
série (f)	series
télé-réalité (f)	reality television
tournée (f)	tour
vedette (f)	star
voir	to see

Eating out

assiette (f)	plate, dish
boire	to drink
carte (f)	menu
choisir	to choose
commander	to order
goûter	to taste
hors-d'œuvre (m)	starter
plat principal (m)	main meal / dish
pourboire (m)	tip
serveur (m) / serveuse (f)	waiter, waitress

Food

agneau (m)	lamb
*ail (m)	garlic
alimentation (f)	food
*amer / amère	bitter
ananas (m)	pineapple
beurre (m)	butter
bien cuit	well-cooked
bière (f)	beer
bœuf (m)	beef
boisson (f)	drink
bonbon (m)	sweet

*canard (m)	duck	saucisse (f)	sausage	bord (m) de (la) mer	seaside
casse-croûte (m)	snack	*saumon (m)	salmon	bronzer	to sunbathe
chocolat (m)	chocolate	sel (m)	salt	carte (f)	map
cerise (f)	cherry	steak (m) haché	burger	carte postale (f)	postcard
champignon (m)	mushroom	sucre (m)	sugar, sweet	colonie (f) de vacances	holiday / summer camp
chou (m)	cabbage	sucré	sugary	crème (f) solaire	sun cream
chou-fleur (m)	cauliflower	tasse (f)	cup	départ (m)	departure
citron (m)	lemon	thé (m)	tea	Douvres	Dover
confiture (f)	jam	thon (m)	tuna	échange (m)	exchange
crêpe (f)	pancake	*truite (f)	trout	à l'étranger	abroad
*crudités (f pl)	raw vegetables starter	*veau (m)	veal	étranger (m)	stranger, foreigner
déjeuner (m)	lunch	viande (f)	meat	faire du camping	to go camping
dîner (m)	evening meal	yaourt (m)	yoghurt	foire (f)	fair
*dinde (f)	turkey			Londres	London
eau (f) (minérale)	(mineral) water	**Sport**		lunettes (f pl) de soleil	sun glasses
*épicé	spicy	basket (m)	basketball	maillot (m) de bain	swimming costume
escargot (m)	snail	centre (m) sportif	sports centre	Manche (f)	English Channel
fraise (f)	strawberry	cheval (m)	horse	nager	to swim
framboise (f)	raspberry	concours (m)	competition	parc (m) d'attractions	theme park
fruits (m pl) de mer	seafood	courir	to run	sable (m)	sand
glace (f)	ice cream	course (f)	race	sac (m) de couchage	sleeping bag
haricots (m pl) verts	green beans	équitation (f)	horse riding	spectacle (m)	show
jambon (m)	ham	escalade (f)	rock climbing	*station (f) balnéaire	seaside resort
lait (m)	milk	féliciter	to congratulate	tour (f)	tower, tour
légumes (m pl)	vegetables	marquer un but / un essai	to score a goal / try	tourisme (m)	tourism
noix (f)	walnut	natation (f)	swimming	trajet (m)	journey
nourrir	to feed, nourish	patin (m) à glace	ice skating	traversée (f)	crossing
nourriture (f)	food	patinoire (f)	ice rink	vacances (f pl)	holidays
nourriture (f) bio	organic food	planche (f) à voile	windsurfing	valise (f)	suitcase
œuf (m)	egg	*plongée (f) sous-marine	underwater diving	voyager	to travel
oignon (m)	onion	piscine (f)	swimming pool	vue sur la mer (f)	sea view
pamplemousse (m)	grapefruit	promenade (f)	walk		
pâtes (f pl)	pasta	skate (m)	skateboarding	**Countries, nationalities and languages**	
pêche (f)	fishing, peach	ski (m) (nautique)	(water) skiing	Afrique (f) / africain	Africa / African
petit déjeuner (m)	breakfast	sports (m pl) d'hiver	winter sports	Algérie (f) / algérien	Algeria / Algerian
petits pois (m pl)	peas	stade (m)	stadium	Allemagne (f) / allemand	Germany / German
poire (f)	pear	*tournoi (m)	tournament	Angleterre (f) / anglais	England / English
poisson (m)	fish	voile (f)	sailing	Belgique (f) / belge	Belgium / Belgian
poivre (m)	pepper	volley (m)	volleyball	Chine (f) / chinois	China / Chinese
pomme (f)	apple			Écosse (f) / écossais	Scotland / Scottish
pomme de terre (f)	potato	**Travel and tourism**		Espagne (f) / espagnol	Spain / Spanish
potage (m)	soup	accueil (m)	welcome		
poulet (m)	chicken	agence (f) de voyages	travel agency		
prune (f)	plum	Alpes (f pl)	Alps		
raisins (m pl)	grapes	arrivée (f)	arrival		
repas (m)	meal	aventure (f)	adventure		
riz (m)	rice	bagages (m pl)	luggage		
salé	salty	(se) baigner	to bathe, swim		

États-Unis (m pl) / américain	USA / American	*événement (m)	event
Grande-Bretagne (f) / britannique	Great Britain / British	frontière (f)	border, frontier
		héberger	to lodge, accommodate
Maroc (m) / marocain	Morocco / Moroccan	horaire (m)	timetable
Méditerranée (f)	Mediterranean	jumelé	twinned
pays (m) de Galles / gallois	Wales / Welsh	laisser	to leave
		lavabo (m)	wash basin
Suisse (f) / suisse	Switzerland / Swiss	lits (m pl) superposés	bunk beds
Tunisie (f) / tunisien	Tunisia / Tunisian	location de voitures (f)	car rental

Transport

aéroport (m)	airport	logement (m)	accommodation
atterrir	to land	*loger	to stay, lodge
auto (f)	car	loisir (m)	free time (activity)
autobus (m)	bus	louer	to hire, rent
autoroute (f)	motorway	partir	to leave
avion (m)	plane	pension (f) complète	full board
bateau (m)	boat	pièce (f) d'identité	means of identification
car (m)	coach		
chemin (m)	way, path	plan (m) de (la) ville	town plan
chemin (m) de fer	railway	projet (m)	plan
conduire	to drive	propriétaire (m/f)	owner
décoller	to take off	*rendez-vous (m)	meeting, appointment
essence (f)	petrol		
(se) garer	to park	*remercier	to thank
se mettre en route	to set off	renseignements (m pl)	information
moto (f)	motor bike		
permis (m) de conduire	driving licence	réserver	to book, reserve
		rester	to stay
route (f)	road, way	retour (m)	return
voiture (f)	car	retourner	to return
vol (m)	flight	revenir	to come back
voler	to fly	séjour (m)	stay, visit
		tarif (m)	price list, rate
		visite (f) (guidée)	(guided) visit
		*voyage (m) organisé	package holiday

Planning and reservations

ascenseur (m)	lift
auberge (f) de jeunesse	youth hostel
*chambre (f) d'hôte	bed and breakfast
chambre (f) familiale	family room
chercher	to look for
clé (f)	key
climatisation (f)	air conditioning
demi-pension (f)	half-board
dortoir (m)	dormitory
dresser	to put up (tent)
emplacement (m)	pitch (tent)

Everyday technology

acheter	to buy
avantage (m)	advantage
bloggeur (m)	blogger
caméscope (m)	camcorder
*clavier (m)	keyboard
cliquer	to click
compte (m)	account
console (f) de jeux	games console
dangereux	dangerous

désavantage (m)	disadvantage		
écran (m)	screen		
*écran (m) tactile	touch screen		
effacer	to delete		
enregistrer	to record		
envoyer	to send		
faire des achats	to shop		
*fichier (m)	file		
forum (m)	chat room		
genre (m)	type, kind		
*imprimante (f)	printer		
imprimer	to print		
inconvénient (m)	disadvantage, drawback		
internaute (m)	internet user		
jeu (m)	game		
lecteur (m) DVD	DVD player		
lecteur (m) MP3	MP3 player		
en ligne	online		
logiciel (m)	software		
mettre	to put		
mettre en ligne	to upload		
moniteur (m)	monitor		
mot (m) de passe	password		
numérique	digital		
ordinateur (m)	computer		
ordinateur (m) portable	laptop		
tablette (f)	tablet		
page (f) d'accueil	homepage		
pile (f)	battery		
recevoir	to receive		
remplir	to fill (in)		
réseau social (m)	social network		
*rester en contact	to stay in contact		
*sauvegarder	to save		
site (m) internet / web	website		
*souris (f)	mouse		
surfer sur Internet	to surf the internet		
taper	to type		
tchatter	to talk online		
télécharger	to download		
texto (m)	text		
*touche (f)	key (on keyboard)		
*traitement (m) de texte	word processing		

Home and the environment

Describing your home

armoire (f)	wardrobe
bain (m)	bath
bâtiment (m)	building
*bricolage (m)	DIY (do it yourself)
cave (f)	cellar
se coucher	to go to bed
cuisine (f)	kitchen, cooking
déménager	to move house
douche (f)	shower
escalier (m)	staircase
étage (m)	floor, storey
faire la grasse matinée	to lie in, sleep in
fenêtre (f)	window
four (m)	oven
foyer (m)	home
immeuble (m)	block of flats
jardinage (m)	gardening
(se) lever	to get up
lit (m)	bed
loyer (m)	rent
lumière (f)	light
maison (f) (individuelle / jumelée / mitoyenne)	house (detached / semi-detached / terraced)
meubles (m pl)	furniture
moquette (f)	carpet
mur (m)	wall
pelouse (f)	lawn
pièce (f)	room
propre	clean, tidy
ranger	to tidy
(se) réveiller	to wake up
rez-de-chaussée (m)	ground floor
sale	dirty
salle (f) à manger	dining room
salle (f) de bains	bathroom
salle (f) de séjour	lounge
salon (m)	living room, lounge
sous-sol (m)	basement

Neighbourhood and town

aire (f) de jeux	play area
animé	lively
bibliothèque (f)	library
boucherie (f)	butcher's shop
boulangerie (f)	bakery
bijouterie (f)	jeweller's shop
*bruit (m)	noise
*bureau (m)	office, study
bruyant	noisy
calme	quiet
centre (m) commercial	shopping centre
charcuterie (f)	delicatessen
circulation (f)	traffic
commerces (m pl)	shops
commissariat (m)	police station
embouteillage (m)	traffic jam
endroit (m)	place
fermeture (f)	closure
gare (f)	railway station
gare (f) routière	bus station
gens (m pl)	people
grand magasin (m)	department store
*grande surface (f)	superstore
habitant (m)	inhabitant
hôtel (m) de ville	town hall
jardin zoologique / zoo (m)	zoo
librairie (f)	bookshop
mairie (f)	town hall
marché (m)	market
musée (m)	museum
parc (m)	park
pâtisserie (f)	cake shop
place (f)	square
poste (f)	post office
quartier (m)	quarter, area
station-service (f)	service station
surchargé	overcrowded

tabac (m)	newsagent's
transport (m) en commun	public transport
se trouver	to be situated
usine (f)	factory
voisin (m)	neighbour
zone (f) piétonne	pedestrian zone

Shopping

aider	to help
besoin (m) (avoir besoin de)	need (to need)
bon marché	cheap
caisse (f)	till
carte (f) bancaire	bank card
choix (m)	choice
chose (f)	thing
démodé	old-fashioned
dépenser	to spend (money)
devoir	to have to
économiser	to save
essayer	to try on
gratuit	free (of charge)
lèche-vitrines (m) (faire du)	window shopping (to go window shopping)
livrer	to deliver
marque (f)	make, label, brand
parfum (m)	perfume
pauvre	poor
portefeuille (m)	wallet
porte-monnaie (m)	purse
prix (m)	price
rayon (m)	department
réduire	to reduce
réduit	reduced
rembourser	to reimburse
soldes (m pl)	sale
vendeur (m) / vendeuse (f)	shop assistant
vendre	to sell
ville (f)	town
vitrine (f)	shop window

  Made a start **Feeling confident** **Exam ready**

Clothing

baskets (f pl)	*trainers*
bijou (m)	*jewel, jewellery*
blouson (m)	*coat, jacket*
ceinture (f)	*belt*
chapeau (m)	*hat*
chaussette (f)	*sock*
chaussure (f)	*shoe*
chemise (f)	*shirt*
cravate (f)	*tie*
écharpe (f)	*scarf*
foulard (m)	*scarf*
*gilet (m)	*waistcoat, cardigan*
jupe (f)	*skirt*
manteau (m)	*overcoat*
mode (f)	*fashion*
nettoyer	*to clean (clothes)*
pantalon (m)	*trousers*
pull (m)	*jumper*
robe (f)	*dress*
sweat (m) à capuche	*hoodie*
veste (f)	*jacket*
vêtements (m pl)	*clothes*

The environment

arbre (m)	*tree*
campagne (f)	*countryside*
champ (m)	*field*
colline (f)	*hill*
en plein air	*in the open air*
environnement (m)	*environment*
ferme (f)	*farm*
fleur (f)	*flower*
herbe (f)	*grass*
île (f)	*island*
lac (m)	*lake*
monde (m)	*world*
montagne (f)	*mountain*
(à la) montagne (f)	*(in the) mountain(s)*
paysage (m)	*landscape*
plage (f)	*beach*
rivière (f)	*river*
*sécurité (f)	*safety, security*

Global issues

agresser	*to attack*
améliorer	*to improve*
allumer	*to switch on*
attaque (f)	*attack*
augmenter	*to increase*
*bande (f)	*gang*
boîte (f) (en carton)	*(cardboard) box*
campagne (f)	*campaign*
centre (m) de recyclage	*recycling centre*
charbon (m)	*coal*
chauffage central (m)	*central heating*
chômage (m)	*unemployment*
couche d'ozone (f)	*ozone layer*
croire	*to believe*
cultiver	*to grow*
déboisement (m)	*deforestation*
effet de serre (m)	*greenhouse effect*
effrayant	*frightening*
égal	*equal*
emballage (m)	*packaging*
empêcher	*to prevent*
en danger	*in danger*
endommager	*to damage*
énergie renouvelable (f)	*renewable energy*
ennui (m)	*problem, worry*
entouré	*surrounded*
état (m)	*state*
éteindre	*to switch off*
déchets (m pl)	*rubbish*
détruire	*to destroy*
disparaître	*to disappear*
faire du recyclage	*to recycle*
gaspiller	*to waste*
gaz (m) carbonique	*carbon dioxide*
gaz (m) d'échappement	*exhaust fumes*
guerre (f)	*war*
*harceler	*to bully, harass*

harcèlement (m)	*bullying, harassment*
immigré (m)	*immigrant*
incendie (m)	*fire*
inconnu	*unknown*
inondation (f)	*flood*
inonder	*to flood*
s'inquiéter	*to worry*
jeter	*to throw (away)*
lourd	*heavy, serious*
lutter	*to struggle*
manifestation (f)	*demonstration*
marée (f)	*tide*
mentir	*to lie*
mondial	*worldwide*
niveau (m)	*level*
ordures (f pl)	*rubbish*
paix (f)	*peace*
pauvreté (f)	*poverty*
perte (f)	*loss*
pétrole (m)	*oil*
piste cyclable (f)	*cycle lane*
(se) plaindre	*to complain*
pollué	*polluted*
poubelle (f)	*dustbin*
produire	*to provide*
produits (m pl) bio	*green products*
protéger	*to protect*
ramasser	*to pick up*
*réchauffement (m) de la Terre	*global warming*
reconnaissant	*grateful*
réfugié (m)	*refugee*
risque (m)	*risk*
robinet (m)	*tap*
sac (m) en plastique	*plastic bag*
sans-abri (m)	*homeless person*
*sauver	*to save*
utiliser	*to use*
vie (f)	*life*

Work and education

My studies

allemand (m)	German
anglais (m)	English
théâtre (m)	drama
biologie (f)	biology
chimie (f)	chemistry
couture (f)	sewing
dessin (m)	art
EPS (f)	PE (physical education)
espagnol (m)	Spanish
études (f pl) des médias	media studies
français (m)	French
géographie (f)	geography
histoire (f)	history
informatique (f)	IT (information technology)
instituteur (m)	primary school teacher (male)
institutrice (f)	primary school teacher (female)
instruction (f) civique	citizenship
langue (f)	language
langues (f pl) vivantes	modern languages
mathématiques / maths (f)	maths
matière (f)	subject
musique (f)	music
physique (f)	physics
professeur (m)	teacher
*proviseur (m)	headteacher
religion (f)	religious studies
sciences (f pl)	sciences

School life

apprendre	to learn
bien équipé	well-equipped
bulletin (m) scolaire	school report
calculette (f)	calculator
car (m) de ramassage scolaire	school bus
collège (m)	secondary school
comprendre	to understand
couloir (m)	corridor
cours (m)	lesson
demander	to ask
devoirs (m pl)	homework
difficulté (f)	difficulty
*diplôme (m)	qualification

directeur (m)	headmaster
directrice (f)	headmistress
discuter	to discuss
distribuer	to give out
*doué	gifted
droit (m)	right
école (f) (primaire / secondaire)	(primary / secondary) school
*échouer	to fail
élève (m/f)	pupil
emploi (m) du temps	timetable
en seconde	in year 11
*enseigner	to teach
*études (f pl)	studies
étudiant (m)	student
examen (m)	examination
faire attention	to pay attention
incivilités (f pl)	rudeness
injure (f)	insult
leçon (f)	lesson
lecture (f)	reading
lire	to read
mal équipé	badly equipped
maquillage (m)	make-up
maternelle (f)	nursery school
note (f)	mark
oublier	to forget
passer un examen	to sit an exam
pause (f)	break, pause
penser	to think
permettre	to allow, permit
porter	to wear, carry
*pression (f)	pressure
récré(ation) (f)	break
redoubler	to repeat the year
règle (f)	rule
règlement (m)	school rules
rentrée (f)	return to school
répéter	to repeat
réponse (f)	reply
résultat (m)	result
réussir un examen	to pass an exam
salle (f) de classe	classroom
savoir	to know
scolaire	school (adj)
tableau (m)	board
terrain (m) de sport	sports ground
trimestre (m)	term
trouver	to find
retenue (f)	detention

Jobs and careers

agent (m/f) de police	police officer
à peine	scarcely
assis	sitting
à temps partiel	part-time
avocat(e) (m/f)	lawyer
boucher (m) / bouchère (f)	butcher
boulanger (m) / boulangère (f)	baker
*boulot (m)	job
candidat(e) (m/f)	candidate
coiffeur (m) / coiffeuse (f)	hairdresser
comptable (m/f)	accountant
compter (sur)	to count (on)
croisière (f)	cruise
débouché (m)	prospect, job prospect, opportunity
debout	standing
dessinateur (m) / dessinatrice (f) de mode	fashion designer
disponible	available
élargir	to widen
employé(e) (m/f)	employee
employeur (m) / employeuse (f)	employer
entreprise (f)	firm, enterprise
entretien (m)	interview
enrichissant	enriching, rewarding
facteur (m) / factrice (f)	postman / postwoman
fermier (m) / fermière (f)	farmer
gagner	to earn, win
idée (f)	idea
infirmier (m) / infirmière (f)	nurse
informaticien(ne) (m/f)	IT worker
ingénieur(e) (m/f)	engineer
interprète (m)	interpreter
journal (m)	newspaper
livre (f) (sterling)	pound (sterling)
maçon (m)	builder
mécanicien(ne) (m/f)	mechanic
mettre de l'argent de côté	to save money
outil (m)	tool
patron(ne) (m/f)	boss

 Made a start   **Feeling confident** ☑ **Exam ready**

petit job (m)	casual job
plombier (m)	plumber
*policier (m) / policière (f)	police officer
recevoir	to receive
tâche (f)	task
travailler	to work
varié	varied
venir de	to have just
vétérinaire (m/f)	vet

Ambitions

| avenir (m) | future |
| espérer | to hope |

espoir (m)	hope
prêt	ready
rêve (m)	dream
rêver	to dream

Education post-16

année (f) sabbatique	gap year
*apprenti(e) (m/f)	apprentice
avoir envie de	to want to
avoir l'intention (de)	to intend (to)
bac(calauréat) (m)	A-level(s)

conseiller (m) d'orientation	careers adviser
en première	in year 12
en terminale	in year 13
épreuve (f)	test
établissement (m)	establishment
étudier	to study
*faculté (f)	university, faculty
former	to train
*laisser tomber	to drop
liberté (f)	freedom
*licence (f)	degree
lycée (m)	sixth form college

French life and culture

Customs

défilé (m)	procession
église (f)	church
jour (m) férié	public holiday
juif / juive	Jewish
messe (f)	mass
mosquée (f)	Mosque
musulman	Muslim
religieux / religieuse	religious
*réunion (f)	meeting

Festivals and celebrations

cadeau (m)	present
fête (f)	festival, celebration, party
fête (f) des Mères	Mother's Day
fête (f) des Rois	Twelfth Night / Epiphany
fête (f) du travail	May Day
fêter	to celebrate
*feu (m) d'artifice	fireworks (a firework display)

jour (m) de l'An	New Year's Day
Pâques	Easter
Pentecôte (f)	Whitsuntide
poisson (m) d'avril	April Fools' Day, April Fool!
Saint-Sylvestre (f)	New Year's Eve
Saint-Valentin (f)	St. Valentine's Day
Toussaint (f)	All Saints' Day
réveillon (m) de Noël	Christmas Eve

Transcripts

Page v Paper 1: Listening
Exam explainer
 Plusieurs étapes du tour de France ont lieu dans les Pyrénées. Les montagnes présentent un défi énorme pour les cyclistes.

Page 1 Numbers
Practice
Example: 37% des Français aiment aller sur des réseaux sociaux.
- Regarder la télé est l'activité préférée de 84% des gens.
- 63% vont au cinéma pendant leur temps libre.
- 75% préfèrent écouter la radio.

Page 2 The French alphabet
Practice
Example: Nous avons réservé nos places de TGV.

- Le soir, je m'occupe des SDF en travaillant aux Restos du Cœur.
- J'ai trouvé ce livre au CDI du collège.
- Ce que j'adore c'est l'EPS, surtout en été.
- Le collège se trouve en face d'un HLM.

Page 3 Dates
Practice
Example: Le premier jour de la fête des Lumières à Lyon est le huit décembre.

(a) Le dernier jour du festival de Cannes est le vingt-huit mai.

(b) Le dernier jour de la fête du citron à Menton est le premier mars.

(c) La fête de la musique a lieu le vingt-et-un juin chaque année.

Page 4 Telling the time
Practice
(a) - Quand est-ce que le train arrive?
- Ce soir, à six heures moins le quart.

(b) L'exposition est ouverte de neuf heures à dix-huit heures trente.

(c) Ce soir, on va au concert. Il commence à vingt heures quinze.

(d) Je me couche tard, vers onze heures du soir.

Page 5 Greetings
Practice
Example: Bon voyage, prends beaucoup de belles photos!

(a) Bon appétit à tous!

(b) Tous mes meilleurs vœux pour le Nouvel An!

(c) Bonne nuit, dors bien!

Page 8 Describing people
Practice
- Pour moi, cela n'a aucune importance si elle est grande ou petite. Je cherche tout simplement quelqu'un qui me fait rire. En plus les filles qui bavardent tout le temps ne m'intéressent pas. J'aime plutôt les filles qui sont un peu timides.
- Mon copain idéal serait quelqu'un d'aimable qui prend soin de moi. Je ne peux pas supporter des gens impatients.
- J'aimerais une copine qui est mince et bien taillée. Elle serait belle, bien sûr, et elle aurait les cheveux marron.

Page 12 Food
Practice
Example: Voici mes conseils pour une alimentation équilibrée. Au petit déjeuner, vous pouvez manger 100 grammes de fruit et 50 grammes de pain.

(a) Pour le déjeuner, il faut choisir entre 100 grammes de viande ou 150 grammes de poisson.

(b) Vous devriez consommer au moins 200 grammes de légumes. Cependant, si vous mangez des pommes de terre, il faut limiter votre consommation à 125 grammes.

(c) Le soir, on devrait manger 50 grammes de viande seulement.

Page 14 Shopping
Practice
Oui, il y a certainement beaucoup de choix, mais le plus important est que c'est moins cher en ligne. Cependant, ça m'embête quand il faut renvoyer un article qui n'est pas de la bonne taille.

Page 15 Social media
Practice
- On voit des gens assis au café, ils ne se parlent pas parce qu'ils passent tout leur temps en ligne. C'est complètement débile. Pour moi, les réseaux sociaux me permettent de rester en contact avec ma famille et avec des copains que je ne vois pas régulièrement.
- Il faut faire attention à ce qu'on poste sur les réseaux sociaux. Une photo qui semble amusante aujourd'hui pourrait te compromettre dans l'avenir. Mais les réseaux sociaux me sont indispensables et m'aident à organiser ma vie. D'ailleurs, je ne suis pas du tout d'accord avec les gens qui disent que c'est une perte de temps.
- À mon avis, trop de jeunes ne se méfient pas des dangers, comme le vol d'identité par des criminels. Cela dit, on peut bien s'amuser sur les réseaux sociaux.

Page 17 French customs
Practice
Example: La gastronomie fait partie du patrimoine culturel de la France. Pour un vrai repas gastronomique, il faut plusieurs jours de préparation.

1 On fait une blague à ses copains ou aux membres de sa famille en leur accrochant un poisson en papier dans le dos en criant 'Poisson d'avril!'.

2 Le jour de la Toussaint, on apporte des fleurs au cimetière et on les laisse sur les tombes à la mémoire des membres de la famille décédés.

3 Les anniversaires, comme celui de la naissance ainsi que celui du mariage, sont une occasion pour se réunir.

Page 19 Reading
Practice

J'adore la lecture et je lis tous les jours avant de me coucher. Bien sûr, comme je suis étudiante, je dois lire beaucoup mais j'aime bien aussi me détendre avec un bon roman. Beaucoup de mes copains téléchargent des livres électroniques, mais moi, je n'utilise pas de lecteur électronique chez moi. Mais quand je voyage, il est pratique d'en avoir un car je ne suis pas obligée d'emporter plein de livres lourds avec moi!

Page 22 Cinema
Practice

Avant de lire les critiques enthousiastes, mes copains m'avaient déjà parlé de ce film car c'était une super production à ne pas manquer. Au début du film, les vues aériennes qui font la comparaison entre l'Australie et l'Inde sont à couper le souffle. Mais ce sont les scènes tournées dans le train et à la gare qui vous font pleurer, ainsi que la réunion entre le jeune homme et sa mère naturelle.

Page 25 Holiday experiences
Practice 2

- Un jour, on a fait une visite guidée du château le plus historique dans la région, mais le guide ne savait rien! Puis j'ai trouvé un joli vase au grand marché, mais il a fallu négocier car au début, le prix était trop élevé.

- Quand je suis arrivée à l'aéroport, je me suis rendu compte que j'avais oublié mon passeport, alors j'ai dû rentrer chez moi pour aller le chercher. Que j'ai été bête!

- On est allés à un concert en plein air dans un parc où il y avait une foule importante. Quand je suis rentré à l'auberge, j'ai découvert que mon porte-monnaie n'était plus dans mon sac.

Page 26 Travel and transport
Practice

Example: Quand je suis arrivé, j'ai pris un taxi qui était rapide, mais cher.

- Le pire, c'était que le train avait trois heures de retard.

- On a passé deux jours en bateau et j'avais le mal de mer.

- Le voyage en avion était confortable, mais on a perdu nos bagages.

- Le car n'était pas cher, mais il y avait trop de circulation sur l'autoroute.

Page 27 Accommodation
Practice

- On ne pourrait pas trouver un meilleur hôtel. C'était vraiment luxueux avec tout le confort. J'avais lu de mauvaises critiques de cet hôtel, mais en fait, je les ai trouvées injustes. Je n'hésiterais pas à y retourner.

- La chambre avait une belle vue sur la rivière et elle n'était pas chère. Mais j'ai été déçu par la piscine qui n'était pas chauffée.

- Je ne logerais plus jamais dans cet établissement. Ma chambre était bruyante et sale et les employés étaient malpolis.

Page 29 Directions
Practice

Quand tu arrives à Dinan, va tout d'abord au château. Traverse la place et va tout droit. Ce n'est pas loin, peut-être à cinq minutes à pied.

Page 31 Shopping on holiday
Practice 1

Pendant ma sortie scolaire, je suis allé au marché près du centre de loisirs pour acheter des cadeaux pour ma famille. J'ai trouvé un beau sac en cuir pour mon père. Je cherchais aussi un foulard pour ma mère mais malheureusement, il n'y en avait pas de sa couleur préférée.

Page 34 Town and region
Worked example

- Avant j'habitais une ville industrielle, mais il y a six mois, nous avons déménagé dans une maison située dans un petit village à la campagne. La vie ici est beaucoup plus tranquille mais il y a peu de magasins. J'apprécie l'absence de pollution, mais j'ai un trajet plus long pour aller au collège.

- Depuis quatre ans, j'habite au centre d'une grande ville. On peut y profiter d'une vie culturelle, riche et variée, mais le samedi soir, c'est trop bruyant.

- Le pire de la vie dans une grande ville c'est sans doute les embouteillages aux heures de pointe quand les gens vont au travail ou rentrent chez eux le soir. Cependant, les transports en commun sont meilleurs qu'à la campagne.

Page 35 Francophone countries
Practice

Le Cameroun, un pays francophone de l'Afrique de l'Ouest, est un des pays les plus pauvres au monde. Dans le domaine de l'éducation, 91% des écoles primaires au Cameroun n'ont pas d'électricité. Parfois, les cours doivent être annulés parce que les salles sont mal éclairées.

Un autre problème pour les élèves dans 69% des écoles primaires et dans 73% des collèges au Cameroun est le manque d'accès à l'eau potable.

Encore plus grave, c'est l'absence de toilettes dans 59% des écoles primaires. C'est pour cette raison que beaucoup de filles abandonnent leurs études scolaires.

Page 36 Seasons and weather

Practice

Example: Moi, j'adore l'été et la chaleur parce que je peux me bronzer au soleil.

- Ma saison préférée c'est l'hiver car j'adore la neige. J'aime faire du ski.
- Pour moi, les beaux jours de printemps, quand il fait doux, sont idéals parce que j'aime faire des promenades à la campagne.

Page 37 My studies

Practice

Ma passion, ce sont les langues, surtout l'anglais. Le prof rend les cours vraiment intéressants. Il y a plusieurs matières que je n'aime pas, les maths par exemple, car je trouve ça difficile et le prof nous donne trop de devoirs. Cependant, le pire, c'est l'instruction civique, car c'est une perte de temps. En plus, le prof est toujours de mauvaise humeur et il nous critique tout le temps.

Page 38 Your school

Practice

- Dans mon collège, il n'y a pas assez d'installations technologiques modernes. Pourtant, les profs font toujours des efforts pour nous donner des cours stimulants. Mais, pour ceux qui ne sont pas forts en matières scolaires, ce n'est pas le bon collège. Il y a trop de redoublements.
- Le collège nous permet d'être indépendants et de réussir, même si cette réussite n'est pas forcément scolaire. On nous offre un grand choix d'activités périscolaires, comme des activités sportives, musicales, créatives et culturelles. C'est vraiment inclusif car tout le monde peut y participer selon ses intérêts personnels.

Page 40 Using languages

Practice

1 Je voudrais apprendre des langues avec des caractères spéciaux comme le chinois. Mon ami a appris cette langue parce qu'il l'utilise quand il voyage avec son boulot, mais pour moi, ça représente un défi car on doit faire des efforts pour apprendre quelque chose de si difficile.

2 Beaucoup de mes copains sont en train d'apprendre une langue étrangère pour trouver un emploi intéressant. D'autres pensent que leurs compétences linguistiques les aideront à gagner un bon salaire. Cependant, moi, j'apprends une langue parce que ma petite amie vient d'Italie et que je veux pouvoir communiquer avec ses parents quand je vais en Italie. En plus, ça vous aide à mieux découvrir le pays. À mon avis, l'italien n'est pas du tout difficile à apprendre.

Page 41 Ambitions

Worked example

Quand j'étais tout petit, je voulais devenir astronaute. Cependant, au cours de ma scolarité, je me suis rendu compte que je n'étais pas assez fort en sciences. Ensuite, j'ai développé une passion pour les langues, surtout pour celles

qui nécessitent l'apprentissage d'alphabets différents comme le chinois et le russe. Je n'ai pas encore décidé si je prendrai une année sabbatique, bien qu'il y ait plein d'avantages à passer un an à voyager dans le monde et à faire la connaissance d'autres gens et de cultures.

Page 43 Charity and voluntary work

Practice

- Je suis très sportif et en ce moment, je m'entraîne pour une course sponsorisée de 5 km qui aura lieu le week-end prochain.
- J'adore faire de la pâtisserie. Je suis en train de faire des gâteaux pour une vente de gâteaux.
- À mon avis, la meilleure façon de collecter des fonds est d'utiliser les réseaux sociaux pour informer les autres de nos activités.

Page 46 Campaigns and good causes

Practice

Voulez-vous aider des milliards de gens qui n'ont pas toujours accès à de l'eau potable ou à des toilettes adéquates? Saviez-vous que des personnes meurent tous les jours suite aux maladies provoquées par le manque d'eau propre? Dans beaucoup de pays, surtout dans les pays les plus pauvres de l'Afrique ou de l'Asie, les enfants doivent aller chercher de l'eau au lieu d'aller à l'école. Aidez-nous à faire une différence. Faites un don d'argent à notre association ou organisez une collecte pour rassembler des fonds.

Page 47 Global issues

Practice

- Dans les grandes cités du monde, on ne peut plus respirer correctement. On ne voit que du brouillard créé par des gaz d'échappement. Il faut absolument trouver une solution à ce problème.
- À mon avis, notre dépendance au charbon et au pétrole n'est plus durable. Il faut trouver des alternatives en utilisant le vent, le soleil et les vagues.
- On dit que la pollution des mers est le problème le plus grave, mais à mon avis, il faut avant tout arrêter la destruction des forêts tropicales car ce sont les poumons de la planète.
- On ne peut pas éviter les catastrophes comme les tremblements de terre ou l'éruption d'un volcan. Cependant, la protection des animaux et des plantes qui sont en voie de disparition devrait être notre priorité et nous devons les sauver!

Page 48 The environment

Practice

- À mon avis, il faut absolument arrêter le gaspillage alimentaire. Tellement de gens achètent trop de fruits ou de légumes ou d'autres aliments qu'ils jettent à la poubelle parce qu'ils pourrissent ou ne sont plus consommables.
- L'eau est un bien précieux. Alors, il faut éviter le gaspillage autant que possible en prenant une douche au lieu d'un bain et en faisant plus attention à la manière dont nous l'utilisons.

- Je ne comprends pas pourquoi les producteurs utilisent tant d'emballages pour leurs produits. Nous devrions refuser d'acheter des produits emballés dans du plastique ou dans du carton.
- Certes, le développement des sources d'énergie renouvelables est important, mais je pense que nous devons plutôt faire des efforts pour réduire notre consommation d'énergie en éteignant les lumières et les appareils électriques quand nous ne les utilisons pas.

Page 52 General conversation
Practice

- Quelles matières n'aimes-tu pas à l'école?
- Quelles sont les matières les plus importantes?
- Qu'est-ce que tu penses des installations sportives dans ton école?
- Décris un voyage scolaire que tu as fait récemment.
- Qu'est-ce que tu changerais dans ton école si tu étais le directeur ou la directrice?
- Comment serait ton ami(e) idéal(e)?
- Qu'est-ce que tu as fait avec tes ami(e)s récemment?
- Qu'est-ce que tu penses des réseaux sociaux?
- Quels sont les dangers d'Internet?
- Quels sont tes projets pour le week-end prochain?

Page 56 Listening strategies
Practice

Il n'y a pas de doute que les Jeux Olympiques apportent une activité économique importante en attirant plein de visiteurs vers un pays, mais il ne faut jamais oublier que créer une infrastructure pour les Jeux coûte vraiment cher. Il existe beaucoup de pays endettés à cause des Jeux.

Page 57 Listening 1
Worked example

Exemple: Depuis le dix-neuvième siècle, la fête des Lumières a lieu chaque année à Lyon du sept au dix décembre.

Cette fête sert à remercier la Vierge Marie, la mère de Jésus Christ, qui aurait libéré la ville de la peste au seizième siècle. Pendant la fête, les façades des monuments et des bâtiments publics, tout comme celle de la cathédrale, sont illuminées avec des couleurs différentes chaque soir. Traditionnellement, les Lyonnais illuminent aussi leurs fenêtres et leurs balcons avec des bougies placées dans des verres colorés.

La ville de Menton, sur la Côte d'Azur, devient un spectacle en jaune et orange pendant la saison du carnaval chaque février. La fête du citron attire plus de 230 000 visiteurs qui viennent admirer les défilés avec leurs grands véhicules décorés de citrons et d'oranges, ainsi que les sculptures géantes créées avec ces fruits qui sont exposées dans les jardins publics. Quelques-unes de ces structures font plus de dix mètres de haut.

Practice

Exemple: Deux touristes américains sont tombés d'une falaise en Normandie en prenant un selfie. Malgré les efforts de l'ambulance aérienne, leur décès a été constaté à leur arrivée à l'hôpital.

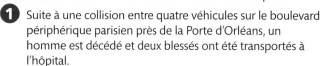 Suite à une collision entre quatre véhicules sur le boulevard périphérique parisien près de la Porte d'Orléans, un homme est décédé et deux blessés ont été transportés à l'hôpital.

Page 58 Listening 2
Worked example

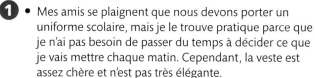
- Mes amis se plaignent que nous devons porter un uniforme scolaire, mais je le trouve pratique parce que je n'ai pas besoin de passer du temps à décider ce que je vais mettre chaque matin. Cependant, la veste est assez chère et n'est pas très élégante.
- Pour moi, les vêtements sont un moyen d'exprimer ma personnalité et ils font partie de mon identité. Alors l'uniforme scolaire m'empêche de faire ça. D'autre part, les profs disent que notre comportement en classe est meilleur quand nous portons un uniforme que quand nous mettons nos propres vêtements.

2 Non, pas du tout. Je n'ai jamais de pièces de monnaie, alors j'utilise ma carte sans contact, c'est plus pratique!

Practice

1
- J'aime bien l'idée de passer ma vie avec une seule personne qui devient mon compagnon constant. D'autre part je ne voudrais pas me marier trop jeune parce que je ne veux pas perdre la liberté de faire ce que je veux.
- Quand on veut fonder une famille je pense que le mariage offre normalement de la stabilité aux enfants. Cependant, la fête elle-même peut devenir incroyablement chère!

2
- C'était affreux, nous nous attendions à une belle vue sur la mer, mais notre appartement donnait sur un chantier de construction. On s'est plaints et le propriétaire nous a promis de rembourser la moitié de la location.
- Quand nous nous sommes installés dans l'hôtel, nous avons remarqué que la douche ne fonctionnait pas, alors nous avons dû changer de chambre.

Page 96 The imperative
Practice 1

- Quand vous arrivez, sortez de la gare et tournez à gauche.
- Allez tout droit jusqu'aux feux, puis tournez à droite.
- Prenez la rue Saint-Martin. Après deux cents mètres, vous arriverez à la place de la Victoire. Traversez la place.
- À l'hôtel de ville, descendez la rue Victor Hugo en direction de la rivière et traversez le pont.

Answers

Page x Understanding rubrics

1 Beware! Each of these words can be used more than once.

2 You must write in full sentences.

3 Write a letter to convince the judges.

4 Write an article to interest readers.

5 Put a cross in the correct box.

6 You must make reference to the following points.

Page 1 Numbers

G 84%; A 63%; B 75%

Page 2 The French alphabet

1 C, D, F, B

2 *Answers will vary.*

Page 3 Dates

(a) 28th May **(b)** 1st March **(c)** 21st June

Page 4 Telling the time

(a) 5:45 p.m. / 17:45

(b) 6:30 p.m. / 18:30

(c) 8:15 p.m. / 20:15

(d) 11 p.m. / 23:00

Page 5 Greetings

(a) at a restaurant **(b)** New Year **(c)** good night

Page 6 Opinions

(a) Loulou **(b)** Selim **(c)** Noah

(d) Karim **(e)** Loulou

Page 7 Asking questions

Model answers:

- Heure du concert (at a box office)
  - *À quelle heure est-ce que le concert commence / finit?*
- Végétarien (in a restaurant with the waiter)
  - *Qu'est-ce qu'il y a sur le menu pour les végétariens?*
  - *Quels plats végétariens avez-vous sur le menu?*
- Projets pour les vacances (talking to a friend)
  - *Qu'est-ce que tu vas faire pendant les vacances?*
  - *Quels sont tes projets pour les vacances?*
- Tarifs pour les étudiants (museum entry)
  - *C'est combien pour les étudiants?*
  - *Est-ce qu'il y a un tarif spécial pour les étudiants?*

Page 8 Describing people

Léo F; Adèle D; Farouk B

Page 9 Family

Model answer:

Est-ce qu'il y a une famille typique en Angleterre? Je ne sais pas, mais je pense que ma famille est comme beaucoup de familles. Le samedi, on passe normalement une journée tranquille à la maison. Je dois faire mes devoirs et mes parents font des tâches ménagères. Cependant, le week-end dernier, nous avons organisé une fête pour l'anniversaire de mon père. Tous mes cousins sont venus et nous avons mangé un déjeuner excellent préparé par ma mère.

À mon avis, il y a plein d'avantages à avoir une famille nombreuse. On peut bien s'amuser ensemble et quand on a beaucoup de frères et de sœurs, on n'est jamais seul car on a toujours quelqu'un avec qui on peut jouer ou parler. Cependant, si on se dispute, par exemple, à propos de ce qu'on regarde à la télé ou si on ne s'entend pas bien, ça peut être désagréable. Je pense que je préfère les familles plus petites et la famille idéale pour moi aurait seulement deux enfants.

Page 10 Friends and relationships

(a) They think he spends too much time at home.

(b) By talking when Marc is trying to work.

(c) She doesn't want to go out every evening with them.

(d) When they comment on what she is wearing.

Page 11 When I was younger

Model answers:

- Quand j'étais petit(e), je jouais souvent avec mes peluches quand il faisait mauvais, mais quand il faisait beau, je jouais dans le jardin avec mon chien.
- À l'âge de sept ans, j'allais à l'école à pied, parce qu'elle était tout près de chez moi. Un de mes parents m'accompagnait car j'étais trop jeune pour y aller tout(e) seul(e).
- Quand j'étais petit(e), je rêvais d'être chanteur (chanteuse), mais maintenant, j'ai envie de faire autre chose.
- Quand j'avais cinq ans, je ne pouvais pas courir très vite. Cependant, je suis maintenant très sportif (sportive) et j'adore l'athlétisme.

Page 12 Food

(a) 100; 150 **(b)** potatoes; 200 **(c)** 50; meat

Page 13 Meals

Model answers:

- Quel est ton repas préféré? Pourquoi?

  Mon repas préféré est le dîner parce que chez nous, c'est un repas chaud. J'aime les aliments salés mais pas trop épicés. Hier, on a mangé des pâtes avec une sauce tomate. C'était délicieux!

- Est-ce qu'il est important de bien manger au petit déjeuner?

  À mon avis, le petit déjeuner est très important parce qu'il nous donne de l'énergie au début de la journée. Cependant, il faut manger un petit déjeuner équilibré: des céréales ou du pain avec des produits laitiers et des fruits.

- Quel repas est le plus important, à ton avis? Pourquoi?

  Ça, c'est une question difficile. Je pense que tous les repas sont importants, à part le goûter parce qu'on mange souvent trop d'aliments sucrés et plein de matières grasses comme les gâteaux et les biscuits. Pour moi, il est important de manger sainement. Au déjeuner, par exemple, je prends souvent une salade et un fruit.

Page 14 Shopping

(a) Things are cheaper.

(b) You have to send something back if it is the wrong size.

Page 15 Social media

Laurent D; Aysha F; Albert A

Page 16 Mobile technology

(a) Léon **(b)** Nora **(c)** Fatima

(d) Léon **(e)** Guy **(f)** Fatima

Page 17 French customs

1 C, E, F

2 Model answers:

- Qu'est-ce qu'il y a sur la photo?

  Sur la photo, on voit des gens qui fêtent peut-être un anniversaire. Ils sont assis à une table dans un jardin ou un parc. Sur la table, il y a de la nourriture et les boissons. Ils sont tous très heureux car ils rient.

- Quel serait ton cadeau d'anniversaire idéal?

  Mon cadeau d'anniversaire idéal, ce serait de l'argent parce que je voudrais une tablette et j'économise en ce moment pour en acheter une.

- Qu'est-ce que tu as fait pour fêter ton anniversaire l'année dernière?

  L'année dernière, j'ai invité mes copains chez moi pour une fête. Ils m'ont offert des cadeaux et ils ont chanté 'Joyeux anniversaire!'. C'était super. Ma mère a fait un gâteau d'anniversaire au chocolat et on a bu du coca. On a dansé et écouté de la musique toute la soirée.

- Comment est-ce que tu fêteras le Nouvel An?

  Quelquefois, on reste à la maison, mais je pense que l'année prochaine nous irons voir un feu d'artifice. Tout le monde dira 'Bonne année!' et on chantera dans la rue. Ça sera génial!

- Est-ce que les fêtes de famille sont importantes?

  Oui, je pense que les fêtes de famille sont très importantes, parce que c'est l'occasion de rassembler toute la famille. L'année dernière, ma grand-mère a eu soixante-quinze ans et nous avons célébré son anniversaire dans un restaurant.

Page 18 French festivals

Model answers:

- Que penses-tu des fêtes françaises?

  À mon avis, les fêtes françaises sont intéressantes, surtout la fête nationale, parce qu'on peut aller voir un feu d'artifice le soir. J'adore les feux d'artifice et c'est formidable de voir le ciel illuminé comme ça.

- Tu es déjà allé(e) à une fête en France? C'était comment?

  Non, je ne suis jamais allé(e) à une fête en France, mais notre prof nous a montré une vidéo d'un carnaval en France. C'est super parce qu'on peut danser et chanter dans les rues et partout on voit des gens déguisés. Je voudrais aller à un carnaval, un jour.

Page 19 Reading

(a) soir **(b)** une œuvre de fiction
(c) imprimés **(d)** légèreté

Page 20 Music

Model answer:

Cher Laurent,

J'adore toutes sortes de musiques, mais celle que je préfère est la pop parce que je trouve que les mélodies sont toujours très rythmiques. Pour moi, la musique est très importante parce que ça m'aide à me concentrer quand je travaille. Il y a quelques années, j'ai entendu la musique d'Ed Sheeran pour la première fois. À mon avis, il est le meilleur chanteur du moment et je l'ai récemment vu en concert sur Internet. Si j'ai de la chance, j'achèterai des billets pour son prochain concert. Ça serait génial!

À bientôt!

Page 21 Sport

Model answers:

- Décris la photo.

  Sur la photo, on voit des gens qui courent. Je pense qu'ils participent à une course, peut-être à un marathon. Les gens au premier plan semblent très heureux. Je pense qu'ils viennent de traverser la ligne d'arrivée.

- Est-ce que les événements sportifs internationaux sont importants à ton avis?

  Ça, c'est une question intéressante! J'aime bien regarder les événements sportifs comme les Jeux Olympiques ou la Coupe du monde de foot, car je trouve l'ambiance vraiment géniale et on peut admirer les efforts des sportifs. Cependant, je pense aussi que ces événements coûtent très cher et il est difficile pour les athlètes des pays pauvres d'y participer.

- Parle-moi d'un événement sportif que tu as vu récemment.

  Récemment, j'ai regardé un match de rugby à la télévision. C'était l'Angleterre contre la France et l'Angleterre a gagné dix-neuf points à seize. À mon avis, c'était un match vraiment passionnant et j'espère que l'Angleterre va gagner le championnat!

- Qu'est-ce que tu feras comme sport pendant tes prochaines vacances?

  J'adore le tennis, alors j'irai au centre sportif au moins trois fois par semaine pour jouer au tennis. Je ferai ça avec mes copains et on ira peut-être aussi à la salle de musculation.

- Est-ce que tu préfères les sports individuels ou les sports collectifs?

  Je préfère participer à un sport collectif parce que j'aime l'interaction sociale avec les autres. On peut se faire de nouveaux amis et j'aime être membre d'une équipe. Je m'entraîne avec l'équipe de basket du collège et, la semaine dernière, nous avons gagné un match. C'était un match vraiment passionnant.

Page 22 Cinema

(a) His friends had talked to him about it.

(b) They are striking (breathtaking) aerial shots.

(c) He was moved to tears / he cried. (He felt emotional.)

Page 23 Television

Model answers:

- Quelles émissions est-ce que tu regardes régulièrement?

  Chaque soir, je regarde les actualités parce que je pense qu'il est important de s'informer de ce qui se passe dans le monde.

- Quels sont les avantages de regarder un film à la télé?

  À mon avis, le plus grand avantage de regarder un film à la télé c'est qu'on n'est pas obligé de sortir et on peut s'installer confortablement sur le canapé! Ce qui m'embête au cinéma, c'est d'avoir des gens très grands assis devant moi qui me bloquent la vue. Je déteste aussi les gens qui mangent du pop-corn pendant tout le film. D'autre part, il est vraiment génial de voir un film sur grand écran.

- Voudrais-tu participer à une émission de télé-réalité?

  Ça dépend de l'émission. Cela pourrait être intéressant de passer une semaine à vivre comme les gens des années cinquante, mais en général, je pense que les émissions de télé-réalité sont débiles, alors je dirais non!

- Qu'est-ce que tu as regardé à la télé hier?

  Je m'intéresse beaucoup aux animaux et hier, j'ai regardé un documentaire très informatif sur les animaux qui habitent en Afrique. On a expliqué que plusieurs espèces sont menacées.

Page 24 Holiday plans and preferences
Model answers:
- Est-ce que tu préfères les vacances d'été ou les vacances d'hiver?

  Je préfère les vacances d'hiver parce que j'adore la neige et que j'aime faire du ski. Cependant, mes parents aiment le soleil, alors nous passons normalement les vacances dans un pays chaud comme la Grèce ou l'Espagne.

- Comment seraient tes vacances idéales?

  Je passerais mes vacances idéales dans un endroit isolé où je pourrais apprécier le paysage et la nature. Je pourrais me détendre en faisant des randonnées et en prenant de belles photos.

- À ton avis, est-ce que les vacances sont importantes? Pourquoi / pourquoi pas?

  À mon avis, les vacances sont importantes car il est essentiel de se détendre et de récupérer un peu; on ne devrait pas travailler tout le temps. Si on ne peut pas partir en vacances, on peut se détendre chez soi et faire des excursions locales.

- Quel type de vacances préfères-tu et pourquoi?

  Je préfère des vacances actives ou culturelles. Je n'aime pas m'allonger sur une plage et ne rien faire. Je pense que les vacances nous donnent la chance de voir le monde.

Page 25 Holiday experiences
1 Advantage – visited a lot of interesting places / all meals included / could exercise on board

Disadvantage – was sometimes seasick

2 Abdou D; Francine E; Hervé B

Page 26 Travel and transport
1 **(a)** train; late **(b)** sea; illness

(c) flight; lost luggage **(d)** coach; traffic

2 **Model answers:**
- Comment vas-tu au collège?

  Normalement, j'y vais à pied, mais hier, j'y suis allé(e) en bus parce qu'il pleuvait.

- Quel est ton moyen de transport préféré? Pourquoi?

  Je préfère voyager en train parce que c'est plus écolo que les autres moyens de transport et que je peux lire ou travailler pendant mon voyage.

- Est-ce que tu es allé(e) en France? Décris ton voyage.

  Oui, j'y suis allé(e) en échange scolaire l'année dernière. Le voyage était assez fatigant car nous avons dû nous lever tôt pour arriver à l'aéroport deux heures avant le départ du vol. L'avion a décollé à l'heure et nous sommes arrivés en France vers dix heures.

- Comment voyagerais-tu si tu avais le choix?

  À mon avis, la voiture est le moyen de transport le plus pratique parce qu'elle donne la liberté d'aller où l'on veut, quand on veut.

Page 27 Accommodation
Nadia C; Bertrand B; Alice E

Page 28 Dealing with problems
(a) Khalid **(b)** Claire **(c)** Alyse

(d) Fabrice **(e)** Khalid

Page 29 Directions
(a) To the castle

(b) Cross the square and go straight ahead.

(c) Not far, about 5 minutes on foot

Page 30 Eating out
(a) 19% **(b)** It's too noisy

(c) a generous amount of food **(d)** poor value for money

Page 31 Shopping on holiday
1 **(a)** in a market (near to the leisure centre)

(b) a leather bag

(c) There wasn't anything in the colour she likes.

Model answers:
2
- Sur la photo, on voit des gens qui sont au marché en France. Ils sont en train d'acheter des fruits et des légumes et d'autres aliments et il y a un homme au premier plan qui porte des sacs. Je pense que c'est l'été parce que les gens portent des vêtements légers.

- Quand je suis en vacances, nous préférons acheter des provisions et faire la cuisine nous-mêmes parce que c'est moins cher que de manger au restaurant.

- Le week-end dernier, je suis allé à un marché à Londres où on peut acheter des vêtements et des bijoux bon marché.

- J'achèterai bientôt un cadeau pour ma sœur car c'est son anniversaire la semaine prochaine. Elle voudrait un collier. Je vais aussi acheter des cadeaux pour mes parents quand je ferai mon échange scolaire.

- À mon avis, ces marchés offrent un choix énorme de marchandises à des prix vraiment intéressants. Cependant, il faut parfois faire attention à la qualité de ces produits.

Page 32 Where I live
Model answers:
- Que penses-tu de ta maison / ton appartement?

  J'aime ma maison, surtout la situation car elle se trouve près du collège et du centre-ville. Elle est assez moderne et tout fonctionne bien. Nous avons une grande cuisine et un salon au rez-de-chaussée, ce qui est bien quand mes copains sont chez moi, mais ma chambre est assez petite. Cependant, c'est une chambre très lumineuse car elle donne sur le jardin.

- Comment serait ta maison idéale?

  Ma maison idéale se trouverait au bord d'une rivière avec une vue sur les collines. Elle ne serait ni grande ni petite et il y aurait une grande cuisine. Elle serait en briques rouges et elle aurait une porte verte et de grandes fenêtres. J'adore lire, alors la maison aurait une salle de lecture avec beaucoup de livres et un fauteuil confortable où je passerais tout mon temps libre. De plus, j'aime organiser des soirées, donc il faudrait que la maison ait une grande salle à manger et au moins deux chambres d'amis.

Page 33 The neighbourhood
Model answer:
Si vous voulez travailler en Angleterre, la ville d'Exeter dans le sud-ouest du pays vous offre une qualité de vie excellente. Dans le passé, la ville était plus petite qu'aujourd'hui, mais elle avait de l'importance grâce à sa cathédrale qui domine encore la cité. Le centre-ville médiéval a été détruit par des bombes pendant la Deuxième Guerre mondiale, mais on a construit de nouveaux magasins et des immeubles à la place des anciens bâtiments. La vie est très agréable à Exeter car il y a quelque chose pour tout le monde: des cinémas et des théâtres ainsi que des restaurants et des centres sportifs. Pour ceux qui s'intéressent à la culture, un festival de musique aura lieu cet été au centre-ville. Pendant une semaine, des musiciens viendront jouer dans des concerts. Il y a quand même des

inconvénients qu'on retrouve dans toutes les grandes villes, surtout les problèmes de pollution car il y a beaucoup de voitures, mais ce problème est moins grave que dans d'autres villes.

Page 34 Town and region

1 Model answer:

J'habite dans une ferme à la campagne depuis trois ans. J'aime vivre ici parce que je peux faire des promenades dans les champs avec mon chien. Cependant, mon frère déteste le village parce que c'est trop petit. Il voudrait habiter dans une grande ville. L'année dernière, il a passé six mois dans une famille aux États-Unis.

2 Model answers:

* Qu'est-ce qu'on peut faire dans ta région?

  J'habite dans le sud-ouest de l'Angleterre. C'est une région très pittoresque où on peut faire des randonnées à la campagne ou au bord de la mer. En été, beaucoup de gens passent leurs vacances dans une des stations balnéaires le long de la côte. On peut y faire des sports nautiques, se bronzer sur les plages ou nager dans la mer. Pour les touristes, il y a quelques vieux châteaux ainsi que des villes intéressantes.

* Où voudrais-tu habiter dans l'avenir?

  Dans l'avenir, je voudrais habiter à la campagne parce que j'aime faire des activités de plein air. Je pourrais faire de l'équitation ainsi que de la pêche. En plus, il y a moins de pollution et la vie est moins stressante. Pourtant, il y aurait des inconvénients parce que je n'ai pas le permis de conduire et il faudrait prendre les transports en commun pour aller en ville.

* Tu aimes habiter dans ta région?

  J'adore habiter dans une grande ville parce qu'il y a tant de choses à faire! On peut se déplacer facilement si on veut retrouver des amis ou aller au cinéma. C'est une ville très historique et il y a beaucoup de choses intéressantes à voir pour les touristes comme la cathédrale médiévale et le vieux quartier. Récemment, j'ai vu une exposition sur les origines de la ville qui était vraiment informative.

* Tu voudrais vivre à l'étranger? Pourquoi / pourquoi pas?

  Je voudrais vivre à l'étranger parce que ça m'intéresse de rencontrer de nouvelles personnes et de découvrir d'autres cultures. Cependant, je ne voudrais pas vivre dans un pays tropical car je n'aime pas tellement la chaleur. D'un autre côté, mes parents aimeraient bien vivre en Espagne parce qu'il y fait plus chaud qu'ici, mais ils ne parlent pas espagnol, alors ce serait difficile pour eux.

Page 35 Francophone countries

(a) The classrooms are badly lit / are too dark because there is no electricity.

(b) There is no access to drinking water.

(c) There are no toilets and girls give up their education.

Page 36 Seasons and weather

(a) snow / skiing

(b) mild / walking

Page 37 My studies

(a) English

(b) The teacher makes the lessons interesting.

(c) Citizenship

(d) The speaker thinks it's a waste of time; the teacher is always in a bad mood; the teacher criticizes them all the time. (any **two**)

Page 38 Your school

(a) no modern technology; it's not good for non-academic pupils / too many pupils have to repeat the year

(b) they are able to succeed in other areas

Page 39 School trips, events and exchanges
Model answers:

* Sur la photo, on voit un groupe d'élèves assis sur des marches au pied d'une colline. Je pense qu'ils sont en train de déjeuner. Peut-être qu'ils mangent des sandwichs. Je pense que le bâtiment sur la colline est le Sacré-Cœur. Les élèves font probablement un échange ou un voyage scolaire à Paris. Les élèves portent tous une casquette rouge.

* À mon avis, les échanges scolaires sont importants parce qu'on a la chance de faire la connaissance de personnes d'une autre culture. En plus, on développe la confiance en soi, et on peut améliorer ses compétences linguistiques.

* L'an dernier, j'ai fait un voyage scolaire en Italie pour étudier les œuvres d'art dans les musées de Venise. C'était un voyage formidable car nous avons vu des peintures très célèbres.

* Dans deux semaines, je participerai à un tournoi sportif avec d'autres écoles de la région. Le tournoi aura lieu dans un autre collège et nous irons en car.

* Moi, je préfère les voyages scolaires parce qu'on reste avec ses amis et qu'on peut bien s'amuser ensemble. Je suis un peu timide et j'ai le mal du pays quand je suis à l'étranger avec des gens que je ne connais pas bien. Bien sûr, si on veut améliorer ses compétences linguistiques, il vaut mieux faire un échange.

Page 40 Using languages

1 (a) B   **(b)** C

2 (a) D   **(b)** A

Page 41 Ambitions
Model answers:

* Tu veux aller à l'université ou commencer à travailler? Pourquoi?

  Je voudrais aller à l'université avant de commencer à travailler parce que je voudrais continuer mes études et que je pense que je trouverai un meilleur emploi si j'ai un diplôme. En plus, je ne sais pas encore ce que je voudrais faire comme travail.

* Est-ce que tu voudrais étudier à l'étranger dans l'avenir? Pourquoi / pourquoi pas?

  Dans l'avenir, je voudrais aller à l'université à l'étranger parce que je pense qu'on peut bénéficier de nouvelles expériences et améliorer ses compétences linguistiques, surtout si on étudie à une université dans un pays européen.

* Tu voudrais prendre une année sabbatique dans l'avenir? Pourquoi / pourquoi pas?

  Je n'ai pas encore décidé parce que je pense qu'on devrait avoir une bonne idée de ce qu'on voudrait faire pendant cette année, par exemple voyager à l'étranger ou faire du bénévolat, sinon on pourrait perdre son temps. Pour le moment, j'ai l'intention d'aller à l'université tout de suite après avoir passé mon bac.

* Qu'est-ce que tu voulais faire comme travail quand tu étais plus jeune?

  Quand j'étais jeune, je rêvais d'être médecin car ma mère faisait ce métier. Malheureusement, il faut avoir de bonnes notes en sciences et je suis très faible dans cette matière. L'important pour moi, maintenant, c'est de faire quelque chose d'intéressant.

Page 42 Education post-16

(a) En septembre, j'étudierai les matières qui m'intéressent le plus.

(b) Je suis content(e) de laisser tomber la géographie parce que c'est ennuyeux.

(c) La plupart de mes amis ont l'intention d'aller à l'université.

(d) Je pense qu'on peut trouver un meilleur emploi si on a fait des études universitaires.

(e) Je voudrais trouver un emploi ou un apprentissage.

Page 43 Charity and voluntary work

Emma F; Guy C

Page 44 Jobs and careers

B, C, E

Page 45 International events

Model answer:

Chaque été, des milliers de gens vont à Londres pour le grand festival de musique qui a lieu à travers la capitale. Le festival a été un grand succès parce que les musiciens les plus célèbres du monde sont venus y jouer. Il y avait quelque chose pour satisfaire tous les goûts musicaux.

Les festivals, tels que celui de Londres, sont très importants pour une ville parce qu'ils attirent de nouveaux touristes. Les hôtels et restaurants en profitent bien sûr ainsi que les autres attractions, comme les monuments et les musées. Cependant, cela peut aussi avoir des inconvénients car il y a plus de gens qui utilisent les transports en commun et si le festival a lieu en plein air, il y a aussi l'impact du bruit et des détritus laissés par les fans sur l'environnement. Dans un mois, il y aura une grande exposition de peintures françaises que j'irai voir. Ça sera un événement à ne pas manquer!

Page 46 Campaigns and good causes

(a) those without access to clean drinking water or proper toilets

(b) People suffer from diseases and die.

(c) poor countries in Africa and Asia

(d) They have to fetch water so don't go to school.

(e) make a donation or organise fundraising

Page 47 Global issues

Fatima G; Noah A; Laure B

Page 48 The environment

Ayesha E; Paul A; Zoë F

Page 49 Pronunciation strategies

Access audio QR code on page for model examples.

Page 50 Speaking strategies

Model answers:

• Quels sont les effets du réchauffement de la Terre?

Je ne sais pas exactement, mais je pense que le changement climatique est un problème très grave.
On voit de plus en plus de tempêtes tropicales tandis qu'en Afrique, il ne pleut pas.

• Qu'est-ce qu'on doit faire pour protéger l'environnement?

Il y a beaucoup de choses qu'on pourrait faire. Moi, j'essaie de consommer moins d'énergie et d'utiliser les transports en commun le plus possible.

Page 52 General conversation

Answers will vary.

Page 53 Using a picture stimulus

Model answer:

Sur la photo, on voit un jeune couple qui vient de se marier. La femme porte une robe blanche qui est jolie et assez traditionnelle. Ils sont dans un jardin avec leurs amis qui sont en train de les féliciter.

Page 54 Role play (Foundation)

Model answers:

• Je suis britannique / anglais(e) / écossais(e) / gallois(e) / irlandais(e).

• Je suis en France pour une semaine.

• J'adore la France parce que la cuisine est délicieuse.

• Mon hôtel est confortable et pas trop cher.

• Où est la gare, s'il vous plaît? / Pour aller à la gare, s'il vous plaît?

Page 55 Role play (Higher)

Model answers:

• J'aime ta maison parce qu'elle est très jolie / moderne / grande.

• J'ai écouté de la musique / j'ai joué sur mon portable / aux cartes / j'ai dormi.

• Je voudrais faire du tourisme et voir la campagne.

• À quelle heure est-ce qu'on mange ce soir? / Quand est-ce qu'on dîne?

• Est-ce qu'on peut regarder la télévision?

Page 56 Listening strategies

• The Olympic Games are good for the economy; the games attract more visitors / increase the number of visitors to the country.

• The cost of creating the infrastructure for the games is high; many countries are in debt as a result.

Page 57 Listening 1

C

Page 58 Listening 2

1 **(a)** jeune **(b)** la famille

2 **(a)** Their flat overlooked a building site; they had expected a view of the sea.

(b) They complained and the ... owner reimbursed them 50% of the rent.

(c) The shower didn't work.

(d) They changed rooms.

Page 60 Reading 1

(a) Fetch water / They had no running (tap) water.

(b) She saw a dance improvisation and a nomadic wedding.

(c) She now appreciates what is important in life / she has changed her daily routine.

Page 61 Reading 2

(a) du nord de la France

(b) lire

(c) une contraction de Voilà Jean

(d) ses parents sont morts / il a perdu son père et sa mère

Page 62 Reading 3

the (school) summer holidays

Page 63 Reading 4

 A   A

Page 64 Translation into English

Model answers:

1 **(a)** With a remote control, you / one / we can change TV programme without leaving your /one's / our chair or the sofa.

(b) I went to the chemist's / pharmacy with the prescription that the doctor had given me to get medicine.

2 I have just spent a week at the seaside/by the sea in this hotel. It has recently been refurbished with new furniture everywhere. On the ground floor, there is a beautiful dining room where dinner is served every evening / night. What I liked most was the heated swimming pool. I would like to go back there next year.

Page 65 Writing strategies

Model answer:

Il y a deux jours, c'était mon anniversaire et j'ai eu seize ans. Le matin, mes parents m'ont offert un nouveau portable comme cadeau et le soir, j'ai invité mes ami(e)s chez moi pour regarder un film. Après avoir regardé la comédie sentimentale, on a mangé de la pizza. Mon anniversaire était super parce que j'ai reçu de beaux cadeaux. À Noël, nous nous réunissons en famille, alors c'est une date importante. Heureusement, tout le monde s'entend vraiment bien dans ma famille. Le week-end prochain, on ira au théâtre à Londres pour voir la comédie musicale *Les Misérables*. J'adore la musique et je connais les paroles de toutes les chansons.

Page 66 Translation into French (Foundation)

Model answers:

1 Mon frère a treize ans.

2 Ma mère va à la bibliothèque en face du supermarché.

3 La semaine dernière, je suis allé(e) au théâtre avec ma famille.

4 Il y a quatre personnes dans ma famille.

5 Ma sœur joue/fait du piano le soir.

Page 67 Translation into French (Higher)

Model answers:

1 Pendant l'été, je suis allé(e) en vacances avec ma famille dans le sud de l'Espagne. L'hôtel était assez petit et ma chambre était sale. Mes parents aiment la nourriture espagnole mais je préfère les plats plus épicés. La semaine prochaine, c'est l'anniversaire de mon frère. Je lui achèterai des chaussettes blanches et un livre.

2 En février, j'ai fait/participé à un voyage scolaire en France. Le voyage était trop long et j'ai eu le mal de mer. Dans l'avenir, je préférerais voyager en avion. J'ai logé chez une famille sympa qui vit dans le centre-ville. L'année prochaine, mon ami(e) français(e) viendra chez moi et nous ferons du tourisme.

Page 68 Writing (Foundation)

Model answer:

En ce moment, je passe mes vacances au bord de la mer dans le sud de la France. Il fait très beau et hier, nous avons nagé dans la piscine et nous sommes allés à la plage.

En France, il fait plus chaud qu'en Angleterre et on achète du pain frais à la boulangerie tous les jours.

L'année prochaine, je voudrais aller à la montagne en Suisse parce que je préfère faire des randonnées ou de l'escalade.

À mon avis, les vacances sont très importantes parce qu'on doit se détendre, sinon on devient trop stressé.

Page 69 Writing (Higher)

Model answer:

Être un(e) bon(ne) ami(e) est très important car on a toujours besoin de copains en cas de problème. Récemment, une de mes meilleures amies a été victime de harcèlement en ligne quand quelqu'un a mis sa photo sur un réseau social et a écrit des choses méchantes et fausses sur elle. J'ai dû la soutenir en passant des soirées avec elle pour la rassurer. Je lui ai conseillé de ne plus utiliser les réseaux sociaux et de changer son numéro de portable. J'étais très heureuse de l'aider car l'année dernière, quand j'avais des difficultés avec mes parents, elle était là pour moi.

Si je gagne la somme de cent euros, j'inviterai mon amie à faire une sortie avec moi. Nous avons envie de passer la journée dans un parc d'attractions, mais ça coûte assez cher. Après y être allé(e)s, nous pourrons manger dans un restaurant italien s'il me reste encore un peu d'argent. À mon avis, ce serait une journée géniale!

Page 70 Articles

1 **(a)** le **(b)** le **(c)** le **(d)** L'; les

(e) le **(f)** L'; l' **(g)** le; la **(h)** La; la; l'

(i) la **(j)** Le

2 **(a)** Il a les cheveux gris et les yeux verts.

(b) Elle est infirmière et elle travaille dans un hôpital.

(c) Il y a des magasins dans le village.

(d) Nous prenons le petit déjeuner dans la cuisine.

(e) J'ai visité l'Espagne l'été dernier.

Page 71 Prepositions

(a) *vers* la gare **(b)** *contre* l'Angleterre

(c) *malgré* la pluie **(d)** *parmi* mes amis

(e) *pour* mon anniversaire **(f)** *chez* moi

(g) *sans* lait **(h)** *sauf* le mardi

(i) *selon* un sondage

Page 72 The preposition *à*

1 **(a)** au **(b)** aux **(c)** à l'

(d) à la **(e)** au

2 **(a)** I would like a ham sandwich.

(b) It's the girl with blue eyes.

(c) My flat is on the third floor.

(d) I had a stomach ache.

(e) They are playing volleyball.

3 **(a)** J'ai mal à l'oreille.

(b) C'est combien, la glace au café?

(c) Ils jouent aux cartes.

(d) J'adore la soupe à l'oignon.

Page 73 Partitives and preposition *de*

Model answers:

(a) J'ai acheté du lait, de la viande et des œufs.

(b) Il n'a pas de poisson.

(c) Le copain / Le petit ami de ma sœur est assez grand.

(d) Le parc est à côté du château.

(e) J'ai essayé de faire mes devoirs.

Page 74 Nouns

(a) mercredi (m) **(b)** pharmacienne (f)

(c) révolution (f) **(d)** chinois (m)

123

(e) rire (m)   **(f)** serveuse (f)
(g) nourriture (f)   **(h)** chou (m)

Page 75 Adjectives

(a) une bonne question
(b) un petit jardin
(c) une amie / copine jalouse
(d) une chemise gris clair
(e) un vieil objet

Page 76 Comparatives and superlatives
Model answers:
(a) Les films d'horreur sont plus passionnants que les films romantiques.
(b) Les feuilletons sont plus divertissants que les actualités.
(c) Les émissions de sport sont aussi intéressantes que les documentaires.
(d) *Amélie* est le film le plus amusant.
(e) C'est l'émission la plus ennuyeuse.
(f) Adele est la meilleure chanteuse.
(g) Il est le pire acteur.
(h) Il a choisi le plat principal le plus cher.
(i) J'ai acheté le souvenir le moins cher.
(j) Ce sont les places les plus inconfortables.

Page 77 Possessive and demonstrative adjectives
Model answers:
(a) Mon père a perdu son portable dans ce magasin-là.
(b) Nous avons rendu visite à nos cousins.
(c) Ses parents et leurs amis ont logé dans cette maison-là.
(d) Mon copain / ami a acheté ce souvenir pour sa sœur.

Page 78 Indefinite and interrogative adjectives

1 **(a)** tous (every day)   **(b)** toutes (all the stations)
   (c) toute (the whole class)   **(d)** tout (all the cheese)
   (e) toute (all the family)
2 **(a)** chaque matin / tous les matins
   (b) chaque étudiant
   (c) quelques personnes
   (d) quelques mots
   (e) quelque temps
3 **(a)** Quelle (What drink do you want?)
   (b) Quelle (What size do you want?)
   (c) Quel (What sport do you like?)
   (d) Quel (What kind of music don't you like?)
   (e) Quelles (What are your favourite subjects?)
   (f) Quel (What is your favourite hobby?)
   (g) quelle (What kind of films do you like?)
   (h) Quels (Which are the best soap operas/TV dramas?)
   (i) Quelle (How lucky!)

Page 79 Adverbs
Model answers:
(a) D'habitude, je quitte la maison de bonne heure.
(b) Parfois / Quelquefois, nous allons / on va au café.
(c) Je joue mieux du piano que mon frère.

(d) Il parle plus doucement que moi.
(e) Malheureusement, il faisait mauvais temps.

Page 80 Quantifiers and intensifiers
Model answers:
(a) Il y a beaucoup d'arbres dans le jardin.
(b) J'ai mangé trop de gâteaux.
(c) On voit tant de sans-abri dans les rues.
(d) Après quelques jours, j'avais vu assez de monuments.
(e) Mes parents sont tellement embêtants / agaçants!

Page 81 Subject and object pronouns
(a) <u>Ils</u> <u>lui</u> donnent un vélo.
(b) <u>Il</u> <u>leur</u> a parlé.
(c) <u>Elle</u> est en train de <u>le</u> lire.
(d) <u>Nous</u> voulons <u>le</u> voir.
(e) <u>Je</u> <u>les</u> ai achetés.

Page 82 Stressed and possessive pronouns
Model answers:
(a) My marks are better than yours.
(b) Our holidays were great. What were yours like?
(c) Have you got your mobile phone? I can't find mine.
(d) He hasn't got a cap? He can borrow mine.

Page 83 Relative and demonstrative pronouns
Model answers:
(a) The shop which is next to the museum is closed.
(b) The man I saw was wearing a black pullover / jumper.
(c) The children I look after are sweet / cute.

Page 84 Pronouns *y* and *en*
Model answers:
(a) Vous voulez encore de la salade?
(b) Oui, j'en veux.
(c) Non, je n'en veux pas.
(d) Avez-vous besoin d'argent?
(e) Oui, j'en ai besoin.
(f) Il rentre du concert. Il en rentre.
(g) Je suis allé en France.
(h) J'y suis allé.
(i) Tu penses venir?
(j) Oui, j'y pense!

Page 85 Conjunctions and connectives
Model answers:
(a) Je déteste habiter en ville parce qu'il y a trop de pollution.
(b) Nous devons arrêter le déboisement de nos forêts, sinon on verra plus d'inondations.
(c) On voit beaucoup de sans-abri dans les rues à cause des problèmes de chômage et de pauvreté.
(d) Je pense qu'on devrait acheter des produits verts tandis que mes parents pensent que nous devons consommer moins d'énergie.

Page 86 The present tense
Model answers:
(a) J'envoie des textos / SMS à mes copains / amis tous les jours / chaque jour.

(b) Nous lisons des poèmes en classe, en ce moment.

(c) Nous allons au cinéma aujourd'hui.

(d) Je ne le connais pas bien.

(e) J'apprends le français depuis cinq ans.

Page 87 Key verbs
Model answers:

1 **(a)** I want to go out. **(b)** Are you hungry?

(c) We needed help. **(d)** They are thirsty.

(e) We were unlucky. **(f)** You are right.

(g) She is afraid of snakes.

2 **(a)** She is in the middle of / in the process of doing the cooking.

(b) He has had a cold for three days.

(c) We had to / were obliged to leave before the end of the concert.

(d) I don't agree with you.

(e) We are about to leave.

(f) I am back.

Page 88 The perfect tense
Model answer:

Hier, j'ai fêté mon anniversaire. Mes parents m'ont donné beaucoup de cadeaux que j'ai ouverts le matin. Le soir, on a fait une fête et beaucoup de mes copains sont venus. Nous avons bu du coca et après, nous avons dansé. Qu'est-ce que tu as fait le week-end dernier?

Page 89 The imperfect tense
Model answers:

(a) Je faisais mes devoirs quand ma mère m'a demandé de descendre.

(b) J'étais en train de lire mon livre quand quelqu'un a frappé à la porte.

(c) Nous traversions la rue quand l'accident s'est passé / est arrivé.

(d) Nous venions d'arriver quand il a commencé à pleuvoir.

Page 90 The pluperfect tense
Model answers:

(a) My brother had gone to the café to meet his friends but no one came.

(b) I had chosen my meal before going to the restaurant.

(c) I had never seen this person before.

(d) When I arrived at the market I noticed that I had forgotten my purse.

(e) We had left early but arrived late at our hotel.

Page 91 The immediate future tense
Model answers:

(a) Nous allons visiter un musée pendant l'échange.

(b) Ils vont voir un film ce soir.

(c) Il va y avoir du vent.

(d) J'espère qu'il va bientôt neiger.

(e) La France va gagner le match.

Page 92 The future tense
Model answers:

(a) Je le verrai demain.

(b) Nous devrons prendre le bus.

(c) Elle aura vingt ans.

(d) Est-ce que tu feras du vélo demain?

(e) Comment est-ce qu'il viendra? / Comment viendra-t-il?

(f) Nous irons au théâtre.

(g) Il n'achètera rien.

(h) Qu'est-ce que vous mangerez?

(i) Quand est-ce que tu sortiras?

(j) Je ne prendrai pas d'entrée.

Page 93 The conditional
Model answers:

(a) S'il était riche, il ne travaillerait pas.

(b) Je préférerais aller en Espagne.

(c) Si j'allais à Paris, je pourrais monter en haut de la tour Eiffel.

(d) Si mon portable ne fonctionnait plus, j'en achèterais un nouveau.

(e) Si je n'avais pas d'argent, je trouverais un emploi.

Page 94 Negative forms
Model answers:

(a) Il n'y a plus de beurre.

(b) Je ne suis jamais allé(e) en France.

(c) Nous ne somme pas allé(e)s au cinéma.

(d) Nous n'y allons pas.

(e) Il n'a parlé à personne.

Page 95 Reflexive verbs
Model answers:

(a) Je ne me lève pas tôt / de bonne heure.

(b) Ils ne se disputent jamais.

(c) Ils se sont lavé les mains.

(d) Nous voulons bien nous amuser.

Page 96 The imperative

1 **(a)** turn left **(b)** turn right
(c) cross the square **(d)** cross the bridge

2 **Model answers:**

(a) For a healthy life…

(b) … drink eight glasses of water a day.

(c) … eat at least five portions of fruits and vegetables each day.

(d) … don't smoke.

(e) … avoid foods that are rich in fat.

(f) … exercise regularly.

(g) … don't stay sitting for too long.

Page 97 Impersonal verbs
Model answers:

1 **(a)** Il reste de l'argent.

(b) Il y avait du vent.

(c) Il manque des informations.

(d) Il s'agissait d'une histoire vraie.

2 **(a)** Because of the strike we / I / they had to walk to school.

(b) You just need to talk to him.

(c) It is forbidden to walk on the lawn.

GCSE French / Answers

Page 98 The infinitive
Model answers:

1 **(a)** Il déteste faire ses devoirs.

(b) Elle adore écouter de la musique.

(c) J'ai essayé d'apprendre les nouveaux mots.

(d) Je sais nager.

2 **(a)** We were invited to participate in a survey.

(b) After having eaten we went to the cinema.

(c) They decided to leave early.

(d) He left without saying a word.

Page 99 The present participle
Model answers:

(a) Being afraid of violence, she didn't go to see that war film.

(b) He was able to buy a new bicycle by saving his pocket money.

(c) He found himself in trouble / difficulty while swimming.

(d) I cut my finger while preparing dinner.

(e) On hearing the noise, we woke up.

Page 100 The passive voice
Model answers:

(a) The castle was built in the sixteenth century.

(b) The road is blocked by a tree.

(c) The buildings have been destroyed by the earthquake.

(d) The thieves have been arrested.

(e) The prices will be reduced.

Page 101 The subjunctive mood
Model answers:

(a) I prefer to go on foot, although I have a car.

(b) I sent him an email so that he knows the time of the meeting.

(c) I will stay near the phone until he comes back.

(d) Although he is rich, he is not generous.

Published by BBC Active, an imprint of Educational Publishers LLP, part of the Pearson Education Group, 80 Strand, London, WC2R 0RL.

www.pearsonschools.co.uk/BBCBitesize
© Educational Publishers LLP 2018
BBC logo © BBC 1996. BBC and BBC Active are trademarks of the British Broadcasting Corporation.

Produced, typeset and illustrated by Elektra Media Ltd
Cover design by Andrew Magee & Pearson Education Limited 2018
Cover illustration by Darren Lingard / Oxford Designers & Illustrators

The right of Liz Fotheringham to be identified as author of this work has been asserted by her in accordance with the Copyright, Designs and Patents Act 1988.

First published 2018

21 20 19 18
10 9 8 7 6 5 4 3 2 1

British Library Cataloguing in Publication Data
A catalogue record for this book is available from the British Library.

ISBN 978 1 406 68593 0

Printed and bound in Slovakia by Neografia.
The Publisher's policy is to use paper manufactured from sustainable forests.

Note from the publisher
1. While the publishers have made every attempt to ensure that advice on the qualification and its assessment is accurate, the official specification and associated assessment guidance materials are the only authoritative source of information and should always be referred to for definitive guidance.
Pearson examiners have not contributed to any sections in this resource relevant to examination papers for which they have responsibility.
2. Pearson has robust editorial processes, including answer and fact checks, to ensure the accuracy of the content in this publication, and every effort is made to ensure this publication is free of errors. We are, however, only human, and occasionally errors do occur. Pearson is not liable for any misunderstandings that arise as a result of errors in this publication, but it is our priority to ensure that the content is accurate. If you spot an error, please do contact us at resourcescorrections@pearson.com so we can make sure it is corrected.

Acknowledgements
The authors and publisher would like to thank the following individuals and organisations for their kind permission to reproduce copyright material.

Text Credit(s): BBC: 1–6, 8–10, 12–18, 20–22, 24–28, 30, 32–38, 41–44, 47–48, 51, 59, 70–71, 72–99 © 2018
Photographs: (Key: T-top; B-bottom; C-centre; L-left; R-right)
Getty Images: Morsa Images vi, 53t; **123rf:** Jacek Chabraszewski viii; margouillat 18t, Nataliya Yakovleva 32, Jozef Polc 53b;
Alamy Stock Photo: Louis-Paul st-onge Louis 9, Paris Market 31, Adrian Sherratt 43, Stefan Auth/imageBROKER 101;
Shutterstock: Monkey Business Images 13, 23, Rawpixel.com 17, DreamSlamStudio 18b, George Rudy 19, Bikeworldtravel 21, Mastapiece 39, Chris Pelle 76, Andrey Skutin 91, Rido 100;
Bananastock: 68

All other images © Pearson Education

Websites
Pearson Education Limited is not responsible for the content of third-party websites.